NATIONAL INCOME VISUALIZED

NATIONAL INCOME VISUALIZED

A Graphic Portrayal of How Economic Activity Is Measured

by ARTHUR O. DAHLBERG

COLUMBIA UNIVERSITY PRESS, NEW YORK, 1956

Published in Great Britain, Canada, India, and Pakistan
by Geoffrey Cumberlege: Oxford University Press,
London, Toronto, Bombay, and Karachi

Library of Congress Catalog Card Number: 56-8558

Manufactured in the United States of America

PREFACE

This book pioneers a new method for visualizing economics. In the process of doing so it also tries to broaden the understanding of national income accounting. There have of course been other books on national income, some more technical and comprehensive, but none of them have tried to explain national income predominantly with visual techniques. The technique used in this book to visualize, integrate, and transmit the subject matter is both new and different.

Recent decades have seen the growth and spread of many efforts to "humanize" knowledge. Economists, as well as others, seeking to satisfy the popular yearning for understanding, have tried to convey their special information with light touch and simple terms. Valuable as these efforts have been, they still have not overcome the historic handicap of economics: lack of a graphic means for showing how economic structures and processes are interlaced. The new graphic technique applied in this book helps peculiarly to reveal such integration and coordination.

Many years ago I concurrently did graduate work in economics and taught engineering at one of our big Midwestern universities. One day, probably as a result of my double exposure to two fields of study, it occurred to me that engineers—in contrast to economists—were relatively lucky in having a secondary or auxiliary tool of communication. For the engineers could first describe in words the physical structures and processes with which they dealt, and then—with their engineering drawing techniques—supplement their verbal descriptions with graphic depictions. This the economists could not do. They had no such auxiliary language. Even though they had their own social structures and processes to deal with, they were limited in describing them by mainly verbal means. Living with this observation, I gradually saw the possibility of devising for economics an auxiliary communication tool similar to that which mechanical drawing provides for engineering.

Economics always relates to a world of property and movement. It always relates to the production, exchange, and distribution of wealth. Every morning we see people going to work in streetcars, autos, and buses, and then returning home again at night. An actual physical surge of human beings from home to work and back again is an observable part of the economic process. The continuous movement of raw materials from the earth to the receiving platforms of plants and factories is also an observable movement. So too is a third one—the flow of finished goods to those who purchase them.

Apart from the people themselves, there is the labor energy which people derive from their food and rest and which they expend daily as they apply themselves to the work of the world. This daily flow of man-hours, of labor energy applied to production and distribution, is also an observable process distinct from the movement of people as such.

The movement of the money which lays claim to the finished goods is an observable process also. As coins are placed on the counter, and currency and checks are passed from hand to hand, industry's goods and services flow out to the claimants of the nation. Money is something that one can measure in motion.

And, of course, economics always relates to the world of property. Either directly or indirectly, someone owns every asset of this world. Besides permitting the private ownership of property, our system permits citizens to enter into debtor agreements with one another and then helps with the enforcement of the agreements. Our laws of property and contract thus permit people both to owe and to own—to create certificates of indebtedness as well as certificates of ownership. The movement of these certificates which witness ownership and indebtedness can also be seen in constant flux.

Despite the dynamic nature of its problem, economics has never been able to portray with visual means the interlacing of its elements. The verbal means by which it has been forced to describe its social structures and movements can be quite effective, it is true. For they are the organizational means that have been used in teaching all of us what we already know. Still, they are not always efficient tools. It is possible, for example, for one man to explain to another the structure and dynamic operation of an automobile engine by means of words alone. But the speaker would have to be expert in exposition, the listener very attentive, and the description probably repeated over and over. In contrast, if one engineer explains the engine to another, he can do it quickly and effectively because he possesses—in his engineering drawing—a visual means of communication superbly designed for describing structure and process. The verbal techniques of economics simply cannot show such integration easily. As a result, economists have often been forced to leave their component explanations dangling before the reader with the implication that he provide his own synthesis.

The written or spoken word tends to put a tremendous load upon the memory of the learner. Just how the contents of "Chapter One" of any economic treatise fits into the general scheme of things is therefore often already vague and partly forgotten by the time "Chapter Two" is read. The symbolism that I devised years ago helps to ease that situation by enabling one to save graphic, instead of memory, pictures of the contents. The essentials of that symbolism are described at some length in the Conclusion of this book.

As head of a business research and consulting firm for the past decade, I have used my graphic integrations very effectively as business tools. They have been very useful in explaining to clients the business cycle analysis and national income forecasting work in which we engage, because graphic portrayals that integrate theory and data enable people to see swiftly how key portions of our economy are made and function.

Several men, who had observed the facility with which the graphic portrayals could clarify economic process and aid group discussion of problems and policy, believed that the technique would also be useful for extending the popular understanding of economics. In this belief they recommended to the Alfred P. Sloan Foundation that a project be set up to explore the development and application of a new tool of communication in the field of economics. So through the sponsorship of these businessmen, and that of Dean Harry Carman and Professor Horace Taylor of Columbia University, the Alfred P. Sloan Foundation established at Columbia the Visual Economics Laboratory. An advisory committee of men experienced in business, government, and university work was appointed. It consists of Professor Lester V. Chandler, Professor Harold Clark, Mr. Stephen M. DuBrul, Professor Albert Gailord Hart, Professor Mabel Newcomer, Professor Horace Taylor (chairman), Dr. George Terborgh, Mr. Donald Warning, Dr. Theodore Yntema, and Professor Kimball Young. To these members I am deeply indebted for valuable suggestions on how best to apply my graphic technique to economic material.

* * * * * * *

This book, more than most, came about through the assistance of others. From the very beginning, Professor Horace Taylor of Columbia University helped continuously, first in sponsoring the project and then, as chairman of the Laboratory's Advisory Committee, with expert counsel and continuous encouragement.

I also had the good fortune of having the imaginative aid of two very able associates: the Assistant Director, Mrs. Tor Norberg, and the Economic Analyst, Mrs. Norma Pace. I am deeply grateful to them both. From the very beginning Mrs. Norberg helped enlist support for the Laboratory project. Then, with artistry and unstinted application, she put the charts into a standard pattern. It was her versatility that made the Laboratory into a smoothly working organization. Mrs. Pace's assistance, because of her special familiarity with both government data and that whole complex of premises, definitions, and procedures that lies behind national income accounting, was invaluable to me in aligning the graphic depictions and verbal explanations with statistical truth and official accounting practice.

My deep and sincere gratitude also goes to the Alfred P. Sloan Foundation for its willingness to support a venture as uniquely different as is ours. One of the aims of that foundation is to provide risk capital for new ventures in economic education. Our Visual Economics Laboratory was fortunate enough to receive such capital—three years of generous aid to help us on our way toward self-support. Without that aid this project would never have been begun.

During the past year the Earhart Foundation also contributed to the support of our Laboratory. In addition, it has generously supplied the funds to make the publication of this book possible.

In a book like this, which attempts to write an economic story in both words and pictures, there is a double chance of making errors. I hope they are not too serious or numerous. In any event, my advisers are not responsible for them. I have had so much independence of action that the blunders are all mine.

Columbia University
New York, June 1, 1956

Arthur O. Dahlberg, Ph. D.
Director Visual Economics Laboratory

INTRODUCTION TO NATIONAL INCOME ACCOUNTING

How many people if asked to name the important inventions of recent decades would mention as one of them the system of national income accounting developed by the National Bureau of Economic Research and the Department of Commerce? Probably not many. Still there is reason to believe that it is one of them.

Prior to the introduction of national income accounting, economists had very poor gauges for appraising the performance of the national economy. The figures they watched—carloadings, bank loans, interest rates, department store sales, and other limited indicators—had not been set up as parts of an integrated whole. Each gave a picture, more or less accurate, of how only one part of the economy was doing. Consequently, economists did not have at any moment in time reliable indicators of how the economy as a whole was functioning. Today that situation has changed, and the practical usefulness of economics has taken a long step forward. The Department of Commerce now has a vast amount of industrial data very well integrated.

Because national income accounting is of far-reaching importance, because it is statistical by nature, and because it involves a broad coverage of both economic theory and data, it was decided to make an extended application of the visualizing technique to analyzing national income accounting. Then too the writer has had considerable association with men vitally interested in changes in national income. As president of an economic research and consulting firm which for a decade has specialized in forecasting the official national income figures, the writer has had occasion to review the problem technically and to learn about those aspects of the problem that seem to puzzle business economists and market research men. The writer concluded that there was a need for a small book especially designed for those economists who use national income figures in their routine work. Of course these men have available the National Income Supplement that is prepared by the United States Department of Commerce. But that source book deals with the subject in elaborate detail. It contains extensive explanations of how the figures were obtained and put together. In an official source book the statistical detail must be there, but some operating men want the ideas without all the statistical verification and background. The writer felt that there would be a market for a book with less detail that limited itself to explaining the logic of national income accounting along with only those tables that are most likely to be used by economists who use national income accounting data in their daily work.

Today businessmen systematically budget their future operations according to their expectations of what the economy as a whole will do. Other people adjust their personal affairs in line with the outlook for business. But how are they to know the state of the economy as a whole? There is only one agency that keeps books on it systematically, and that is the United States Department of Commerce. To understand its reports on the economy's performance, therefore, one must understand how the Department of Commerce measures that performance. Through all the pages that follow, the reader should bear in mind that the primary goal of the government economists and their national income accounting is to measure and report on what is happening to the nation's output. As the nation improves its science, its organization, and its tools, as its population and machines increase, the economists want to report quantitatively what is happening to the nation's real output.

The diagrams in this book are divided into two sets. The first set, Diagrams 1 to 29, is organizational only. It tries to show by easy steps the setting and rationale of national income accounting. The second set does three additional things:

1. It adds quantitative dimension to each element of flux in the economy. By so doing it gives a feeling for the magnitude of each action. By following these the reader can obtain for himself an integrated understanding of the economic relationships focused on in national income accounting.

2. It portrays the logic used by the Department of Commerce in its national income analyses and shows how the Department handled certain difficult conceptual problems such as savings, statistical discrepancy, rent, profit, interest, depreciation, and so forth. Accounting often had to be fitted to the limitations of the data.

3. It presents the Department of Commerce's six basic tables of accounts—statistical building blocks—and converts them into pictures of dynamic process. These six tables—reproduced in Section III—are:

I National Income and Product Account
II Consolidated Business Income and Product Account
III Personal Income and Expenditure Account
IV Consolidated Government Receipts and Expenditures Account
V Rest of the World Account
VI Gross Savings and Investment Account

These basic tables are statistical summaries, interlaced by the Department of Commerce to fit the rationale of its accounting. What that rationale is, and how the various concepts that make it up are interlaced, becomes quite clear when the tables are converted into diagrams.

While national income accounting is an ingenious way of measuring the economic activity of the United States, it is not perfect. One should consequently be careful not to attribute to gross national product figures more significance than they possess. For they measure only activity, not necessarily economic welfare as many writers imply. Because national income accounting deals with only the flow of receipts and expenditures of the major spending groups and does not deal concurrently with the changing assets and liabilities of these groups, it does not show the social price—often the severe price—in expanded debt and altered political power that society often pays for maintaining or lifting the level of gross national expenditures.

National income accounting regards all expenditures made for final goods and services as reflections of a genuine market demand. Dollars spent, for example, under the fixed ceiling-price conditions of an OPA and under the fixed floor-price conditions of an NRA are regarded as measuring an output that is just as genuine as that for which dollars are spent under free market conditions. Our economy could, therefore, conceivably shift from its present relatively free prices to the fixed prices of a communist or fascist state without gross national expenditure figures depicting any of the transition. Under such a condition—and it happened in Hitler's Germany—gross national expenditures could, and possibly would, continue upward. So it is not enough to regard rising dollar figures as reflecting an economic improvement of the community. Obviously we must concurrently watch what is happening both to the financial assets and liabilities of the major spending groups and to their political rights and duties, powers and privileges, liberties and exposures. But, so long as we view national income accounting in its proper sociological setting, it is a helpful invention and a superior gauge of how the economy is doing, for it is based on a very realistic conception of how our big industrial machine works.

The terms and concepts used in national income reporting have now been adopted by the Council of Economic Advisers as the official language for describing the interrelationships and performance of the nation's big industrial machine. Consequently, national income accounting is no longer the exclusive concern of the statistician, but also the understandable concern of the operating men of business and of every responsible citizen. For that reason this book of pictures, explaining the logic and procedures of national income accounting, is aimed particularly at making easily understandable a highly important matter that would otherwise remain in the field of specialists.

▶ Growth has averaged about 3 percent per year

CHART I

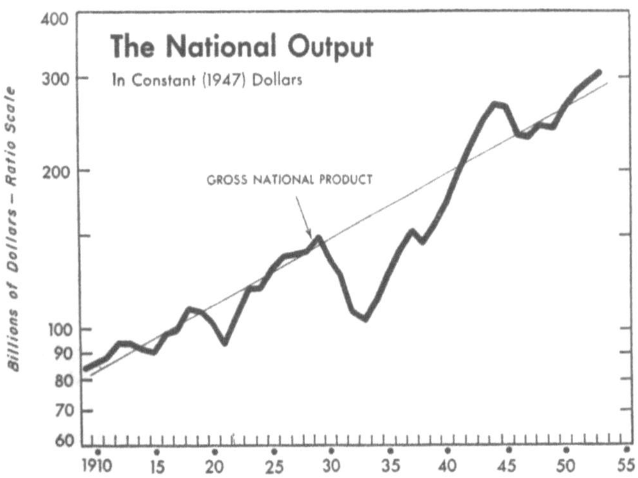

Source: U. S. Department of Commerce

CONTENTS

TABLES AND CHARTS

Section I

GROSS NATIONAL EXPENDITURES
ITS SOURCES AND PARTICIPANTS

PEOPLE ARE PRODUCERS, CONSUMERS, AND PARTICIPANTS IN GOVERNMENT

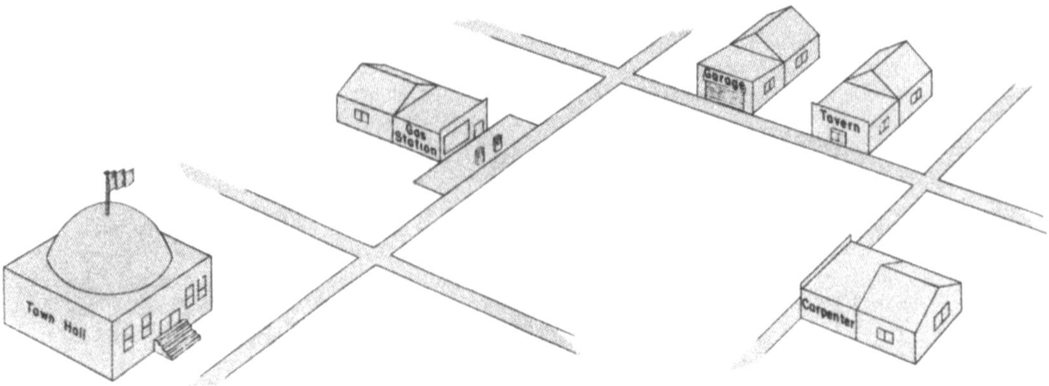

TRIPLE-ROLED PEOPLE CAN BE SYMBOLIZED AS THREE DISTINCT GROUPS

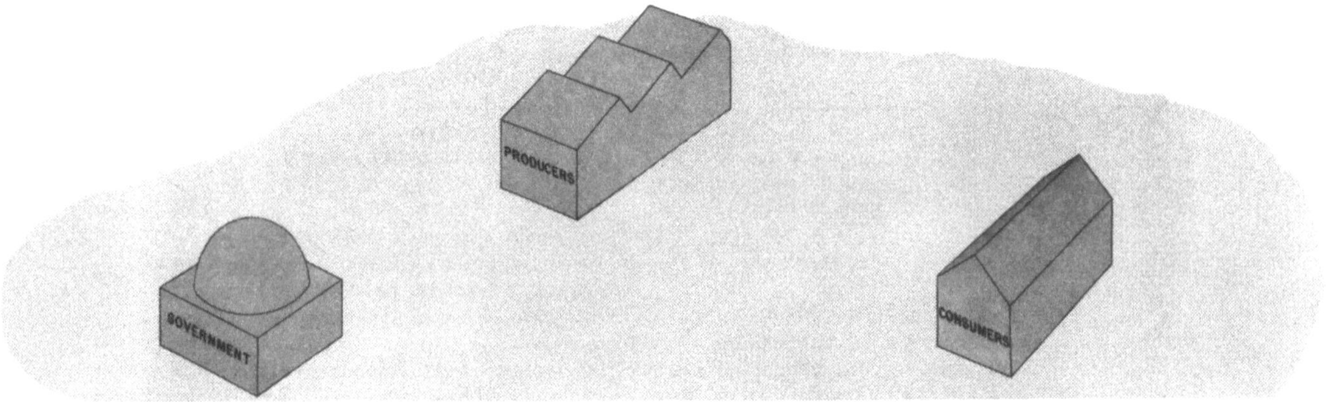

DIAGRAM 1

Scarcely anyone is a jack-of-all trades today. Almost everyone is a specialist. The family chores of our parents' time move increasingly out of the house. Shirts and sheets are laundered outside. Milking is done at the dairies. Dresses are made in the factories. Every producing home-owner offers only one or two highly specialized products to the community, even though he draws on the whole community for a wide variety of items in return. The baker, the laundryman, the garageman, the merchant, each a consumer of small amounts of hundreds of different goods and services, gives up in return big quantities of some specialized product or service. Measuring the changing output of goods and services from millions of producers to millions of consumers is the big concern of national income accounting.

This diagram introduces the system of symbols that we have devised to represent the various groups involved in the production and exchange of goods and services. We begin in the top part of Diagram 1 with a simple symbolic illustration of the dual economic activity of individuals. In the diagram, the same individual who is a specialized producer in the front or shop part of his house (the Carpenter, for example) is also a consumer in the back part of his house of a multitude of products supplied by others. Also shown is the Town Hall, where the political activity of the community takes place, where the voters meet to elect leaders and to pass laws. When voters act as a group through the agency of the Town Hall and their elected representatives, they delegate, as it were, considerable independence of spending action to the community representatives.

The Department of Commerce in its national income accounting keeps tab separately on people as producers and as consumers; for full coverage it must also keep tab separately on the producing and spending of individuals when they act as a government. In the lower part of Diagram 1, the people of the nation are classified separately as Producers, as Consumers, and as Government—as three groups which, according to national income accounting, are invested with discretion over spending.

In this lower part of Diagram 1 we show our system of symbols for the three groups: a single house-like structure to represent all individuals as consuming households, a factory-like structure to represent them as business producers, and a domed structure to represent them as government. With these symbols and a system of connecting pipes to represent economic flows, we are now ready to portray some of the major aspects of national income.

HOW GOVERNMENT CLASSIFIES THE GOODS AND SERVICES PRODUCED

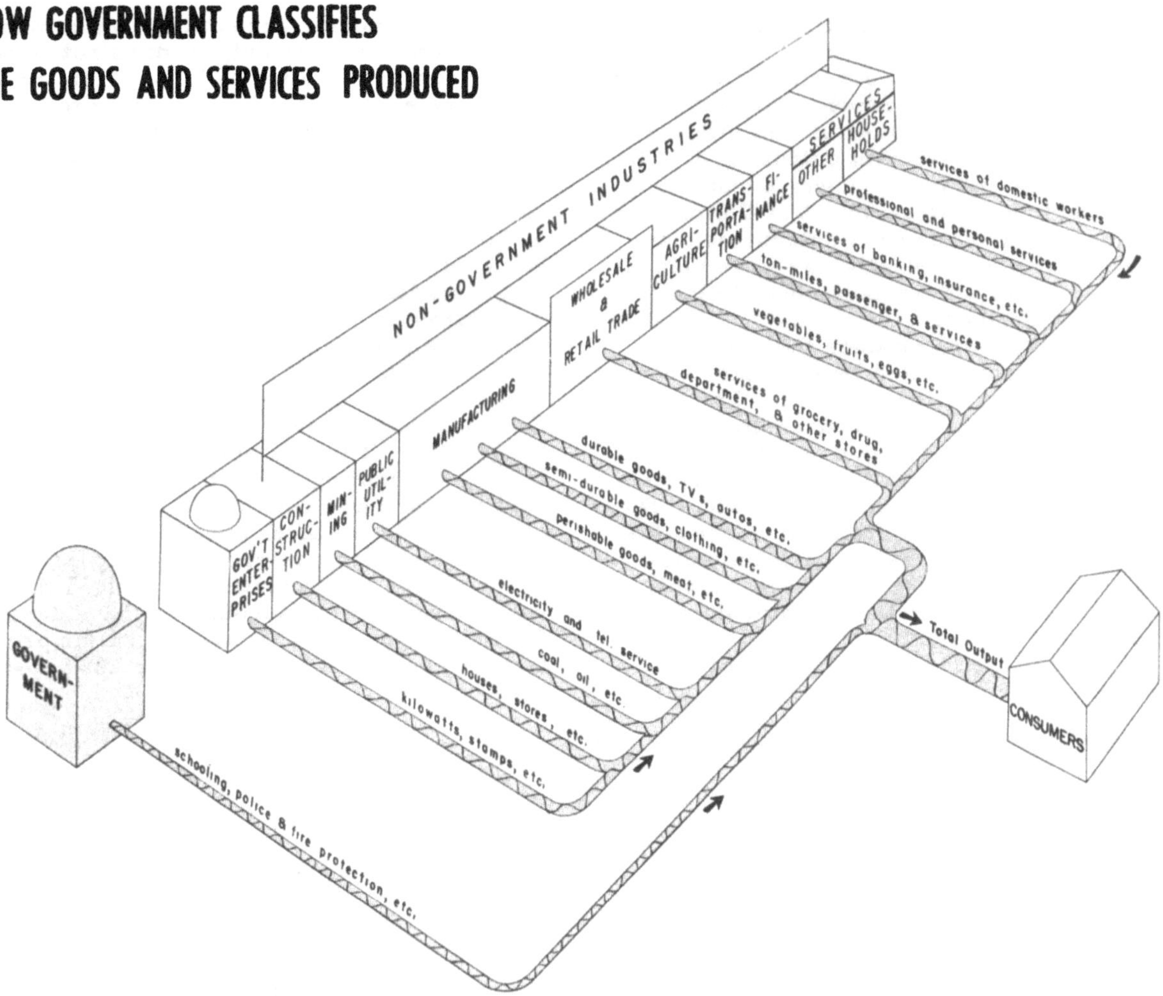

DIAGRAM 2

People acting as Business Enterprises, producing Households, and Government turn out hundreds of thousands of assorted goods and services. A major task for national income accounting is to collect data on this diversified activity in order to measure the total output. To facilitate the compilations and at the same time to provide a meaningful summary of activity, the Department of Commerce grouped the many kinds of economic activity into a small, manageable number of classifications. But, in order to get down to a reasonable number, decisions had to be made as to what constituted logical groups.

Classifying activity is a very difficult thing to do logically, since business does not organize its work to fit man-made definitions. When businessmen adapt resources and processes to turning out goods and services, they do so without any regard whatsoever to how statisticians might later want to define and classify what they do. The industrial groupings which the statisticians compile are based upon classification of the sales and income reports of individual companies. It is not always easy to decide in which category a company belongs, especially when its products cover a range wide enough to span more than one industrial grouping. So long as the classification bands are wide, such as those shown in Diagram 2, there is no big problem. But the finer the industrial breakdown, the more questionable the industry figures become.

How the Department of Commerce currently groups the activities of the nation's millions of producers into industrial classifications is portrayed in Diagram 2. There are nine major nongovernment industrial classifications and two government sectors. In the diagram we have illustrated only in general terms the kind of product that flows from each of these broad producing groups. Notice that the government appears twice as a producer. At the extreme left of the diagram, separated from all the other sectors, is the general Government—federal, and state, and local agencies. The output of the general Government consists of services such as schooling and police and fire protection. This service output of Government is classified separately by the Department of Commerce.

Besides producing these general services that are usually provided for entirely out of taxes, government produces other things as well. This activity is not included in general government, because its output is sold in the markets at a price. This secondary activity is carried on at a profit or a loss, more or less like the activity of private business enterprise. Because of this similarity, secondary government output, e. g., the postal service and public power production, is regarded by the Department of Commerce as being a part of business enterprise. In this diagram, consequently, we have placed the Government Enterprises close to the private enterprises.

Among those who produce the nation's service is a group called Households, shown in the upper part of the diagram. The major output of these producing households is the services turned out by the domestic workers they employ. (The output of housewives is not counted as part of national income.) Do these households differ from the households of consumers? Not really. The only distinction is that they are producers as well as consumers because they employ domestic workers.

Our symbolism is set up to distinguish between producers and consumers so that one can see more clearly the exchange or flow that must constantly go on between them.

National income accounting, which was designed to measure output, does not necessarily concern itself with "flow." Its reports are exclusively in accounting terms. It deals with receipts and expenditures or with profit and loss. These items necessarily imply flow; the income of one group is the outlay of another, or, as the Department of Commerce puts it, an entry in one table has a corresponding entry in another. Our diagrams take these tables one step further by portraying visually the flows of output which are only imputed in the tables.

The entire output of the nation, as classified and summarized by the Department of Commerce, is shown by the rivulets in Diagram 2. It is this output that national income accounting seeks to measure and report on—and how this output changes from one period to another. But how does the government measure changing output? What is the nature of the statistical gauges that its national income accountants have devised for the purpose? What are the major problems encountered and the major assumptions made?

TABLE A.

RELATIVE PRODUCTIVE IMPORTANCE OF MAJOR INDUSTRY GROUPS*

	Government	Government Enterprise	Construction	Mining	Communications & Public Utilities	Manufacturing	Wholesale & Retail Trade	Agriculture, Forestry, & Fisheries	Transportation	Finance, Insurance, & Real Estate	Services	Rest of World	Total Percent
	Percent of Total												
1929	4.9	.9	4.3	2.3	3.3	24.9	15.2	9.4	7.6	14.5	11.8	.9	100
1932	10.4	1.7	2.5	1.6	5.4	16.9	14.9	7.8	7.5	15.9	14.4	.9	100
1939	10.4	1.3	3.2	2.2	3.9	24.6	17.1	8.2	6.4	10.9	11.4	.4	100
1946	11.5	1.0	3.6	1.7	2.7	27.0	19.2	9.7	5.7	8.1	9.6	.3	100
1953	10.3	1.1	5.0	1.8	3.3	31.9	17.2	5.5	5.2	8.7	9.5	.5	100
1954	10.6	1.1	5.2	1.7	3.7	30.2	17.5	5.5	5.0	9.2	9.8	.5	100

*Based on National Income

THERE ARE THREE MAJOR PRODUCERS OF THE NATION'S OUTPUT

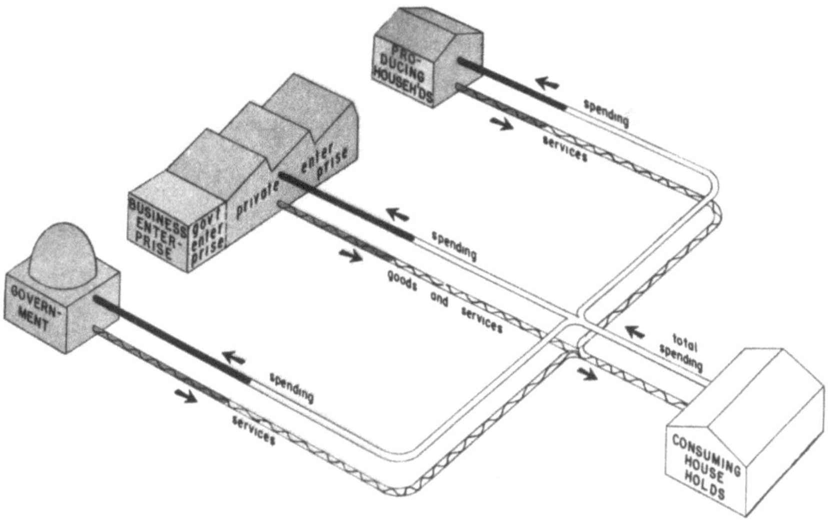

DIAGRAM 3

The output shown in Diagram 2 is the product of three major producers: Business, Government, and Producing Households. Diagram 3 shows that these producers supply their products to Consuming Households. (Foreign countries also contribute to our production, but their contribution percentagewise is so small that in order to simplify the portrayals we have chosen to omit showing it in these early diagrams.)

The output of Business Enterprise is fairly easy to imagine. It consists of the many durable, nondurable, and perishable goods described in the preceding diagram, plus the various services rendered by professional groups, by retail and wholesale establishments, by financial institutions, and so on. It is by far the largest producing group in the nation. Note in Diagram 3 that the Department of Commerce classifies the activity of Government Enterprise as being a parallel to Private Enterprise, and both as being a part of Business Enterprise. The Department of Commerce does this because some government enterprises sell their products and services (such as kilowatt hours and postal services) to consumers at a price and make either a profit or loss in doing so.

The general Government as a producer (shown to the left of Business Enterprise) furnishes the general services of schooling, fire and police protection, defense, and general administration.

There is also a third major producer, called Households. This classification covers Producing Households only, that is, only those comparatively few households which purchase services from paid servants and other workers. The output of housewives, which of course is the major part of private household activity, is excluded. Included in household activity, besides the services of hired domestic help, is the service output of workers who are paid by religious, charity, labor, and other nonbusiness establishments.

Logically one would think that the household services performed by housewives would be considered to be a part of national output along with the services of hired cooks and maids. But housewives do not produce for the market nor receive wages, and thus their contributions do not meet one of the Department of Commerce's key criteria for inclusion. The Department of Commerce, while apologizing for the inconsistency, finds the task of measuring the housewife's contribution to the nation's output so difficult that it has omitted that activity in its coverage. (If a rich bachelor hires a cook and pays her wages, then her services are counted as a part of national output. But if he marries the cook, her contribution is not counted and national output does down.)

Business Enterprise, Government, and Producing Households then are the three major producers of the nation's output, and it is their activity that is measured and reported on by the Department of Commerce.

THE TWO BASIC EXCHANGES IN ECONOMIC LIFE

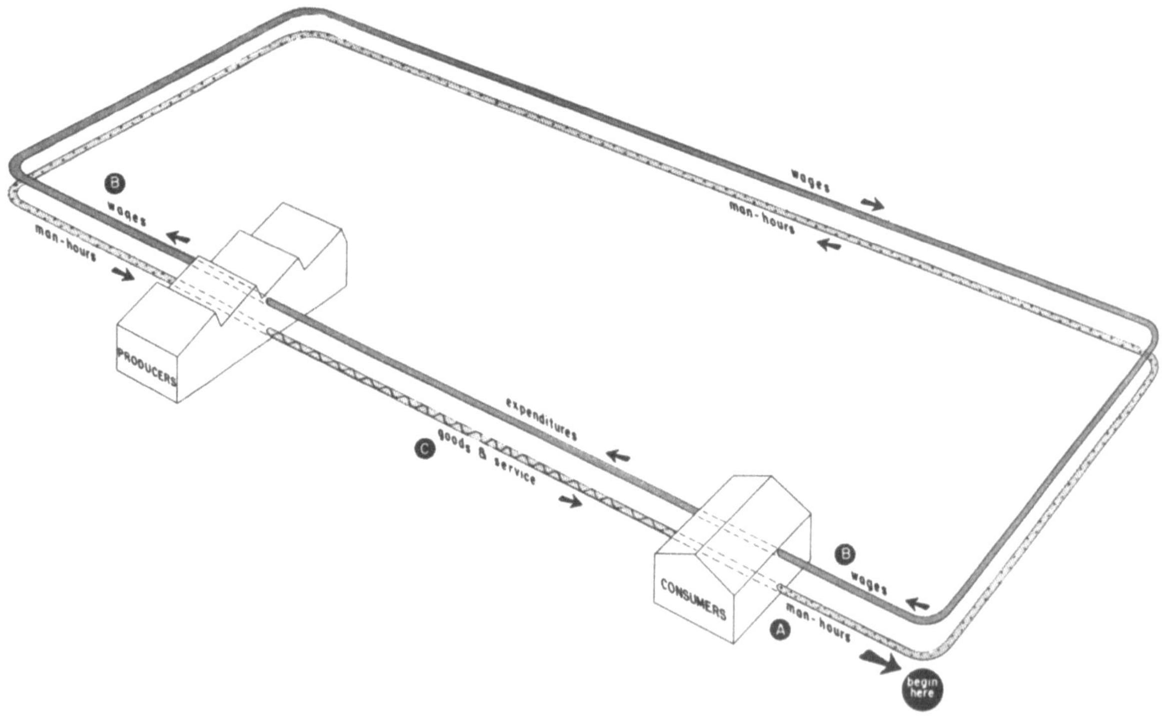

DIAGRAM 4

Diagrams 2 and 3 showed the total output flowing from the nation's producing establishments to the final consumers. These goods and services flow to the consumers mainly in exchange for money. Diagram 4 shows how consumers hand over their money (called expenditures) in order to obtain their goods and services. The interchange of productive services for money incomes and then of these money incomes for goods and services are the basic exchanges of economic life.

Thus there are two basic exchanges that go on continuously in economic life: (1) People first exchange their man-hours and other productive services for wages and other money income, and (2) they then exchange their money income for goods and services. People constantly act in the dual role of producers and consumers, and both roles involve a continuous exchange of money. In Diagram 4, beginning with the Consumers, we see how they bring their Man-Hours (A) to the Producers' factories and in return for these Man-Hours receive Wages (B). The Wages that they bring home constitute consumer buying power. Consumers can now spend these Wages for the Goods and Services (C) turned out by the Producers, thus completing a circuit of basic exchanges. National income accounting is made up of many such exchanges. There are of course other elements besides man-hours needed to produce output—elements such as land and capital—just as there are sources of consumer income other than wages—sources such as rent and interest. As we proceed with the development of national income accounting, it will become clear that the flows of money, man-hours, raw materials, finished goods, and the like are all variations of and additions to the two basic exchange circuits shown. (There are some items in national income which do not involve exchange or flows at all, and it would seem that our symbolism does not apply in those cases. To illustrate, the Department of Commerce includes an item in consumption expenditures called "value of food produced and consumed on farms." In this case, as in all other imputations, there is really no exchange of money for goods. It is only that the Department of Commerce assigns an equivalent market value to the products consumed and in that way imputes a value to them. Our symbolism correspondingly imputes a flow for those items.)

U.S. OUTPUT CAN BE MEASURED IN FOUR DIFFERENT WAYS

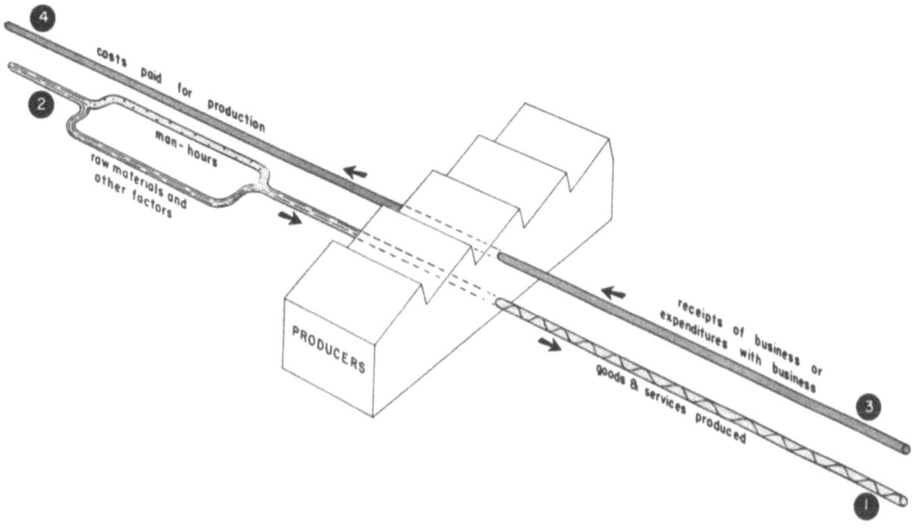

DIAGRAM 5

Because economic activity consists of exchanges, as shown in the preceding diagram, it is theoretically possible to measure the production performance of the nation—the changing volume of goods and services—in different ways. Diagram 5 is an abbreviated adaptation from Diagram 4, and it brings into focus the flow of money and of goods and services in and out of the business building alone. In this diagram the business sector of the economy is used, for the sake of simplicity, to represent all of the nation's productive enterprises.

One could theoretically measure directly the output of goods and services shown coming out of Stream 1 in terms of the number of houses built, coal mined, wheat raised, autos made, operas given, teeth filled, or ingots poured. But, as Diagram 2 showed, the stream of products pouring out at Stream 1 is made up of hundreds of thousands of different kinds of goods and services. Obviously, it is impossible to find a physical or tangible common denominator for measuring the total output of such a wide variety of items in a meaningful way.

Theoretically too the volume of output might be measured by calculating the input of man-hours and other factors shown flowing into the building by way of Stream 2. This may be a fairly reasonable approach in some fields, e.g., textiles and armament production. One could use the input of bales of cotton as a measure of the activity in defense production, but recourse to measuring output through the use of input data is at best very limited. For one thing, the output per man-hour has to be accounted for. And how can one measure this rapidly changing item accurately?

National income economists have concluded that dollar expenditures and accounting transfers involved in the production and distribution of the total goods and services produced provide the only practical common denominator. Consequently they measure the nation's changing output exclusively in dollar (and imputed dollar) terms. These dollar exchanges are sketched in Diagram 5 as Streams 3 and 4. Stream 3 represents all the dollars spent by consumers in the markets to purchase the output of finished goods and services. Stream 4 shows all the dollars paid out as costs in the labor markets, capital markets, and land markets for the labor and other productive factors needed to turn out the goods and services produced. Stream 3, when blown up to full coverage and properly qualified, becomes Gross National Expenditures in national income accounting; and Stream 4, when blown up to full coverage and properly qualified, becomes National Income. In the next few charts we shall discover which groups contribute to the total gross national spending and how the Department of Commerce arrives at its figures.

THE CONSUMER MAKES THE LARGEST EXPENDITURES FOR GOODS AND SERVICES

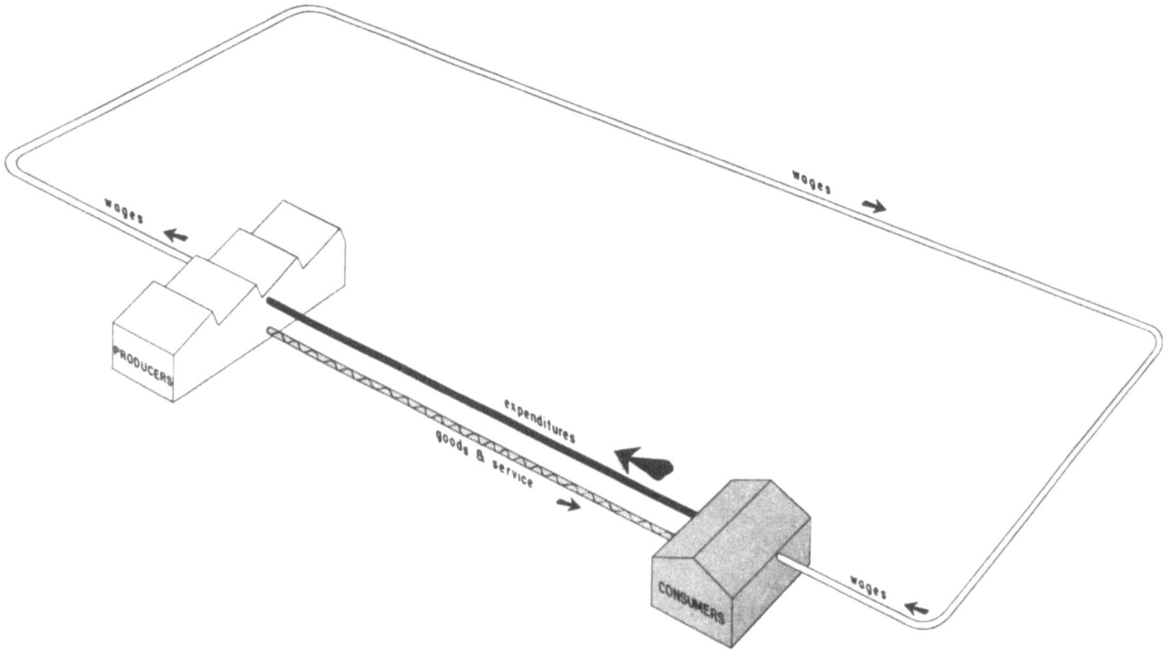

DIAGRAM 6

Consumers are the largest buyer of the nation's output, just as business is the largest producer. They buy about 70 to 80 percent of the total volume of goods and services produced for final use.

What do they buy? The Department of Commerce keeps records on the hundreds of different items consumers purchase and then tabulates the purchases in several ways. The simplest classification used is (a) durable goods items, (b) nondurable goods items, and (c) services.

The Department of Commerce then presents another summary tabulation of consumer expenditures by twelve different classifications: Food and tobacco, Clothing and accessories, Personal care, Housing, Household operation, Medical care, and so on. Then it breaks down each of these classifications into more subgroups.

The availability of such detailed information on consumer spending is very helpful. Where the consumers' money goes, how they allocate their expenditures among various product groups, which groups are being favored and which are losing out are useful facts to know, not only for general economic analysis but for helpful and intelligent decisions in day-to-day living. Which industries offer the best job opportunities, for example, or which offer the most growth opportunity for investment, can be better known because of the availability or information on consumer spending.

TABLE B. —*Personal consumption expenditures, 1929–55*

[Billions of dollars]

Period	Total personal consumption expenditures	Durable goods: Total	Durable goods: Automobiles and parts	Durable goods: Furniture and household equipment	Durable goods: Other	Nondurable goods: Total	Nondurable goods: Food excluding alcoholic beverages	Nondurable goods: Clothing and shoes	Nondurable goods: Gasoline and oil	Nondurable goods: Other	Services: Total	Services: Housing	Services: Household operation	Services: Transportation	Services: Other
1929	79.0	9.2	3.2	4.8	1.2	37.7	19.5	9.4	1.8	7.0	32.1	11.4	4.0	2.6	14.0
1930	71.0	7.2	2.2	3.9	1.1	34.0	18.0	8.0	1.7	6.3	29.8	11.0	3.9	2.2	12.7
1931	61.3	5.5	1.6	3.1	.9	28.9	14.7	6.9	1.5	5.7	26.9	10.3	3.5	1.9	11.2
1932	49.3	3.6	.9	2.1	.6	22.8	11.4	5.1	1.5	4.8	22.9	9.0	3.0	1.6	9.3
1933	46.4	3.5	1.1	1.9	.5	22.3	10.9	4.6	1.5	5.3	20.7	7.9	2.8	1.5	8.5
1934	51.9	4.2	1.4	2.2	.6	26.7	12.2	5.7	1.6	7.2	21.0	7.6	3.0	1.6	8.8
1935	56.3	5.1	1.9	2.6	.7	29.3	13.6	6.0	1.7	7.9	21.9	7.6	3.2	1.7	9.4
1936	62.6	6.3	2.3	3.2	.8	32.8	15.2	6.6	1.9	9.1	23.5	7.9	3.4	1.9	10.3
1937	67.3	6.9	2.4	3.6	1.0	35.2	16.4	6.8	2.1	9.8	25.1	8.4	3.7	2.0	11.1
1938	64.6	5.7	1.6	3.1	.9	34.0	15.6	6.8	2.1	9.5	25.0	8.8	3.6	1.9	10.7
1939	67.6	6.7	2.2	3.5	1.0	35.1	15.7	7.1	2.2	10.1	25.8	9.0	3.8	2.0	11.0
1940	71.9	7.8	2.7	3.9	1.1	37.2	16.7	7.4	2.3	10.8	26.9	9.3	4.0	2.1	11.4
1941	81.9	9.7	3.4	4.9	1.4	43.2	19.4	8.8	2.6	12.3	29.0	10.0	4.3	2.4	12.3
1942	89.7	7.0	.7	4.7	1.6	51.3	23.7	11.0	2.1	14.5	31.5	10.8	4.8	2.7	13.1
1943	100.5	6.6	.8	3.9	1.9	59.3	27.8	13.4	1.3	16.7	34.7	11.3	5.2	3.4	14.7
1944	109.8	6.8	.8	3.8	2.2	65.4	30.6	14.6	1.4	18.7	37.7	11.9	5.9	3.7	16.3
1945	121.7	8.1	1.0	4.6	2.5	73.2	34.1	16.5	1.8	20.8	40.4	12.4	6.4	4.0	17.5
1946	146.6	15.9	3.9	8.7	3.3	84.5	40.4	18.2	3.0	22.8	46.2	13.6	6.7	5.1	20.8
1947	165.0	20.6	6.3	11.0	3.4	93.1	45.6	18.8	3.6	25.1	51.3	15.4	7.4	5.5	23.0
1948	177.6	22.2	7.3	11.5	3.4	98.7	49.4	19.6	4.3	25.5	56.7	17.5	8.0	5.9	25.2
1949	180.6	23.6	9.5	10.9	3.2	96.9	48.8	18.5	4.7	24.9	60.1	19.4	8.5	5.8	26.4
1950	194.0	28.6	12.4	12.9	3.3	100.4	51.0	18.5	5.0	25.9	65.0	21.4	9.4	5.8	28.5
1951	208.3	27.1	10.9	12.7	3.5	111.1	58.3	19.8	5.5	27.4	70.1	23.4	10.3	6.4	30.0
1952	218.3	26.6	10.4	12.5	3.7	116.0	61.3	20.1	6.0	28.6	75.7	25.6	11.1	6.8	32.1
1953	230.6	29.8	13.2	12.8	3.9	118.9	63.0	19.8	6.6	29.5	81.8	27.9	12.1	7.3	34.6
1954	236.5	29.3	12.5	12.9	3.9	120.9	64.5	19.7	7.2	29.5	86.4	29.8	12.6	7.3	36.8
1955	252.4	35.3	16.9	14.3	4.2	125.9	67.1	20.6	7.7	30.6	91.1	31.2	13.6	7.4	38.9

CHART 2 PERSONAL CONSUMPTION EXPENDITURES

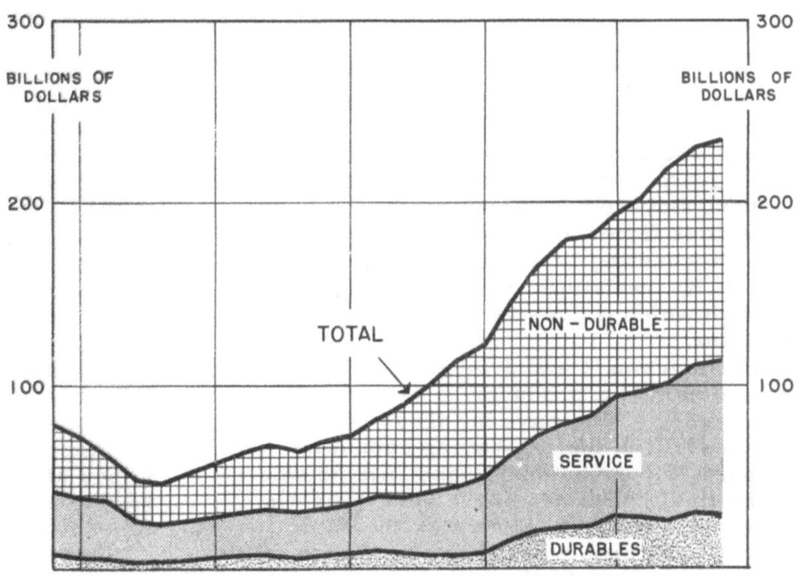

THE GOVERNMENT IS A MAJOR SPENDER FOR GOODS AND SERVICES

A. THE CONSUMER PAYS FOR GOVERNMENT SERVICES VIA TAXES

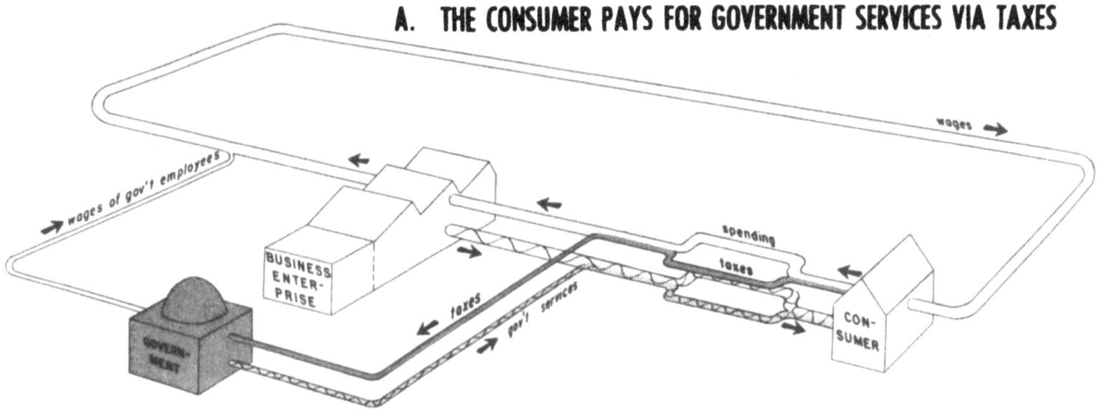

B. BUT THE GOVERNMENT SPENDS THE CONSUMER'S TAX MONEY FOR HIM

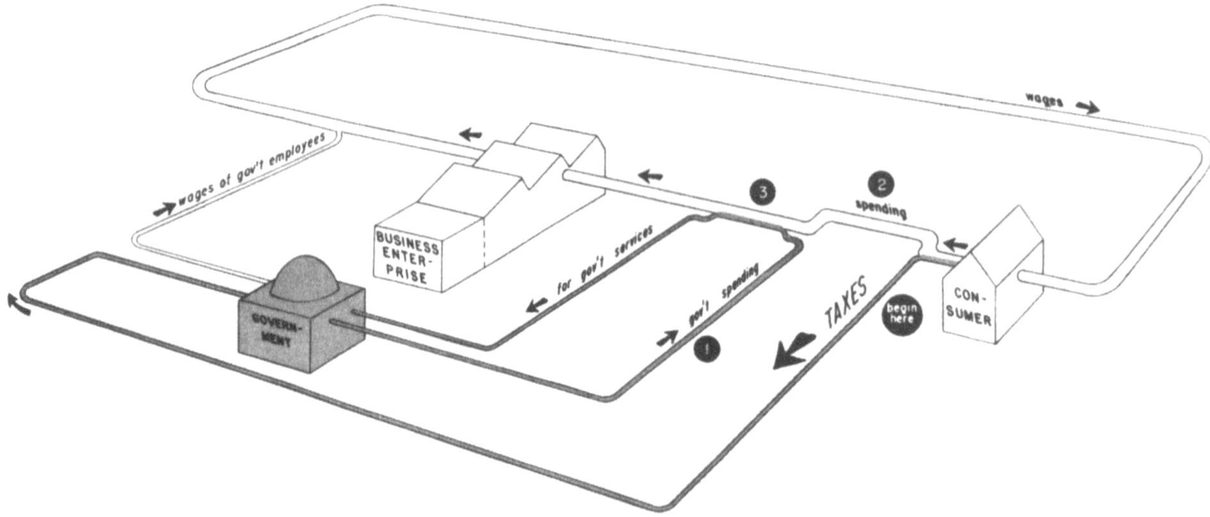

DIAGRAM 7

Government as well as household Consumers buys a part of the nation's output. Spending thus can be considered to be a second economic function of Government. In Diagram 7, A and B, we concentrate on showing Government as a spender or buyer. What does Government buy? In national income accounting Government buys the Services of its own employees. The channels through which it does this are shown in the two panels.

In Diagrams 2 and 3 we showed how the government is a producer of services for its citizens. Who pays for these services? Obviously it is the tax-paying consumer who supports the government, and it is he who is the final consumer of the government's services. Panel A illustrates the basic reality. As people set up governments, they divert tax money to them and receive services in return. This is a simple and realistic exchange of government services for the taxes of contributors. But in national income accounting taxpayers are not regarded as the purchasers of government service.

In national income accounting, people in their role of participants in government are regarded as a separate spending group, a group with discretion of its own in buying more or less goods and services. Consequently, the Department of Commerce regards Government and not household Consumers as the purchaser of the government produced Services. It is Government which disburses the tax money into the total spending stream, as shown in the lower panel of Diagram 7. Government Spending (1) obtained from taxes is, for example, added to the Consumers' Spending for goods and services (2) In the diagram the two are joined at (3) to provide a subtotal of two of the big expenditures contributing to total expenditures.

Thus, instead of buying the services of government workers directly, as was suggested by the top panel of Diagram 7, people buy them indirectly, as is shown in the lower panel. The tax money of household Consumers, for example, flows to the Government as receipts. Then the Govern-

CHART 3 PERSONAL TAXES, 1929-1954

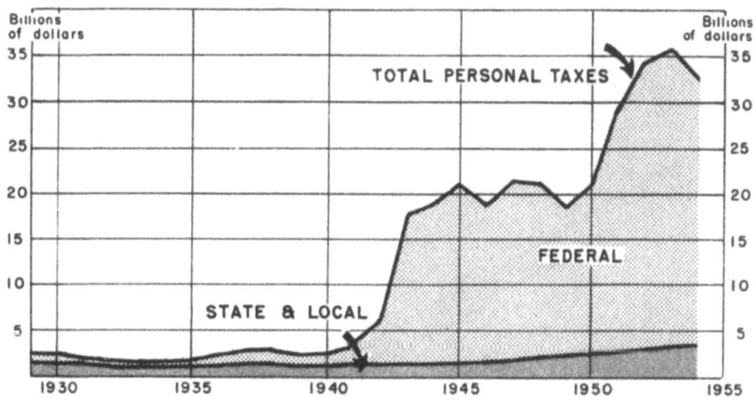

For data see Table 3 in Appendix

ment—not the household Consumer—pours the tax revenues into the total spending stream (3) and proceeds to pull off from that total the part that it uses to pay the wages and salaries of the employees who render the services. The amount of total spending in both of the situations pictured is the same. It is only that the route by which the funds get into the total spending stream is different. In the lower panel it becomes clear that the spending decisions lie with the Government and not with the Consumer.

GOVERNMENT SPENDS TO BUY GOODS AND SERVICES FROM BUSINESS

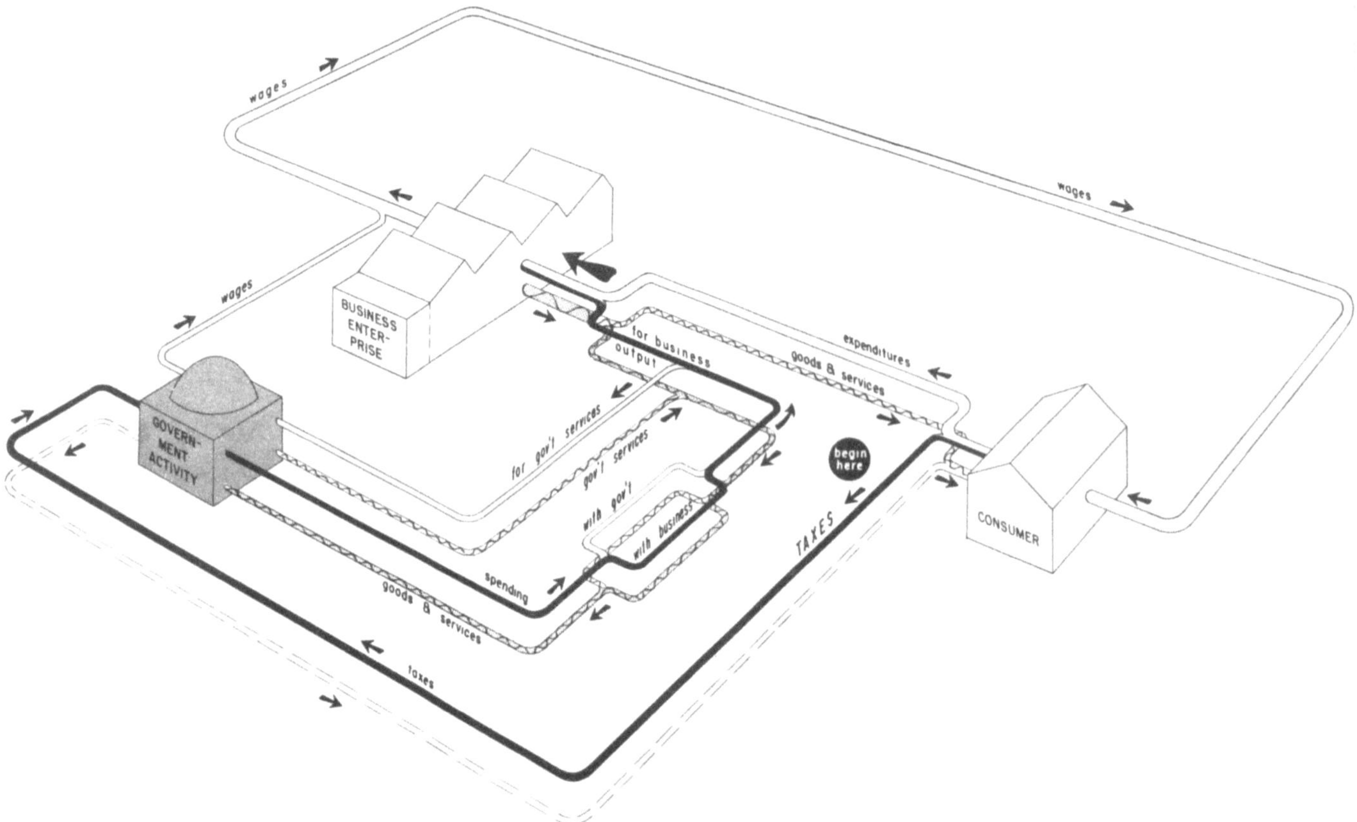

DIAGRAM 8

Taxes provide for more than the employment of government workers—that is, for more than the production of government services. Legislators keep taxes high enough to permit the government to purchase other things too—that is, to substitute its own demands for goods and services for the demands that the consumers would otherwise express directly in buying goods from business.

Diagram 8 shows how taxes provide not only enough money to pay the teachers, soldiers, policemen, and judges who produce the government services, but much more besides. Legislators collect extra amounts so that government can buy from private business items like highways, aircraft, tanks, and the like, which are considered essential to taxpayers' welfare and security. Thus the taxpayer uses his government to some extent as his agent for buying goods and services from private business.

The goods purchased by government from private business are bought for the benefit of the citizens and are really used by them, not by the government. But because government is the spender, it can also implicitly be regarded as a final "consumer." Consequently, in Diagram 8 we show the return stream of business product purchased by Government ending in the government building and not continuing to flow all the way back to the Consumer, as is suggested by the broken line.

We see now that, in terms of national income accounting, Government carries on four separate activities:

1. It is a producer of government services,
2. It is a substitute spender for the household consumer in buying services from government employees,
3. It is a substitute spender for the household consumer in buying goods and services from private business,
4. It is implicitly a consumer of all the goods and services it purchases.

GOVERNMENT SPENDING FOR GOODS & SERVICES, 1929-1954

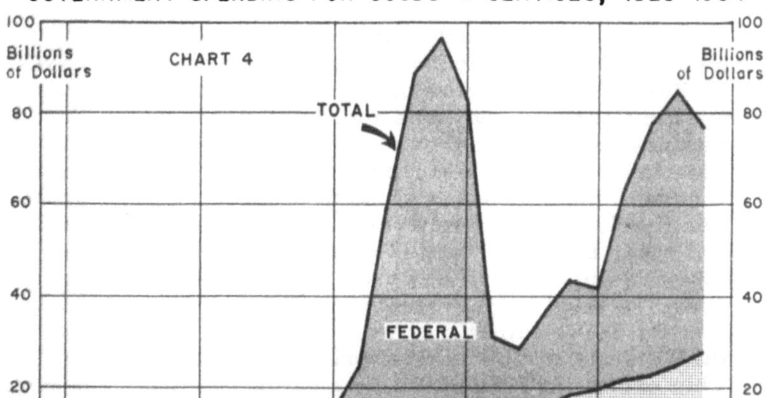

For data see Table 2 in Appendix

BUSINESS IS A THIRD MAJOR SPENDER FOR GOODS AND SERVICES

(IT TOO ACTS AS SUBSTITUTE SPENDER FOR CONSUMERS)

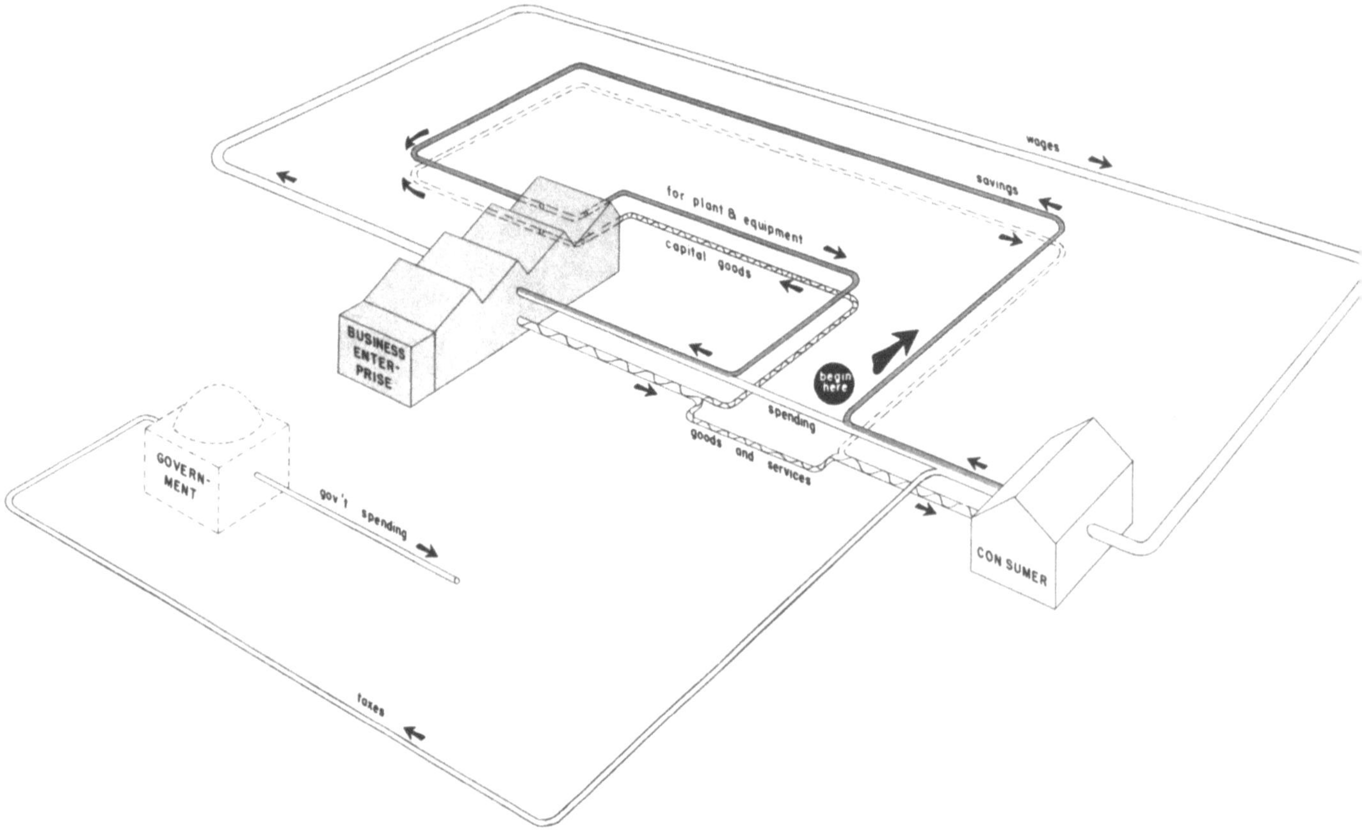

DIAGRAM 9

Just as Government buys goods and services for the Consumer with his tax money, so Business Enterprise buys some goods for the Consumer with his money savings. Business spending here is confined to business investment in plant and equipment, and it covers the purchases of (1) new construction (residential, commercial, industrial and other building), and (2) machinery and other equipment. In a sense, Business also "buys" a third item, namely, inventories. For Business sometimes produces more than it sells to Consumers and Government. This excess of production over sales is kept in inventory bins and, because Business finances the goods held in inventories until they are sold, the Department of Commerce figures that these inventories are temporarily purchased by Business.

When Business invests Consumers' savings in plant and equipment, we do not usually think of it as being substitute spending for the household Consumer. But it is essentially that. Individuals do entrust a large part of their savings to banks and insurance companies, which in turn invest the savings for them in plant and equipment. Often, too, individuals invest directly in the business by turning over their savings in exchange for securities. In both instances the individuals' funds are handed over to business, either directly or indirectly, and business exercises the discretion over spending them. Sometimes business is tardy in respending the funds as rapidly as it receives them. At other times business spends more than it receives from savers by borrowing new money from the commercial banks and spending that money too for plant and equipment. Although the volatility of such spending behavior reflects itself in both gross expenditure and national income totals, the source of the money spent is not reported fully in national income accounting.

TABLE C. *—Gross private domestic investment, 1929–55*

[Billions of dollars]

Period	Total gross private domestic investment	Nonfarm producers' plant and equipment			Farm equipment and construction			Residential construction (nonfarm)	Other private construction	Net change in business inventories		
		Total	Equipment	Construction	Total	Equipment	Construction			Total	Nonfarm	Farm
1929	16.2	9.3	5.2	4.1	0.9	0.6	0.3	3.6	0.7	1.7	1.8	−0.2
1930	10.3	7.2	4.0	3.3	.7	.5	.2	2.1	.7	−.4	−.1	−.3
1931	5.5	4.4	2.6	1.8	.4	.3	.1	1.6	.5	−1.3	−1.6	.3
1932	.9	2.4	1.4	1.0	.2	.1		.6	.2	−2.6	−2.6	
1933	1.4	2.2	1.5	.8	.2	.1		.5	.1	−1.6	−1.4	−.3
1934	2.9	2.9	2.1	.9	.3	.3	.1	.6	.1	−1.1	.2	−1.3
1935	6.3	3.7	2.7	1.0	.5	.4	.1	1.0	.1	.9	.4	.5
1936	8.4	5.0	3.6	1.4	.7	.5	.2	1.6	.2	1.0	2.1	−1.1
1937	11.7	6.5	4.5	2.1	.8	.6	.2	1.9	.2	2.2	1.7	.5
1938	6.7	4.7	3.1	1.5	.7	.5	.2	2.0	.3	−.9	−1.0	.1
1939	9.3	5.3	3.7	1.6	.7	.5	.2	2.7	.3	.4	.3	.1
1940	13.2	6.9	4.9	2.0	.8	.6	.2	3.0	.3	2.2	1.9	.3
1941	18.1	8.6	6.1	2.5	1.1	.8	.3	3.5	.3	4.5	4.0	.5
1942	9.9	5.3	3.7	1.6	.9	.7	.3	1.7	.2	1.8	.7	1.2
1943	5.6	4.6	3.5	1.1	.8	.6	.3	.9	.1	−.8	−.6	−.2
1944	7.1	6.2	4.7	1.5	1.0	.7	.3	.8	.1	−1.0	−.6	−.4
1945	10.4	9.2	6.9	2.3	1.0	.7	.3	1.1	.2	−1.1	−.6	−.5
1946	27.1	14.8	10.0	4.8	1.6	.7	.9	4.0	.6	6.1	6.4	−.2
1947	29.7	20.7	15.0	5.7	3.0	1.6	1.4	6.3	.7	−1.0	1.3	−2.3
1948	41.2	23.5	16.8	6.7	2.9	2.3	1.5	8.6	1.0	4.2	3.0	1.1
1949	32.5	21.7	15.3	6.4	4.0	2.5	1.5	8.3	1.3	−2.7	−1.9	−.9
1950	51.2	25.5	18.5	7.0	4.2	2.6	1.6	12.6	1.5	7.4	6.4	.9
1951	56.9	29.1	20.4	8.8	4.7	2.8	1.8	11.0	1.7	10.4	9.0	1.4
1952	49.6	29.7	20.6	9.1	4.4	2.5	1.9	11.1	1.6	2.8	2.1	.6
1953	51.4	32.3	21.9	10.3	4.2	2.5	1.7	11.9	1.8	1.2	1.9	−.7
1954	47.2	30.8	20.2	10.6	3.7	2.1	1.6	13.5	2.1	−2.9	−3.2	.4
1955	59.4	33.3	21.3	12.0	3.8	2.5	1.4	16.6	2.3	3.3	3.1	.2

Source: Economic Report of the President, 1956

Today, business itself finances a large part of its capital expenditures through depreciation reserves and earnings; business does not have to rely solely upon the savings which individuals make available to it. But, even so, the nation's plant and equipment (except in some isolated cases of government ownership) are the collective property of individuals who possess the ownership claims to both corporate and noncorporate business.

Like the Government, Business too is considered in the accounting of the Department of Commerce to be the final consumer of the plant and equipment that it purchases, even though, realistically, both plant and equipment are owned collectively by the groups in the community who have passed their savings on to the business managers. One can therefore consider that the capital goods bought by Business flows on to Consumers, as indicated by the broken line in the diagram.

Thus we see that, in the Department of Commerce's accounting, Business—like Government—carries on several distinct activities:

1. It is a producer of a wide variety of goods and services,

2. It is a substitute spender for consumers,

3. It is a consumer of the goods bought with funds diverted to it by individuals.

THE THREE SPENDERS ARE THE THREE FINAL CONSUMERS

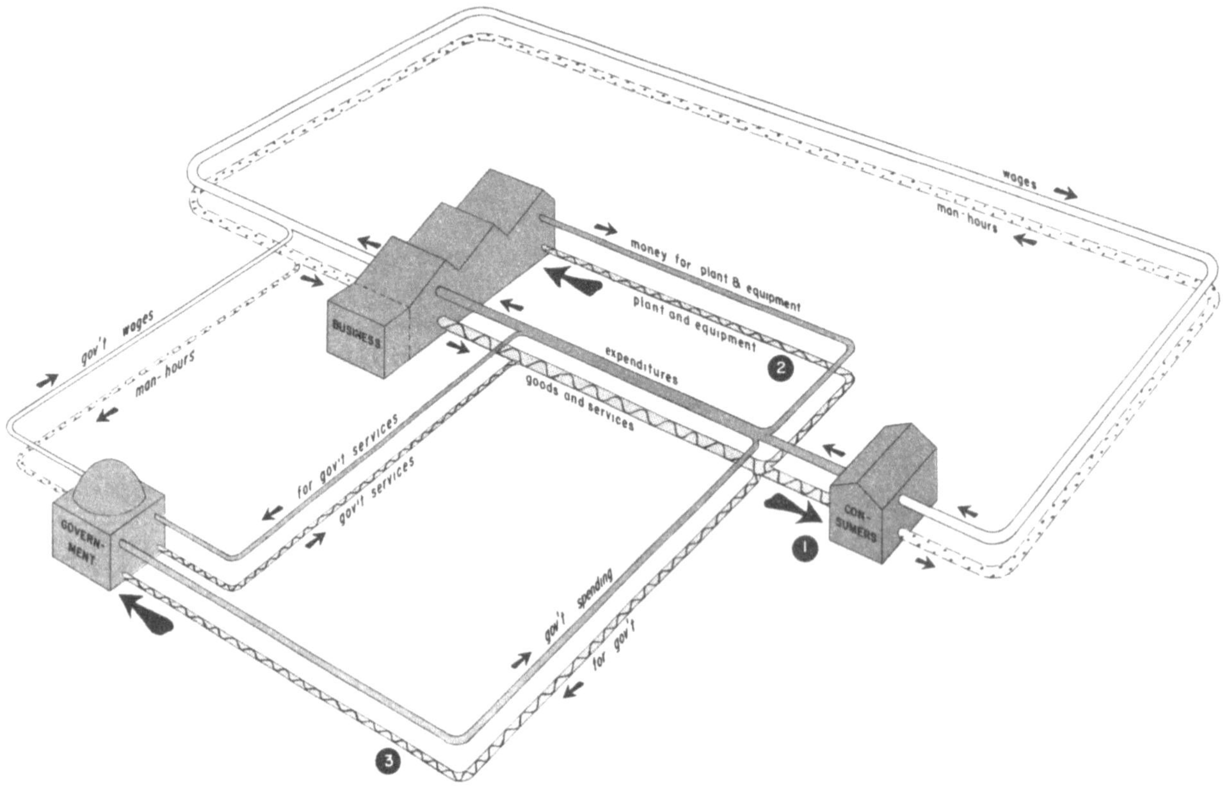

DIAGRAM 10

Diagram 3, which pictured the three major producers of the nation's output, portrayed the consumer in the households as being the only recipient of the total output. In the long run he is. But at any particular time (as shown in Diagrams 8 and 9) the two other groups (business and government) which act as spending agents for the consumer can also be considered as being final consumers. This is shown in Diagram 10, where the return flow of goods (Streams 1, 2, and 3) exchanged for the money spent terminates in the very three building where the spending originates.

Business corporations and governments, being inanimate, cannot, of course, consume anything. It is human beings who use and wear out both the buildings and equipment that organized business buys for them with their savings, and the tanks and aircraft that the government buys for them with their taxes.

But, because of organizational arrangements, both the managers of business and the officials of government have considerable discretion over how much they will spend of the money entrusted to them, when they will spend it, and for what they will spend it. Because the volume of goods and services returning to business and government is synchronized with their expenditures, it is as easy and convenient from a statistical point of view to regard Business and Government as consumers as it is to regard them as spenders.

Diagram 10 integrates the spending and implied consuming roles (Streams 1, 2, and 3) of the three organizational groups: Consumers, Business, and Government.

THE RELATIVE FLUCTUATIONS IN SPENDING, 1929 - 1950

Domestic investment per capita has shown the widest swings in the general business fluctuations since 1929 in real terms . . .

CHART 5

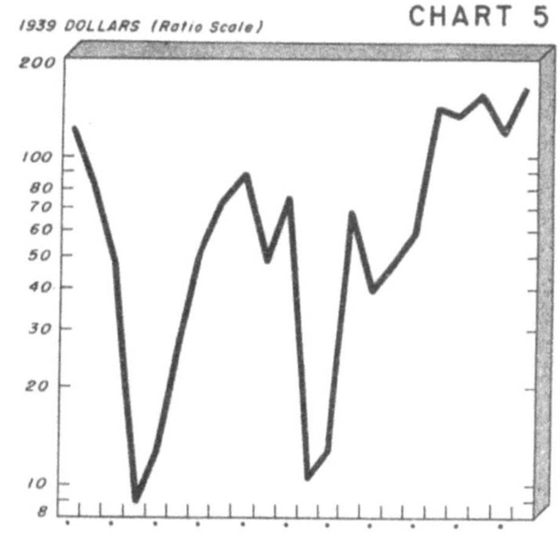

while real consumption expenditures per capita have been relatively stable, but expanding substantially since mid-nineteen thirties.

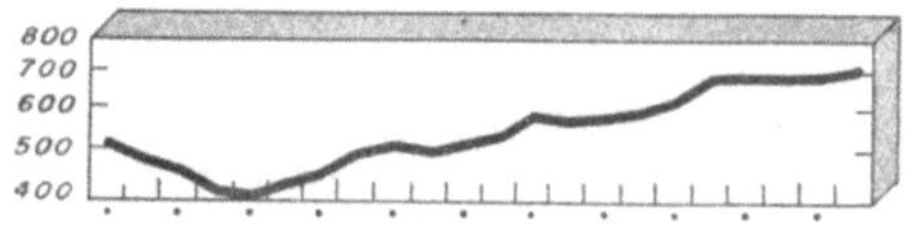

Except for the World War II years, real government expenditures per capita have tended steadily upward.

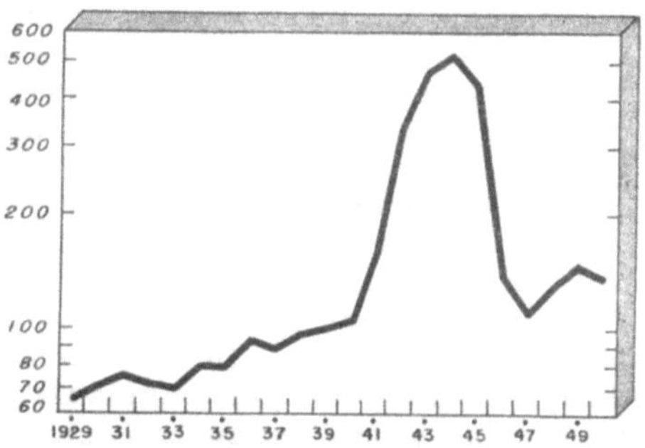

Source: Survey of Current Business, 1950

THE TOTAL SPENDING OF THE THREE GROUPS IS CALLED "GROSS NATIONAL EXPENDITURES"

(THIS TOTAL SPENDING IS ONE OF THE MAJOR MEASURES OF U.S. OUTPUT)

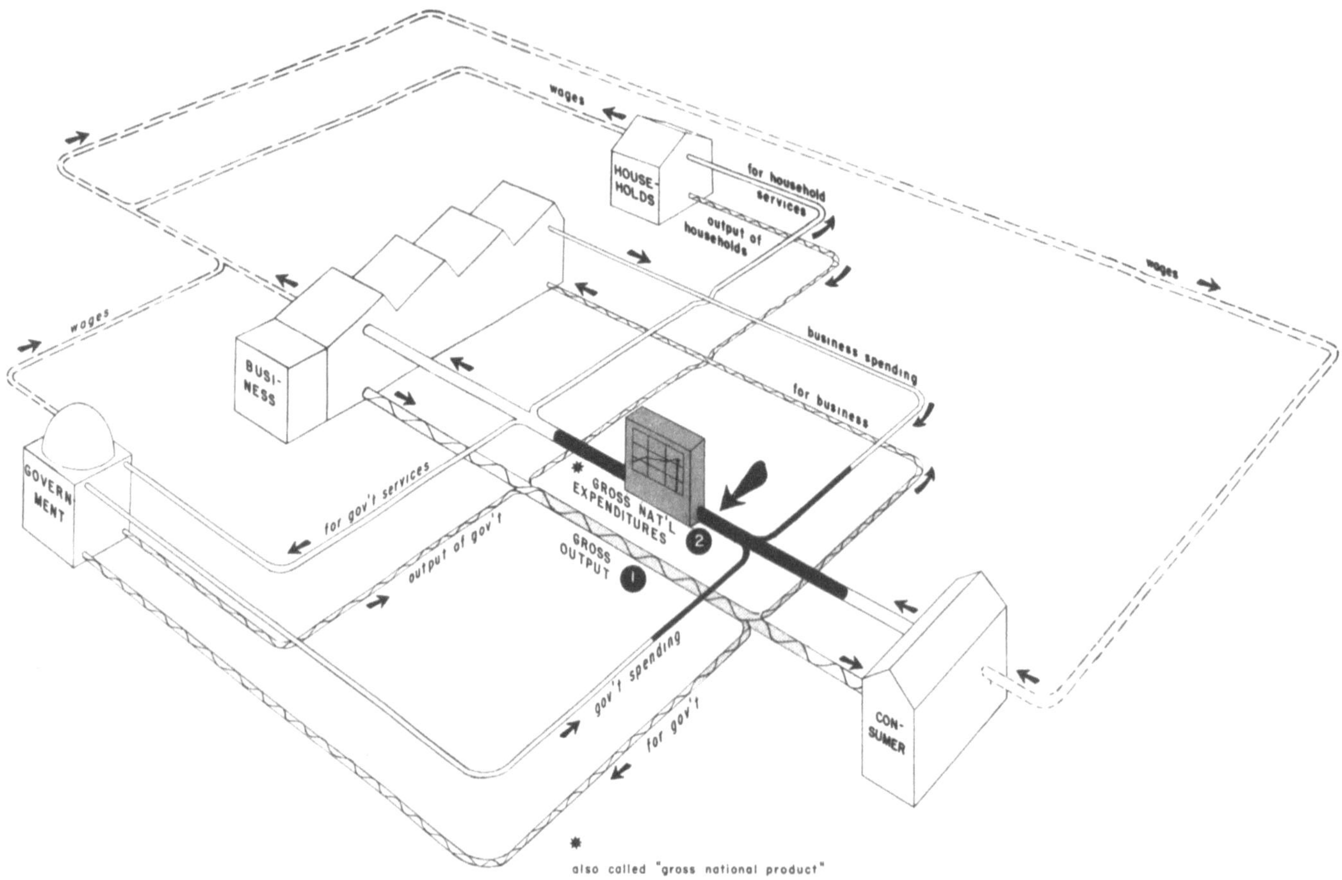

DIAGRAM 11

Gross National Expenditures is the sum of all expenditures by the three major spending groups.[1] Logically, the total value of all the goods and services purchased by these groups can be viewed as the total value of all the goods and services produced for these groups. When viewed in this second way—that is, when expenditures are viewed as the value (or exchange) equivalent of production—the total expenditures are called Gross National Product.

The common practice of using the term "Gross National Product" quite interchangeably with "Gross National Expenditures" has led to considerable confusion. For the two terms are only numerical value equivalents. They are not conceptual equivalents. Semantically the term "expenditures" suggests money outlays, whereas "product" suggests the volume of goods and services produced. What makes the term "product" particularly confusing is the fact that the Department of Commerce uses it to mean not the volume but the value of the goods and services produced. Diagram 11 helps to resolve the confusion. It shows how the two terms "expenditures" and "product" (Stream 2), as used by the Department of Commerce, are really dollar equivalents and how they are related to a stream of real (or volume) output shown at Stream 1. But, as stressed in Diagram 5, no measure of gross output at Stream 1 is directly available.

Diagram 11 is one of the major summary diagrams, for it recapitulates key steps in the development and presentation of the Department of Commerce's measure of output called "Gross National Expenditures," and completes this part of the income story.

The diagram highlights the fact that Gross National Expenditures is equal to the sum of the spending by the three major groups—consumer and government spending for goods and services, plus business spending for

[1] Actually, there is a fourth group whose spending contributes to the total, the "Rest of the World" group, but, as explained previously, because its contribution is small we have omitted it in this first section of the book. We will take it up separately later on.

TABLE D. —*Gross national product or expenditure, 1929–55*

[Billions of dollars]

Period	Total gross national product	Personal consumption expenditures[1]	Gross private domestic investment: Total	Gross private domestic investment: New construction: Total	Gross private domestic investment: New construction: Residential (nonfarm)	Gross private domestic investment: New construction: Other	Gross private domestic investment: Producers' durable equipment	Gross private domestic investment: Net change in business inventories	Net foreign investment	Government purchases of goods and services: Total	Government purchases of goods and services: Federal: Total	Government purchases of goods and services: Federal: National security[2]	Government purchases of goods and services: Federal: Other	Government purchases of goods and services: Federal: Less: Government sales	Government purchases of goods and services: State and local
1929	104.4	79.0	16.2	8.7	3.6	5.1	5.8	1.7	0.8	8.5	1.3				7.2
1930	91.1	71.0	10.3	6.2	2.1	4.1	4.5	−.4	.7	9.2	1.4				7.8
1931	76.3	61.3	5.5	4.0	1.6	2.4	2.8	−1.3	.2	9.2	1.5				7.7
1932	58.5	49.3	.9	1.9	.6	1.2	1.6	−2.6	.2	8.1	1.5				6.6
1933	56.0	46.4	1.4	1.4	.5	1.0	1.6	−1.6	.2	8.0	2.0				6.0
1934	65.0	51.9	2.9	1.7	.6	1.1	2.3	−1.1	.4	9.8	3.0				6.8
1935	72.5	56.3	6.3	2.3	1.0	1.3	3.1	.9	−.1	10.0	2.9				7.1
1936	82.7	62.6	8.4	3.3	1.6	1.7	4.2	1.0	−.1	11.8	4.8				7.0
1937	90.8	67.3	11.7	4.4	1.9	2.5	5.1	2.2	.1	11.7	4.6				7.2
1938	85.2	64.6	6.7	4.0	2.0	2.0	3.6	−.9	1.1	12.8	5.3				7.5
1939	91.1	67.6	9.3	4.8	2.7	2.1	4.2	.4	.9	13.3	5.2	1.3	3.9		8.2
1940	100.6	71.9	13.2	5.5	3.0	2.5	5.5	2.2	1.5	14.1	6.2	2.2	4.0		7.9
1941	125.8	81.9	18.1	6.6	3.5	3.1	6.9	4.5	1.1	24.8	16.9	13.8	3.2		7.8
1942	159.1	89.7	9.9	3.7	1.7	2.0	4.3	1.8	−.2	59.7	52.0	49.6	2.7	0.2	7.7
1943	192.5	100.5	5.6	2.3	.9	1.4	4.0	−.8	−2.2	88.6	81.2	80.4	1.5	.6	7.4
1944	211.4	109.8	7.1	2.7	.8	1.9	5.4	−1.0	−2.1	96.5	89.0	88.6	1.6	1.2	7.5
1945	213.6	121.7	10.4	3.8	1.1	2.7	7.7	−1.1	−1.4	82.9	74.8	75.9	1.0	2.2	8.1
1946	209.2	146.6	27.1	10.3	4.0	6.3	10.7	6.1	4.6	30.9	20.9	21.2	2.5	2.7	10.0
1947	232.2	165.0	29.7	14.0	6.3	7.7	16.7	−1.0	8.9	28.6	15.8	13.3	3.8	1.3	12.8
1948	257.3	177.6	41.2	17.9	8.6	9.3	19.1	4.2	2.0	36.6	21.0	16.0	5.6	.5	15.6
1949	257.3	180.6	32.5	17.5	8.3	9.2	17.8	−2.7	.5	43.6	25.4	19.3	6.6	.4	18.2
1950	285.1	194.0	51.2	22.7	12.6	10.1	21.1	7.4	−2.2	42.0	22.1	18.5	3.9	.3	19.9
1951	328.2	208.3	56.9	23.3	11.0	12.4	23.2	10.4	.2	62.8	41.0	37.3	4.2	.4	21.8
1952	345.2	218.3	49.6	23.7	11.1	12.6	23.1	2.8	−.2	77.5	54.3	48.8	5.8	.4	23.2
1953	364.5	230.6	51.4	25.8	11.9	13.8	24.4	1.2	−2.0	84.5	59.5	51.4	8.5	.4	25.0
1954	360.5	236.5	47.2	27.8	13.5	14.3	22.3	−2.9	−.3	77.0	49.2	43.2	6.3	.4	27.8
1955	387.4	252.4	59.4	32.4	16.6	15.8	23.8	3.3	−.3	75.9	45.8	40.8	5.3	.3	30.1

Source: Economic Report of the President, 1956

construction, equipment, and inventory change. But it shows more. It shows that this spending flows on to the nation's producers and becomes the business receipts, as it were, of the three major producers, business, government, and producing households. Furthermore, the diagram shows that it is in the receipts of the producers that income (here shown only as wages) originates and flows on to the individuals. Finally, the volume of output of the three producers is shown flowing to the three buyers in exchange for their spending.

THE SPENDING OF ALL GROUPS STEMS FROM THE INCOME OF CONSUMERS

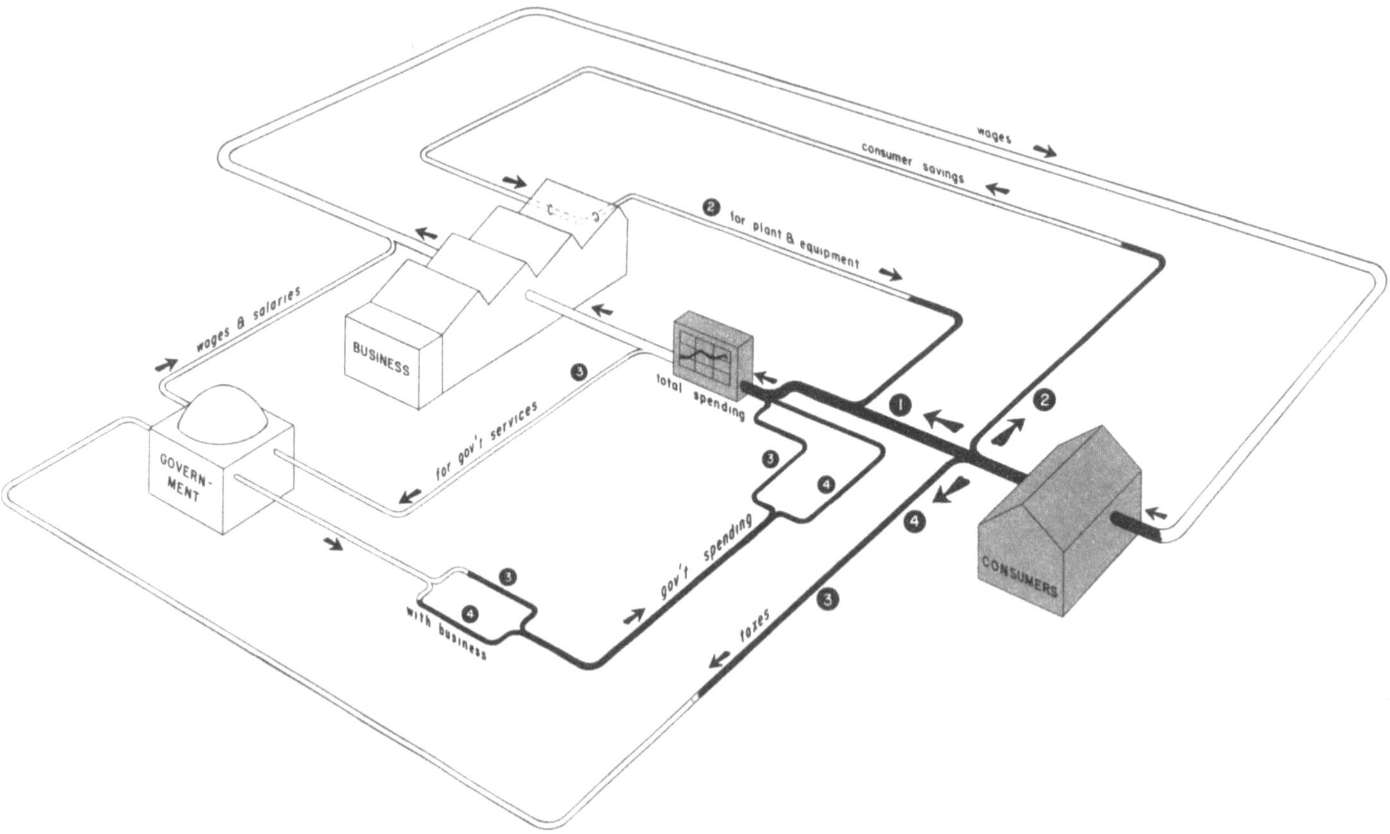

DIAGRAM 12

We saw in Diagram 8 how the Government is an agent or substitute spender for the individual—the Household Consumer—in buying some of the goods and services produced by Business Enterprise. We also saw in Diagram 9 how, like Government, Business too is to some extent a substitute spender of the Household Consumer's money or savings. For business collects some of the consumers' income (through the selling of securities or borrowing) and spends (or invests) it for new plant and equipment. In this investing way business acts as an agent for the individual consumer.

The spending stream of all groups—Consumers, Government, and Business—therefore originates mainly in the income of individual consumers. Because national income accounting does not isolate or explicitly show the current spending that has its roots in the new money created by the banks (see Diagram 39), all spending seems to have its distant roots in the income of individual consumers.

There are four major routes by which the money from Household Consumers travels into the total demand stream to ask for goods and services:

Route 1. Money is spent directly by Household Consumers with Business (and with themselves as Producing Households—see Diagrams 3 and 11) for the products of Business and Producing Households.

Route 2. Money is entrusted by consumers to business groups to act as investing agents for them. Then it is invested by business.

Route 3. Tax money is diverted to government. Some of it is spent by the government to pay for the services that the government produces.

Route 4. The remaining tax money is used by the government to purchase privately produced goods and services.

Section II
THE DISBURSEMENT CIRCUITS INVOLVED IN NATIONAL INCOME ACCOUNTING

U. S. OUTPUT CAN BE MEASURED IN FOUR DIFFERENT WAYS

Now that we have completed our portrayal of one major measure of output—Gross National Expenditures—it is advisable to refer again to Diagram 5, which shows the four possible ways of measuring output. That diagram also highlights the issue with which the next seventeen charts will deal, namely: how to measure national output by measuring certain "factor" disbursements made by producers instead of by measuring their receipts.

In Diagram 5 we explained why the Department of Commerce in measuring output had to limit its efforts to measuring the money paid for the output (and accounting transfers) (Streams 3 and 4). (Measuring output through Streams 1 and 2 was either too difficult or infeasible.) Stream 3 measures output by adding up all the receipts of the producers (only the Business producer is shown in the diagram) or the equivalent sum of all the money that is spent with the producers. The first twelve diagrams developed and explained this total sum which is Gross National Expenditures. Stream 4 in the diagram measures output in a second major monetary way—by summing up all the costs paid out by the producers in turning out the goods and services for the nation's consumers.

We shall now analyze how national output is calculated by measuring the monetary (and accounting transfers) Stream 4. We shall deal with the many items of cost that enter into the total disbursement streams. We shall see that there is reason for including some disbursements and excluding others.

Understandably those costs of producing goods that are compiled by the Department of Commerce are based upon the accounting records of business. But because it is not always easy to understand what these costs are and what is behind the accounting terminology, we have devised a series of illustrative charts that first try to show functionally what the various "economic" costs of doing business are. We begin our illustration by setting up a new business. Then we trace the contributions made by what are commonly called the "economic factors" to producing the sales product of the business. After seeing the nature of these "economic" costs, it is perhaps easier to understand national income accounting costs and conventions. This will be the concern of the next few diagrams.

THE FOUR WAYS OF MEASURING OUTPUT ARE INTERRELATED THROUGH EXCHANGE RATIOS

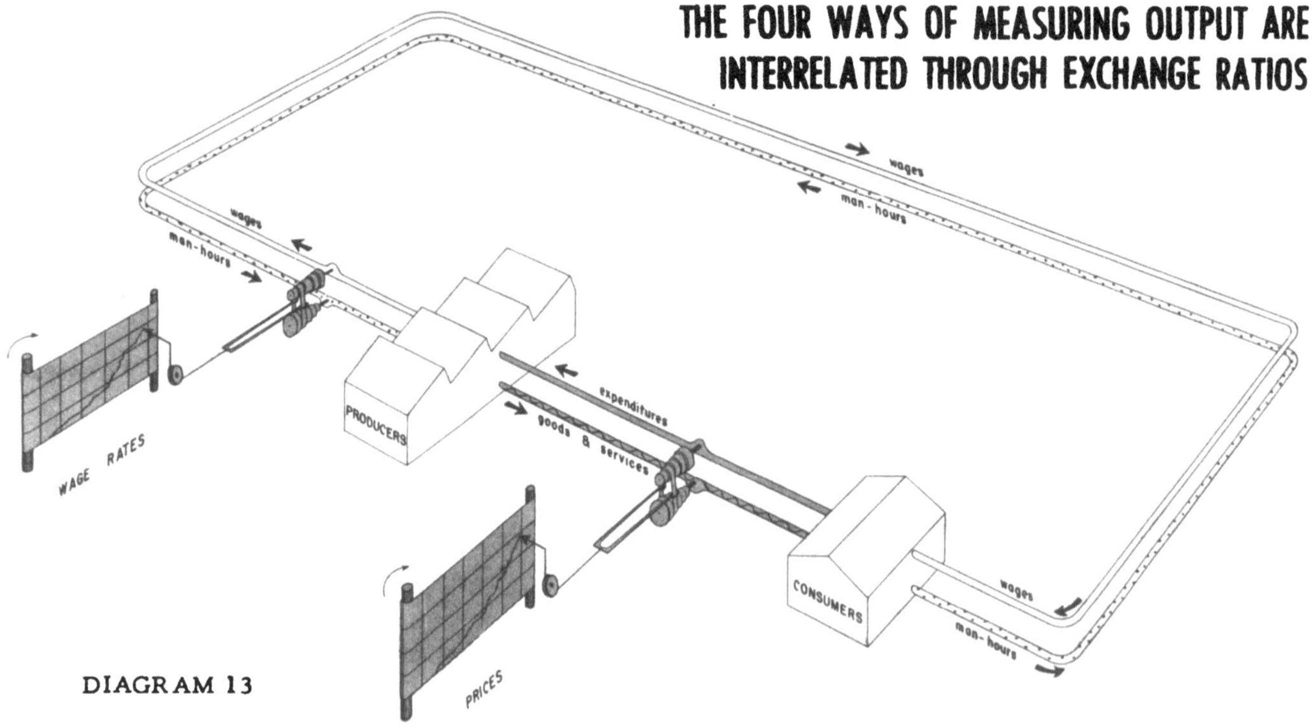

DIAGRAM 13

This chart introduces the concept of exchange ratios, a concept one must necessarily possess if one is to understand fully both the significance and the limitations of the monetary measures of U. S. output used by the Department of Commerce. Thus far we have omitted dealing with the relation of units of money to units of output, that is, with price relationships. But we can not ignore them.

First, let us review what the term "price" means. Suppose in a simple economy that Mr. A. specializes at making lumber, Mr. B. at making butter, and other people at making hats and shoes. At what ratios should the products exchange for one another? Should Mr. A. give five or ten or twenty feet of lumber for each pound of butter? Five or ten or twenty feet for each pair of shoes? How should the ratios involved be determined? What should the exchange ratios be? How much toothpaste is worth a diamond ring, how much rouge is worth one cigar—these are basic questions. Answering them takes us straightway into the theory of value. Yet in all economies the question somehow does get answered, inasmuch as goods do exchange for one another at ascertainable exchange ratios and mechanisms like free markets do get established for deciding the ratios. The resultant exchange ratios are the essence of price. Because we use a system of monetary exchange, it is well to think of "price" as being the particular exchange ratio that exists between units of money and units of other kinds of goods.

Between the production of goods and the consumption of goods stands the process of exchange, and money is the medium used for carrying it out. We acquire this money by first exchanging our man-hours for it. Then we obtain our goods and services by exchanging our money for them. These basic exchanges were sketched in Diagram 4 In modified form these basic exchanges also provide the basis for Diagram 5, which showed four possible ways of measuring output.

When dealing with the process of exchange one is necessarily forced to deal concurrently with the exchange ratios prevailing. One must consider, for example, how many units of money are at the moment being paid for each man-hour of effort purchased, and how many units of money are at the moment being paid for each unit of product acquired. Prevailing exchange ratios help us to express this.

One exchange ratio, the wage rate, reflects how the market evaluates man-hours in terms of the unit of money in use. The other ratio, price, reports on the quantity of goods and services that can be obtained for a given amount of money and reflects how buyers evaluate them. Such ratios are always changing, reflecting as they do ever-changing economic conditions. Sometimes more money is needed to purchase a given amount of goods—and prices rise. Sometimes man-hours command a higher wage than at other times—and wage rates rise.

Diagram 13 shows that when the number of dollars needed to pump output from producers to consumers changes, the exchange ratio—or price—also changes. In our symbolism, when the number of dollars needed does change, the belt moves to a new location on the step-pulleys shown and by activating the string on the pulley causes the stylus to register a different reading on the price meter. In a relatively free market system it is the physical supply of and the monetary demand for goods which are the main forces that make for the different positions of the belt on the pulleys and for the varying prices that the different positions of the belt record on the price meter via the stylus shown.

Because most people are both producers and consumers—as Diagram 1 brought out—they are all interested in having particularized exchange ratios that work to their advantage. We all want a high price for our own products and a low price for the product of others. All societies must and do devise some mechanism for operateing under that violent conflict of interest.

In the United States we rely predominately on the market mechanism where the pressures of private supply or private demand move the belt back and forth. We try to devise, through laws and working rules, social control mechanisms that are as automatic as possible and that will keep the exchange ratios relatively fair. In Soviet Russia they rely on government officials—who have police power and discretion—to move the belts back and forth by hand as they think best.

TABLE E. —*Average gross hourly earnings in selected industries, 1929–55*

Period	Manufacturing			Bituminous coal mining	Building construction	Class I railroads	Telephone	Wholesale trade	Retail trade (except eating and drinking places)	Laundries	Agriculture
	Total	Durable goods	Nondurable goods								
1929	$0.566			$0.681							$0.241
1930	.552			.684							.226
1931	.515			.647							.172
1932	.446	$0.497	$0.420	.520							.129
1933	.442	.472	.427	.501							.115
1934	.532	.556	.515	.673	$0.795					$0.378	.129
1935	.550	.577	.530	.745	.815			$0.648		.376	.142
1936	.556	.586	.529	.794	.824			.667		.378	.152
1937	.624	.674	.577	.856	.903		$0.774	.698		.395	.172
1938	.627	.686	.584	.878	.908		.816	.700		.414	.166
1939	.633	.698	.582	.886	.932	$0.730	.822	.715	$0.542	.422	.166
1940	.661	.724	.602	.883	.958	.733	.827	.739	.553	.429	.169
1941	.729	.808	.640	.993	1.010	.743	.820	.793	.580	.444	.206
1942	.853	.947	.723	1.059	1.148	.837	.843	.860	.626	.482	.268
1943	.961	1.059	.803	1.139	1.252	.852	.870	.933	.679	.538	.353
1944	1.019	1.117	.861	1.186	1.319	.948	.911	.985	.731	.605	.423
1945	1.023	1.111	.904	1.240	1.379	.955	.962	1.029	.783	.648	.472
1946	1.086	1.156	1.015	1.401	1.478	1.087	1.124	1.150	.893	.704	.515
1947	1.237	1.292	1.171	1.636	1.681	1.186	1.197	1.268	1.009	.767	.547
1948	1.350	1.410	1.278	1.898	1.848	1.301	1.248	1.359	1.088	.817	.580
1949	1.401	1.469	1.325	1.941	1.935	1.427	1.345	1.414	1.137	.843	.559
1950	1.465	1.537	1.378	2.010	2.031	1.572	1.398	1.483	1.176	.861	.561
1951	1.59	1.67	1.48	2.21	2.19	1.73	1.49	1.58	1.26	.92	.625
1952	1.67	1.77	1.54	2.29	2.31	1.83	1.59	1.67	1.32	.94	.661
1953	1.77	1.87	1.61	2.48	2.48	1.88	1.68	1.77	1.40	.98	.672
1954	1.81	1.92	1.66	2.48	2.60	1.93	1.76	1.83	1.45	1.00	.661
1955	1.88	2.01	1.71	2.55	2.66	1.95	1.82	1.91	1.50	1.01	.675

Source: Economic Report of the President, 1956

TABLE F. —*Consumer price indexes, 1929–55*

For city wage-earner and clerical-worker families

[1947–49=100]

Period	All items	Food	Housing		Apparel	Transportation	Medical care	Personal care	Reading and recreation	Other goods and services
			Total	Rent						
1929	73.3	65.6		117.4	60.3					
1930	71.4	62.4		114.2	58.9					
1931	65.0	51.4		108.2	53.6					
1932	58.4	42.8		97.1	47.5					
1933	55.3	41.6		83.6	45.9					
1934	57.2	46.4		78.4	50.2					
1935	58.7	49.7		78.2	50.6					
1936	59.3	50.1		80.1	51.0					
1937	61.4	52.1		83.8	53.7					
1938	60.3	48.4		86.5	53.4					
1939	59.4	47.1		86.6	52.5					
1940	59.9	47.8		86.9	53.2					
1941	62.9	52.2		88.4	55.6					
1942	69.7	61.3		90.4	64.9					
1943	74.0	68.3		90.3	67.8					
1944	75.2	67.4		90.6	72.6					
1945	76.9	68.9		90.9	76.3					
1946	83.4	79.0		91.4	83.7					
1947	95.5	95.9	95.0	94.4	97.1	90.6	94.9	97.6	95.5	96.1
1948	102.8	104.1	101.7	100.7	103.5	100.9	100.9	101.3	100.4	100.5
1949	101.8	100.0	103.3	105.0	99.4	108.5	104.1	101.1	104.1	103.4
1950	102.8	101.2	106.1	108.8	98.1	111.3	106.0	101.1	103.4	105.2
1951	111.0	112.6	112.4	113.1	106.9	118.4	111.1	110.5	106.5	109.7
1952	113.5	114.6	114.6	117.9	105.8	126.2	117.2	111.8	107.0	115.4
1953	114.4	112.8	117.7	124.1	104.8	129.7	121.3	112.8	108.0	118.2
1954	114.8	112.6	119.1	128.5	104.3	128.0	125.2	113.4	107.0	120.1
1955	114.5	110.9	120.0	130.3	103.7	126.4	128.0	115.3	106.6	120.2

Source: Economic Report of the President, 1956

THE "ECONOMIC FACTORS" NEEDED FOR A NEW BUSINESS

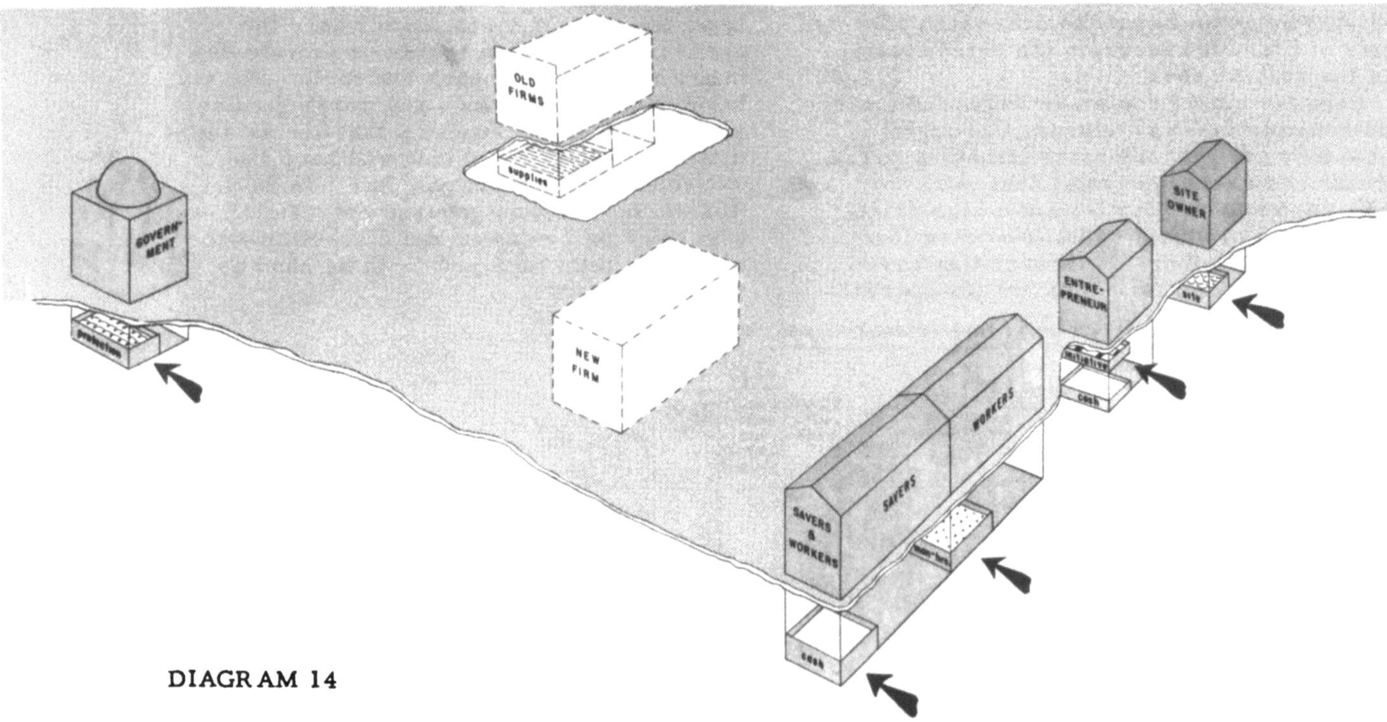

DIAGRAM 14

In making its measurements of national income the Department of Commerce keeps tab on the dollars paid out for the so-called factors of production—wages, rent, interest, profits, and the like. It concerns itself extensively with such a breakdown of total outpayments. And in its reports it differentiates between the kinds of reward for different kinds of economic or "factor" contribution—"wages" for man-hours, "interest" for secured capital, and so forth. To help present clearly the focus of the Department of Commerce's interest we have inserted a series of diagrams (14 through 17) that illustrates the nature and function of the different kinds of dollar payments that a business organization makes in its operations.

The major purpose of a business firm is to turn out a finished product—to turn it out by combining and coordinating the materials, assets, and services of many contributors. Let us picture this organizing process in a series of steps. By so doing we can show more clearly how the nation's output can be measured by totaling the costs incurred in producing that output.

The Department of Commerce's accounting definitions of such items as profit, interest, depreciation allowances, and rent illustrated by this section of the book do not necessarily correspond to the functional classical definitions, as later diagrammatic portrayals of these terms will bring out. Whether a particular dollar paid to a contributor for helping with production is interest, profit, rent, or wages is not, as we shall see, always easy to decide.

The term "factors of production" is commonplace in economic discussion. But what does the term mean? Perhaps it is best to think of the "factors" as being the economic building blocks needed for the creation of a new business. Factors of production are the economic elements that go into the establishment of every new business organization. They are the items which dynamic individuals in the community assemble, organize, and weld into new-producing organizations.

This diagram shows separately each of the building blocks (or economic factors) lying around in the basement bins of potential contributors. The savers have money, the workers have man-hours, the entrepreneur has initiative (and sometimes cash), the landlord has land sites or office space, the government has available the service of contract enforcement and property protection. The entrepreneur reaches out, collects, and welds these ingredients together when he sets up a new enterprise. He believes he can make a profit for himself by integrating these building blocks or "factors" to produce items which consumers by their dollar voting in the market place will indicate they want in appreciable volume.

This diagram also illustrates how in every community there is available for sale to new firms the materials and supplies of old firms. While these supplies are necessary ingredients for the operation of the new firm, they are not, as we shall see, "factors of production."

The next three diagrams illustrate how the entrepreneur organizes the material, assets, and services of many contributors to turn out a new finished product and how this calls for the making of "factor payments."

HOW A NEW BUSINESS IS PRIMED WITH WORKING CAPITAL AND ENTREPRENEURSHIP

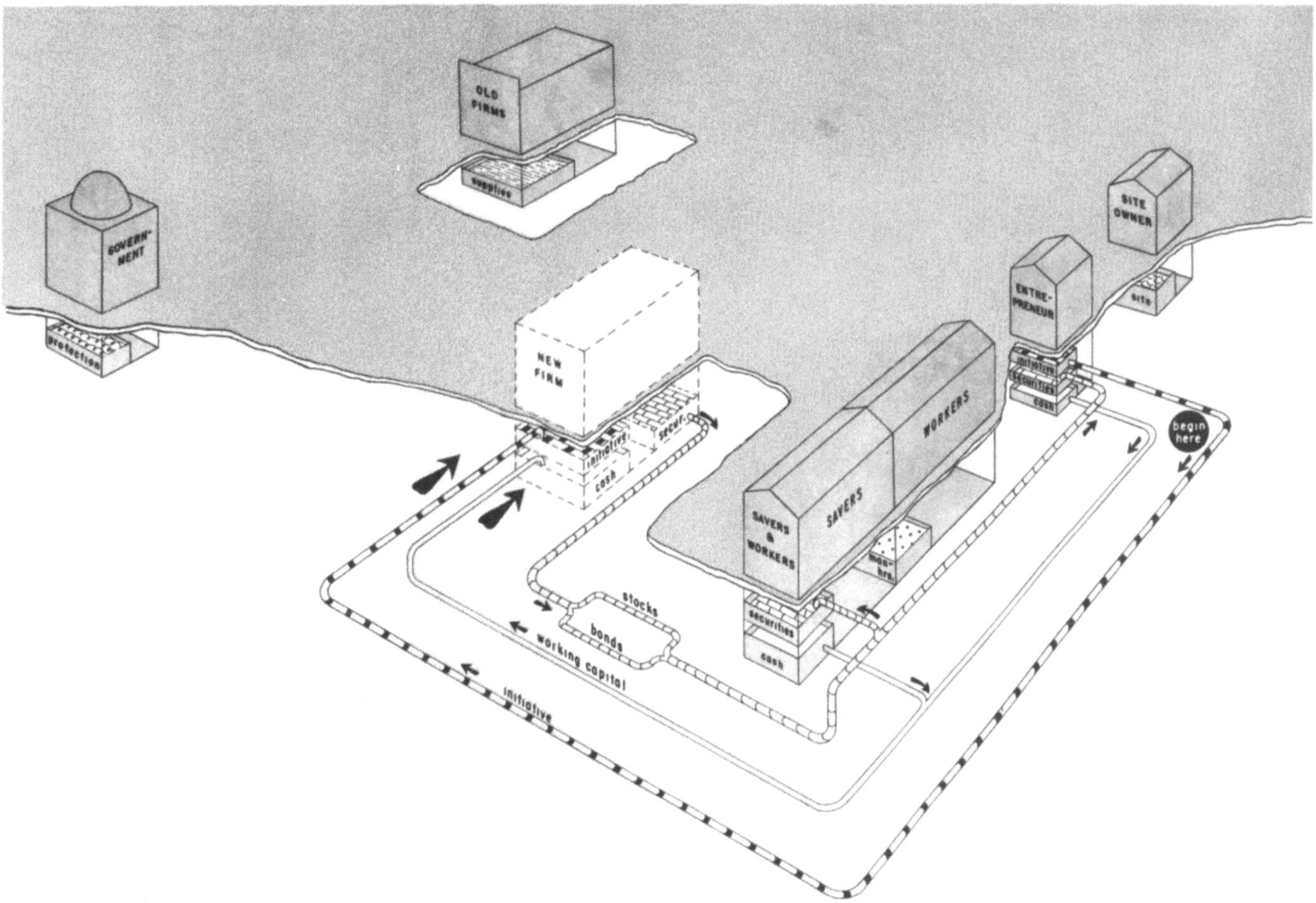

DIAGRAM 15

The entrepreneur is the initiator who organizes the new business venture and integrates the economic factors. It is he who directs the factors to produce some new product aimed at some real or suspected want of the community. His economic contribution is initiative, man-hours risked, direction, judgment, and occasionally a part of the risk-capital. The Entrepreneur's Initiative is therefore, because of his dynamic organizational role, one of the key building blocks, a key factor of production. The diagram illustrates how the Entrepreneur's Initiative is transferred to the new firm to become a part of the new firm's assets.

But the risk-capital (the money needed to run the business until it is self-supporting), whether provided by the entrepreneur or by other members of the community, is also a highly essential building block. The diagram illustrates that Working Capital—a second vital element in business operations—also becomes an asset of the new firm. To undertake a new business always costs money, because expenditures of considerable magnitude must be made even before the business gets into production and begins to offer its product for sale to the public. Sometimes the entrepreneur has enough risk capital of his own to meet all the initial costs of setting up the business and of keeping it going until the business is on a self-sustaining basis. More often than not, however, he must secure the capital from those other people who have cash and who view his proposed new venture favorably enough to invest in it. In return for the cash, these investors receive claims to the business which may take the form of stocks, bonds, or other claims. The diagram shows the Cash of Savers (Working Capital) being exchanged for the Securities of the New Firm.

Only when a new business possesses the know-how and drive of an entrepreneur and adequate working capital obtained from the savings of risk-taking investors is it primed to begin operations. These two elements are the essential ones needed for the birth of a new business. For with working capital the entrepreneur can buy the raw material he needs, he can hire the labor he requires, and he can pay his rent and taxes. He is set to begin operations.

THE PROPERTY ITEMS (FACTORS OF PRODUCTION) WHICH BUSINESS OPERATIONS CONVERT INTO GOOD AND SERVICES

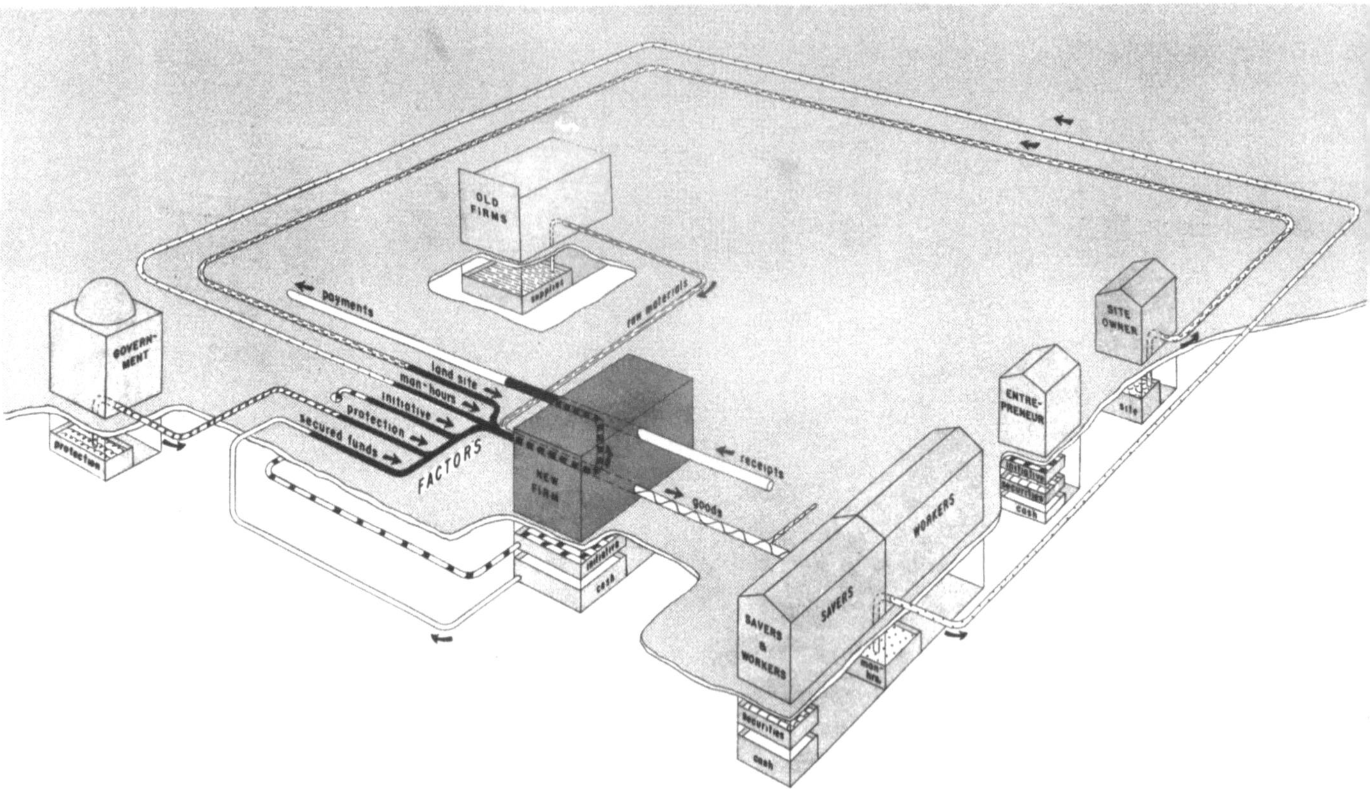

DIAGRAM 16

The entrepreneur in setting up operations is now ready to join his two assets of initiative and working capital with the other economic factors needed to produce goods.

This diagram shows how the entrepreneur combines his own initiative and his acquired working capital with other property contributions into a producing concern. Once the entrepreneur has at hand both the initiative, which drove him into the new undertaking, and enough working capital to tide him through the early stages of his new venture, he can begin to purchase and assemble those other factors of production which are also necessary for the establishment and operation of a business.

The entrepreneur always needs a land site—or a building already located on a land site. The diagram illustrates how he obtains a third ingredient, a location or Land Site from which to operate the new venture. Thus land is a third building block needed for the establishment of any new business.

A new business naturally needs employee too. It will not run itself. The entrepreneur needs the assistance of people who for wages are willing to work under his direction. The diagram illustrates how the workers' Man-Hours are combined with other factors to produce the goods of the New Firm. Man-hours are thus a fourth factor of production.

Fortunately when the entrepreneur begins his activities in the community he finds a government already in operation, one that uses its police power and courts to protect both his property and his contracts. These services rendered by government also constitute an essential building block or factor in the production and sale of goods. The diagram illustrates how the Protection and aid of government joins with the other factors of production. (The contribution of government to production is not usually regarded

Diagram 16 shows another contribution necessary to the production of goods, that is, the supplies and Raw Materials furnished by the Old Firms already in existence. These supplies are not regarded or shown here as being factors of production. A later diagram will show why they are not factors. as a factor of production, but the writer believes that a good case can be made functionally for so regarding it. In its accounting, the Department of Commerce treats corporate taxes as a factor cost but justifies it on grounds other than as a payment for services rendered by the government.)

Thus for a single firm there are five major factors of production:

1. Initiative
2. Risk capital
3. Land
4. Man-hours
5. Government aid and protection

The cash or working capital (the Secured Funds) that was raised by the entrepreneur is shown in the diagram flowing upward from the cash bin in the basement of the New Firm to join the other factors that feed into the firm's big intake stream. Thus working capital is one of the key factors or ingredients for producing the new product. This Cash flows upward and outward into the firm's cash Payments Stream to the left of the building. It is the outflow of this cash which enlists the assistance of all the factors of production until the Receipts obtained from the sale of the Goods produced are themselves adequate to take care of the payments. The next diagram will show the specific payments which the entrepreneur pours out as compensation for the various factor contributions.

THE PAYMENT FOR EACH KIND OF PROPERTY CONTRIBUTION (OR FACTOR) HAS A DIFFERENT NAME

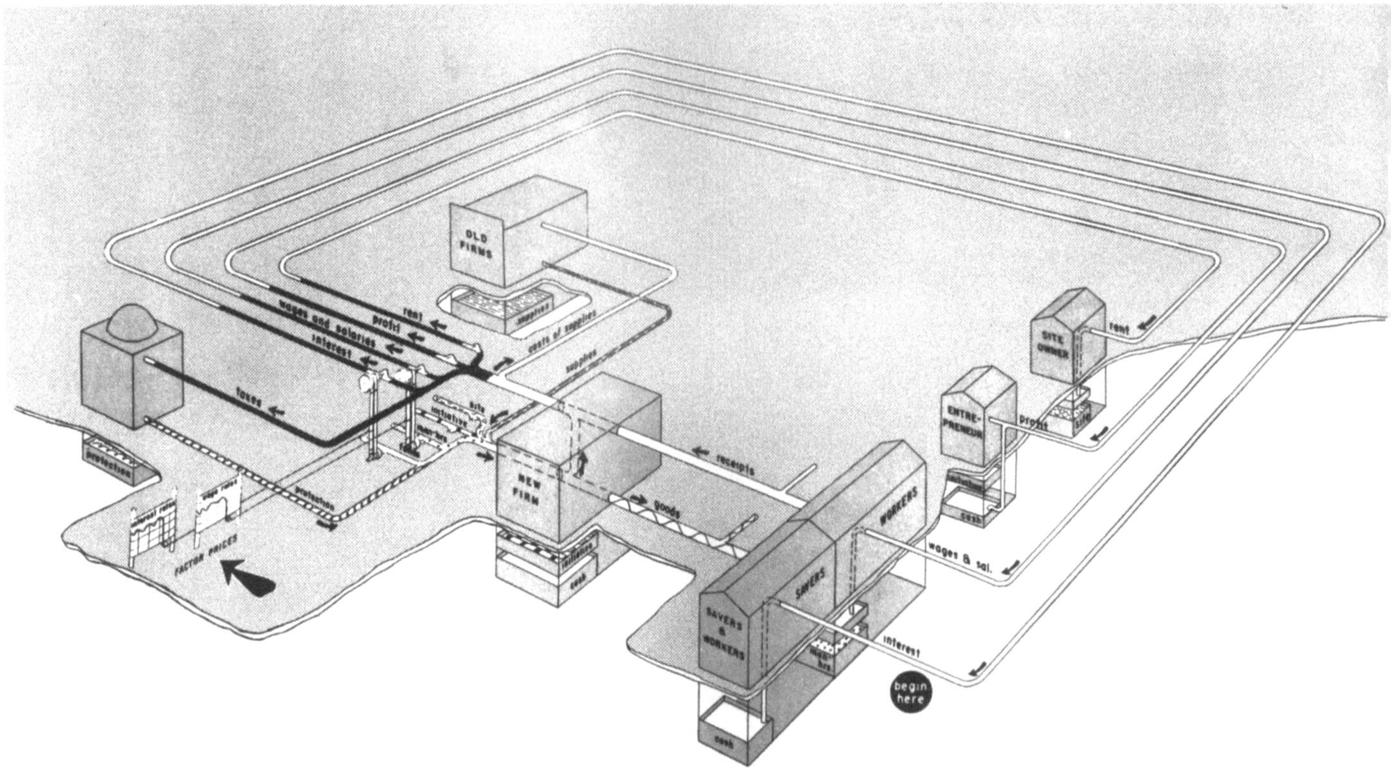

DIAGRAM 17

It is up to the entrepreneur of a new firm to integrate the productive forces of the community and to make superior use of them. It is he who must induce various contributors to provide the ingredients needed for the production of his product. He must compensate each contributor out of his working capital. He must then turn around and sell to consumers the special product that his organization produces. Consumers by their freedom of choice in spending money decree through their dollar voting whether his output is wanted at the prices charged in preference to other items available to them. Through continuous sales he hopes to obtain compensation and a reward for his effort.

This diagram matches up the dollars paid out for each kind of economic contribution with the factor contributed. The diagram also highlights the name or label in economic literature usually assigned to each kind of factor payment. In economic literature

"rent" is the name for the use of the site—that is, of the factor land,

"interest" is the name of the payment for that part of the working capital which is secured by first claims against the assets of the new venture (bonds),

"profit" pays for the factor of initiative-and-entrepreneurial-risk-capital, that is, the part of the working capital which is not secured by first claims against the business,

"wages" is the name of the payment for the man-hour contributions of the employees, and

"taxes" (mainly state and local) is the name of the payment made to government. As mentioned under Diagram 16, taxes are not usually regarded as a factor cost but the writer believes that to a high degree it is one, because in an organized community production, exchange, and distribution can not be carried out without state rendering the service of protecting property and enforcing contracts. Also it is obvious that unless the night policeman, for example, walked his beat protectively, many producers would have to hire their own night watchman and pay out more money for wages, that is, pay out more money in the form of another factor cost.

The other terms as illustrated are classical in concept. As we shall see later when we get to the statistical portrayal of specific national income accounts, the Department of Commerce's definitions of such terms as rent, interest, and profit differ from the classical ones.

Note that the payments made for supplies and raw materials to the already established firms of the community are merely referred to in the diagram as "costs of supplies," not as factor payments. We shall see in the next chart that these costs in turn themselves break down into factor payments for working capital, labor, land, and governmental protection.

FACTOR PRICES

All these exchanges of money by the single firm with those who contribute to production go on at a Factor Price. The entrepreneur theoretically bargains in the labor market over the wage rate he pays for the man-hours contributed by workers. In the capital market he carefully negotiates the interest rate paid for the working capital contributed; in the local government market—if it can be called that—he quarrels with the tax assessors over tax rates and appraisals or moves, when feasible, to areas where the tax rates are lower; in the real estate market he makes terms over the rent he pays; and in the commodity market he bids for his materials and supplies, just as consumers bargain with him in the retail market over the prices they pay him for his product.

If these factor costs were the only ones involved in production, then prices charged to consumers would be a composite of these factor prices. In such a case, receipts from consumers would cover only the factor costs and the goods and services flowing to consumers would probably reflect on the factor prices. As a matter of real life, however, the firm has to provide in its prices two major additional outlays: excise taxes and depreciation. How these additional charges figure into the final prices paid by consumers will be shown in later diagrams.

THE OUTPAYMENTS OF THE FIRM ARE SPLIT BETWEEN SUPPLIERS AND FACTORS

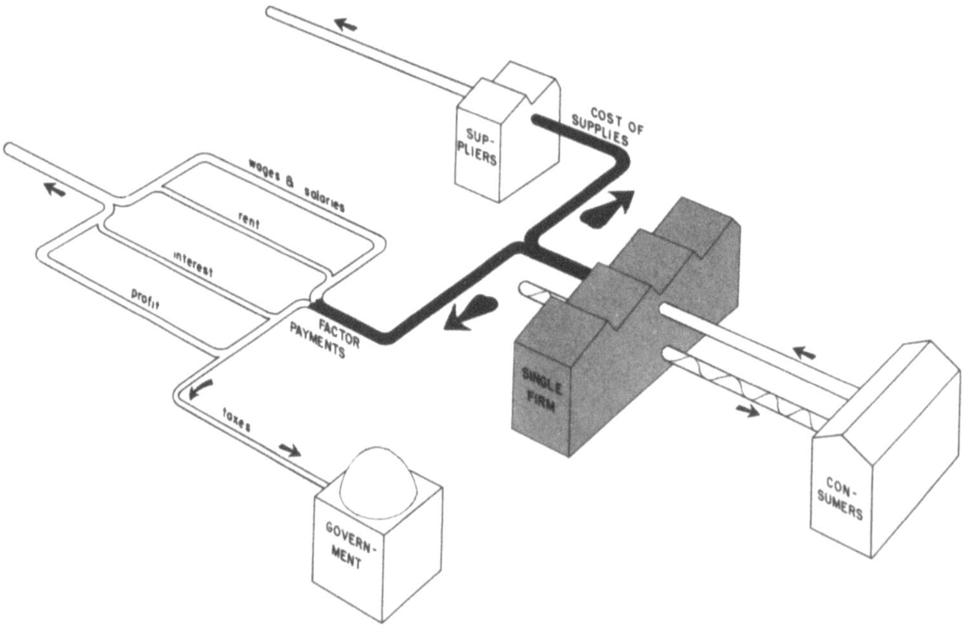

DIAGRAM 18

In practice, the outpayments of every firm are split between Costs of Supplies on the one side and Factor Payments on the other. This chart highlights that breakdown.

When the single firm reports its operations to the Bureau of Internal Revenue for tax purposes, it usually separates out its payments to suppliers of material. In national income accounting, however, these outlays for materials do not appear in the accounts at all. The reason is that national income accounting is concerned only with the sale of final products to final consumers. All sales transactions of intermediate products are washed out of the sales totals. It is only natural to wonder at this point what happens to these payments to suppliers. How are they counted in the government's calculation of national output? How do they figure in the total scheme of national income accounting?

HOW ALL PAYMENTS FOR SUPPLIES BECOME FACTOR PAYMENTS

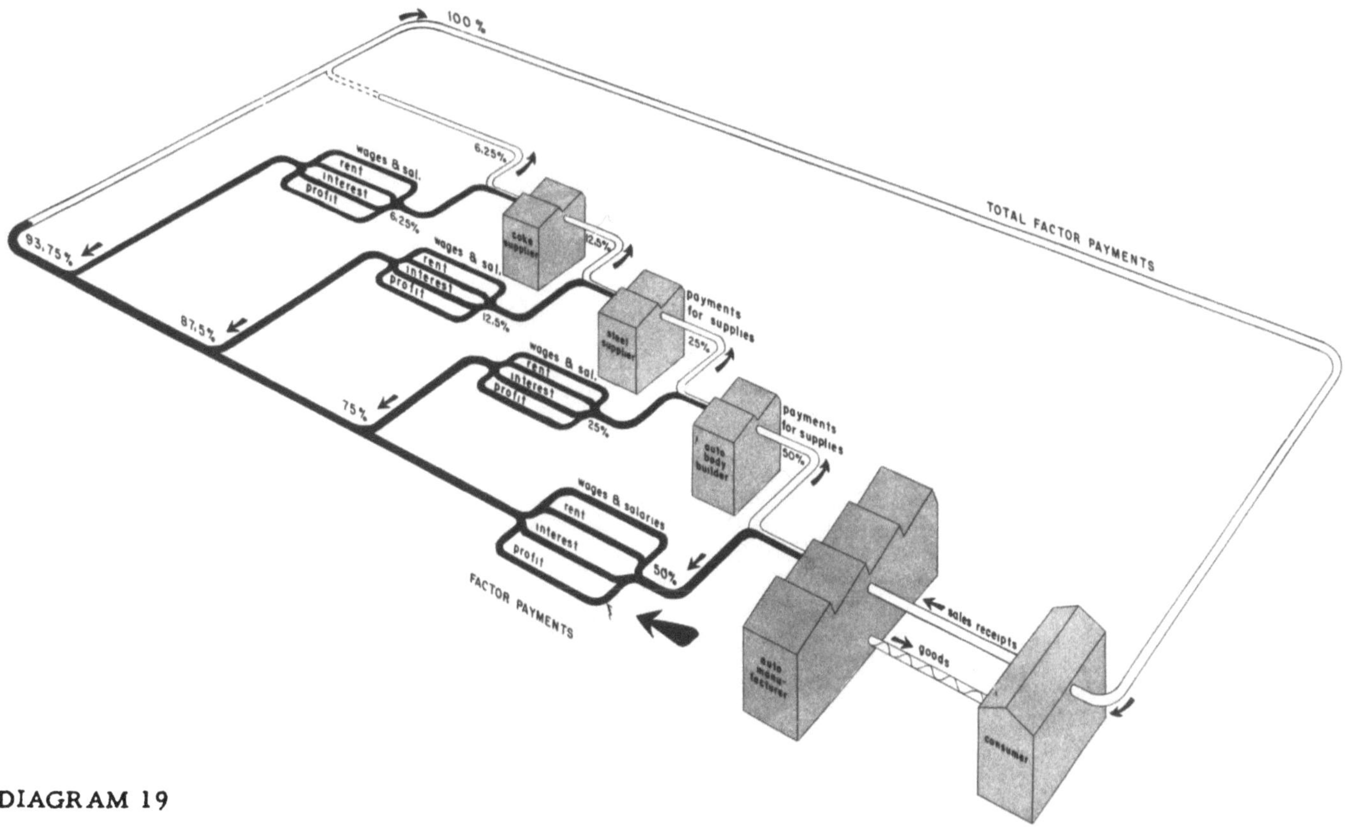

DIAGRAM 19

When we look at and analyze the payments of all the firms in a community instead of only one firm, it becomes clear that all the payments of the single firm to other firms for materials and supplies turn eventually into factor payments too. Diagram 19 charts the process by which the payments to suppliers become factor payments The single firm's payments to supplier firms make up the gross receipts of the supplier firm. These gross receipts in turn become factor payments: rent, profits, wages, interest, and taxes. In the diagram we illustrate the operations of an auto company and of the supplying companies which back up the line with supplies. The Auto Manufacturer sells autos to the final Consumer, for which he receives cash. To produce the autos the company buys materials from an Auto Body Builder and pays factor costs too. The body manufacturer in turn disburses his receipts for two kinds of payments. He buys steel from the Steel Supplier and then makes factor payments to those who contribute to his production. The steel companies then use their sales receipts to buy coke from Coke Suppliers and also to make payments to those who supply their factors of production. The diagram thus shows how all the outpayments of the many manufacturers who back up the line of automobile production turn into "factor payments." The sum total of all these factor payments of a final producer and his payments to suppliers is equivalent to the value of the cars supplied to the consumer.

The Department of Commerce is basically concerned only with the nation's output sold to the final consumer, as the chart brings out. It collects data only on the expenditures by consumers for final products. That is the same as saying that the Department of Commerce limits itself to the net sales receipts of those who sell the goods directly to consumers. In computing gross expenditures it omits the network of intermediate sales of all supplies needed in production from the basic raw materials up to the finished products sold to the consumer. But these intermediate payments to suppliers are important and do contribute to the total volume of income disbursed to individuals because they too all become factor payments as described above.

Thus the Department of Commerce, when it proceeds to calculate output by adding up all the costs of producing goods, has to add up the factor payments of all firms, including the suppliers, to get the value of the nation's product or sales to all the final consumers. But at any moment of time the total money used in payment in all transactions greatly exceeds both the total sales receipts from the final consumer or the equivalent total factor payments made by the producers during that moment of time.

HOW THE CONSUMERS' EXPENDITURES FOR FINAL PRODUCTS RECIRCULATE TO GENERATE A MUCH LARGER GROSS SALES FIGURE

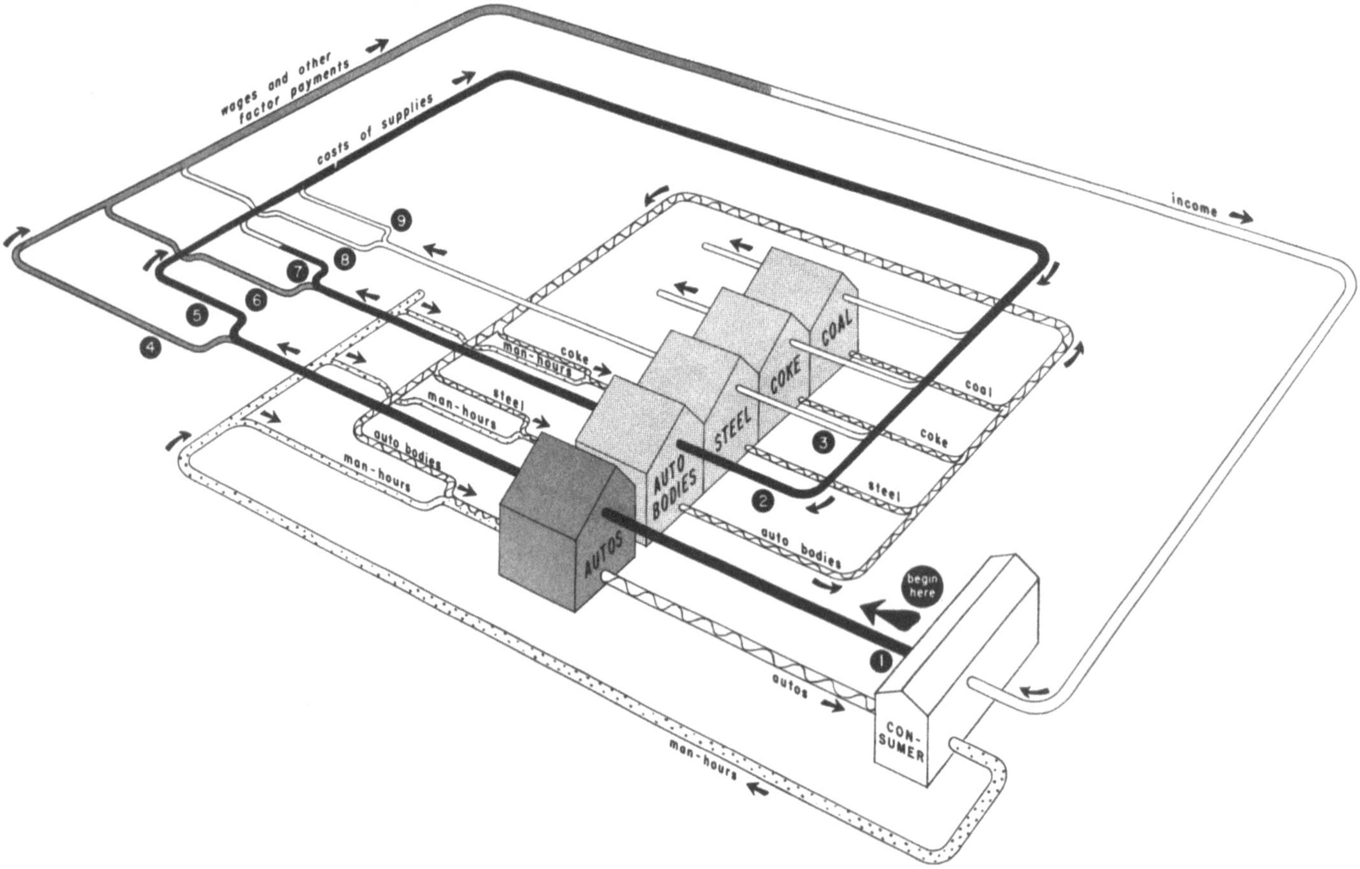

DIAGRAM 20

The gross sales of the economy and the net sales to the consumers differ appreciably. In the previous diagram we explained how the Department of Commerce, because it is interested in measuring only the net stream of output that flows to the final consumer, records only the expenditures made with the producers of final products. In its national income accounting it does not concern itself with inter-industry gross streams of payments. Considerable confusion exists in understanding this point. In the many reports published, for instance, on the gross annual sales of American industry, we may read how the sales of the steel industry and other primary metals in 1953 totaled about $30 billion and how the gross sales of the electrical machinery industry totaled about $28 billion. As a matter of fact, sales of all manufacturing industries alone in 1953 were about $300 billion. If the sales of nonmanufacturing industries are added, the total would be much higher—probably about $600 billion. Still, total Gross National Expenditures in 1953 were only $365 billion. The explanation of course is that the gross national expenditure figures record only the expenditures of those who buy the final products of the nation. Diagram 19 illustrates why the total gross sales of the nation are much larger than gross national expenditures by consumers for final product.

Using the auto manufacturer as an example again, we show Consumers paying Auto Companies for a supply of automobiles. (This is the only payment stream that is part of the gross national expenditures stream.) The Auto Company disburses (as Wages and Other Factor Payments) the money it received for its automobiles to the suppliers of Man-Hours and the other factors of production (not shown here) and (as Costs of Supplies) to the suppliers of Auto Bodies. The Auto Body Company sells nothing to final consumers. Its output of auto bodies flows circuitously into the stream that feeds materials into the automobile companies, as shown. The stream of cash receipts (2) of auto body companies, like that of auto manufacturers, is disbursed partly for man-hours (Stream 6) and other factors and partly in payment to steel companies (Stream 7) for steel. Similarly, in the illustration, the output of the Steel Company flows around circuitously to supply the Auto Body Company. The Steel Company, in turn, leans upon suppliers from the Coke

Company, and so on down the line. On the expenditures side, the Department of Commerce need only concern itself with the spending made with the auto company (Stream 1) in return for the only goods—the autos—delivered to the final consumer. On the payment side, the Department of Commerce obtains an equivalent measure of output by adding all the factor payments of all the companies, whether producers of final products or of intermediate supplies (Streams like 4 plus 6 plus 8 . . . . The other streams, 5, 7, and 9. . . . , which represent payments to suppliers, are omitted.)

There are other inter-industry payments as well as those involving supplies. For industries pay one another rent, interest, and dividends too. The Department of Commerce handles the inter-industry payments for rent, interest, and dividends by "netting" them, a process comparable to the one just described for payments to suppliers. Interest payments recorded by the Department of Commerce are those made to persons only and are obtained by subtracting from the total interest paid in the nation the amount of interest that is paid to industry. In the same way, payments of rent and dividends in national income accounting exclude the inter-industry payments of rent and interest. Total amounts of interest, rent, and dividends actually paid in the economy are much higher than the net reported by the Department of Commerce.

KINDS OF FACTOR PAYMENTS BY DIFFERENT TYPES OF BUSINESS ORGANIZATION

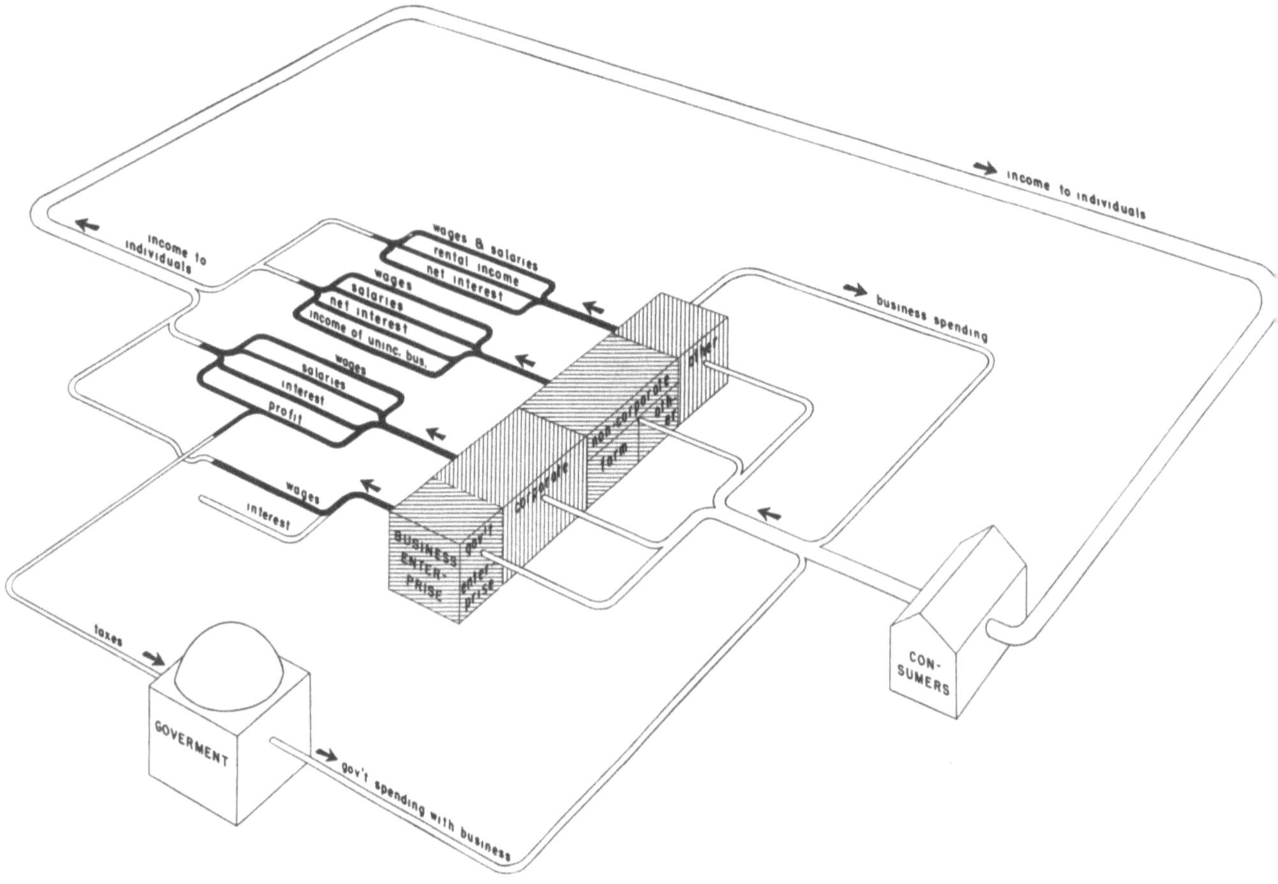

DIAGRAM 21

The single firm whose factor payments to the contributors to production were schematically reviewed in Diagrams 14 to 18 was of the corporate type. But there are several other types of business organization, too, and the Department of Commerce keeps books on how much income each type produces by measuring the factor payments handed out by each. It keeps records on Noncorporate Business, both Farm and Other, and on Other business organizations which include Individual Property Owners, Cooperatives, and Mutual Financial Institutions.

In Diagram 21 we illustrate the Department of Commerce's major classifications of business organization and the kinds of factor payments made by each. The terms used to describe the various factor payments of each kind of business organization are also shown.

For example, the payment (or charge against production) for entrepreneurial service which the Department of Commerce calls Profit relates exclusively to the income stream generated by businesses of the Corporate form. Entrepreneurial income generated by other types of business is called by a different name—Income of Unincorporated Business. In subsequent diagrams, when we show a breakdown of factor payments, for all types of business organizations combined, we will show the reward or return for the entrepreneur's initiative and risk capital as consisting of two rivulets. It will be Profit from Corporations and Income of Unincorporated Business from Noncorporate Business.

Note again that Government Enterprises which sell products at a price and on which a profit or loss is made are included under Business Enterprise and not under Government. Notice too that interest paid by Government Enterprise (whether federal, state, or local) is not recorded as being a factor payment.

THE SUM OF ALL FACTOR PAYMENTS BY ALL PRODUCERS IS CALLED "NATIONAL INCOME"

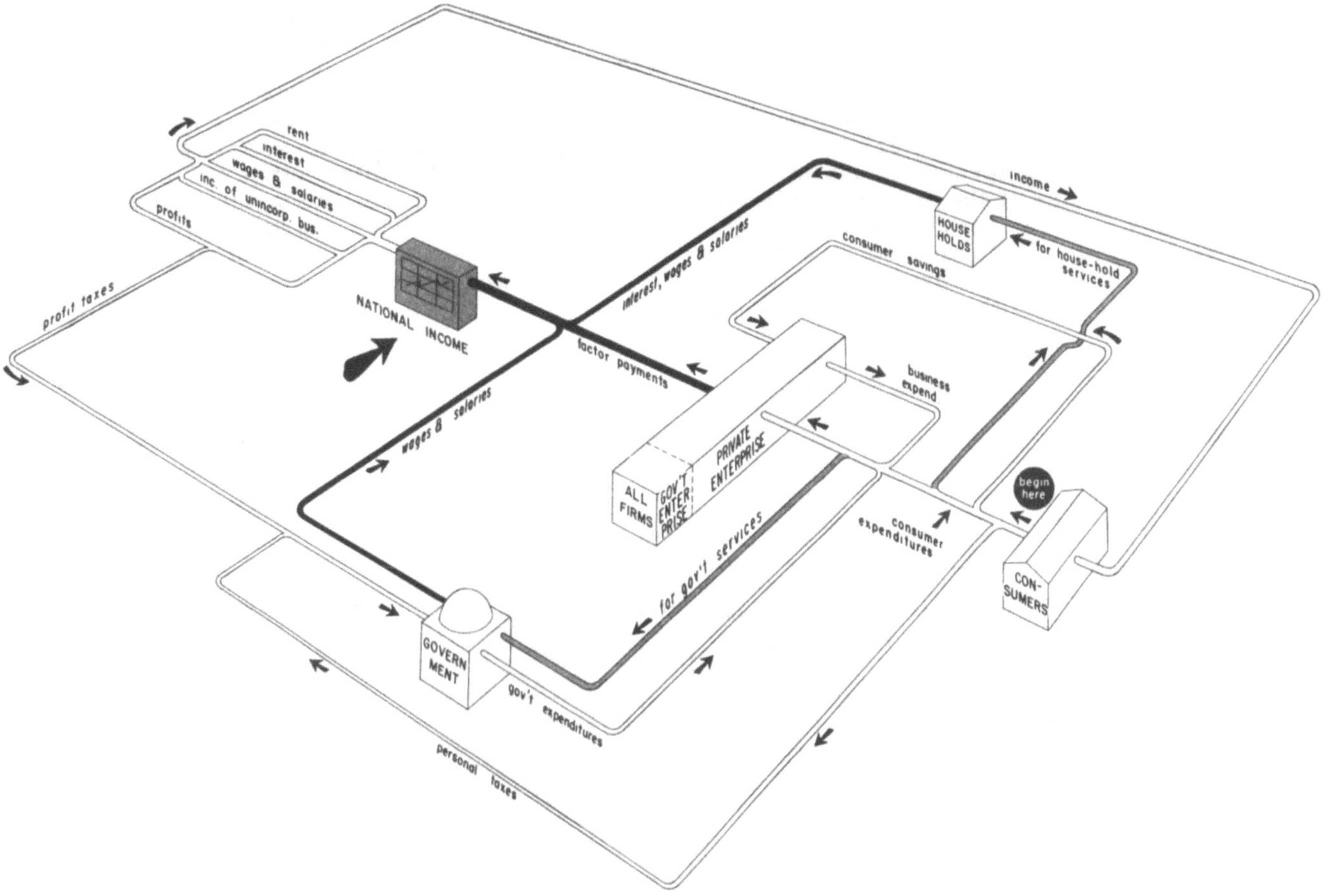

DIAGRAM 22

Diagram 21 showed us the several kinds of factor payments that originate in the various legal forms of business enterprise and then flow on to individuals. All of these factor payments of business make up only a part of the total income generated by the producing organizations of the country. To get the total of all income generated, namely "National Income," we must add to the wages, interest, rent, and profits paid by business enterprise the additional factor payments made by Government and Households, as shown in this diagram.

To see the setting for these two additional income contributions we must realize that the nation's purchasers—the consuming households, governments, and business enterprises—collectively purchase goods and services not only from business establishments but also from Government and producing Households. The production of these services for the nation's consumers results in the generation and distribution of additional streams of income. This added income grows out of the expenditures which Government and Households make mainly with themselves, as shown by the chart.

The diagram shows that Households make two kinds of factor payments—Interest and Wages and Salaries. The Department of Commerce regards the interest payments of Households as being a necessary cost of current production, just as interest payments by business are part of current production costs.

The diagram also shows the Government making only one kind of factor payment, namely, Wages and Salaries, even though we know Government makes rather large interest payments too. The interest paid by federal, state, and local government is not considered by the Department of Commerce to be a factor cost against current production. So it is not included in National Income.

The decision to exclude government interest in measuring current production was made after World War II, when national income accounting was reviewed and revised. Because so much of the federal debt and its resultant interest charges grew out of the large financing requirements of the war, the Department of Commerce does not consider government interest payments (even those paid by state and local governments) as being factor payments. Even though state and local governments in selling bonds for roads, schools, and the like sell their securities competitively with industrial corporations and pay savers for their contributions, their interest payments are regarded as transfer payments and not as payments for a current service rendered

In Diagram 22 the sum of all the expenditures for goods and services by consumers, business, and government, shown on the right-hand side of the producer buildings, is represented in the diagram as being no larger in magnitude than the total national income. Receipts of producers are shown as being equal to the sum of the factor payments made in producing the goods. But in real life the total expenditures are larger than this because they include both the extra payments that consumers must usually make to compensate manufacturers for the wear-out of their plant and equipment and to cover the many excise taxes that the government imposes. Because national income excludes these two extra costs of production it is sometimes regarded as measuring "output at factor prices." In order to arrive at a figure for total output at "market prices," we must add to the national income figure some extra charges for life's real excise taxes and life's real wear-out of plant and equipment.

TABLE G. —*National income by distributive shares, 1929–55*

[Billions of dollars]

Period	Total national income	Compensation of employees	Business and professional income and inventory valuation adjustment			Income of farm proprietors	Rental income of persons	Corporate profits and inventory valuation adjustment			Net interest
			Total	Income of unincorporated enterprises	Inventory valuation adjustment			Total	Corporate profits before taxes	Inventory valuation adjustment	
1929	87.8	51.1	8.8	8.6	0.1	6.0	5.4	10.1	9.6	0.5	6.4
1930	75.7	46.8	7.4	6.7	.8	4.1	4.8	6.6	3.3	3.3	6.0
1931	59.7	39.7	5.6	5.0	.6	3.2	3.8	1.6	−.8	2.4	5.8
1932	42.5	31.1	3.4	3.1	.3	1.9	2.7	−2.0	−3.0	1.0	5.4
1933	40.2	29.5	3.2	3.7	−.5	2.4	2.0	−2.0	.2	−2.1	5.0
1934	49.0	34.3	4.6	4.6	−.1	2.4	1.7	1.1	1.7	−.6	4.9
1935	57.1	37.3	5.4	5.4		5.0	1.7	2.9	3.1	−.2	4.8
1936	64.9	42.9	6.5	6.6	−.1	4.0	1.8	5.0	5.7	−.7	4.7
1937	73.6	47.9	7.1	7.1		5.6	2.1	6.2	6.2		4.7
1938	67.6	45.0	6.8	6.6	.2	4.3	2.6	4.3	3.3	1.0	4.6
1939	72.8	48.1	7.3	7.5	−.2	4.3	2.7	5.7	6.4	−.7	4.6
1940	81.6	52.1	8.4	8.5		4.6	2.9	9.1	9.3	−.2	4.5
1941	104.7	64.8	10.9	11.5	−.6	6.5	3.5	14.5	17.0	−2.5	4.5
1942	137.7	85.3	13.9	14.3	−.4	10.0	4.5	19.7	20.9	−1.2	4.3
1943	170.3	109.6	16.8	17.0	−.2	11.4	5.1	23.8	24.6	−.8	3.7
1944	182.6	121.3	18.0	18.1	−.1	11.5	5.4	23.0	23.3	−.3	3.3
1945	181.2	123.2	19.0	19.1	−.1	11.8	5.6	18.4	19.0	−.6	3.2
1946	179.6	117.7	21.3	23.0	−1.7	13.9	6.2	17.3	22.6	−5.3	3.1
1947	197.2	128.8	19.9	21.4	−1.5	14.5	6.5	23.6	29.5	−5.9	3.8
1948	221.6	140.9	21.6	22.1	−.4	16.7	7.2	30.6	32.8	−2.2	4.5
1949	216.2	140.9	21.4	21.0	.5	12.7	7.9	28.1	26.2	1.9	5.2
1950	240.0	154.3	22.9	24.0	−1.1	13.3	8.5	35.1	40.0	−4.9	5.9
1951	277.0	180.4	24.8	25.1	−.3	16.0	9.1	39.9	41.2	−1.3	6.8
1952	289.5	195.3	25.7	25.5	.2	14.3	9.9	36.9	35.9	1.0	7.4
1953	303.6	209.2	25.9	26.1	−.2	12.3	10.3	37.2	38.3	−1.1	8.8
1954	299.7	207.9	25.9	26.0	−.1	12.0	10.5	33.8	34.0	−.2	9.5
1955	322.2	221.2	27.3	27.6	−.2	11.1	10.7	41.4	43.2	−1.8	10.5

Source: Economic Report of the President, 1956

"NATIONAL INCOME" DOES NOT INCLUDE EXCISE TAXES

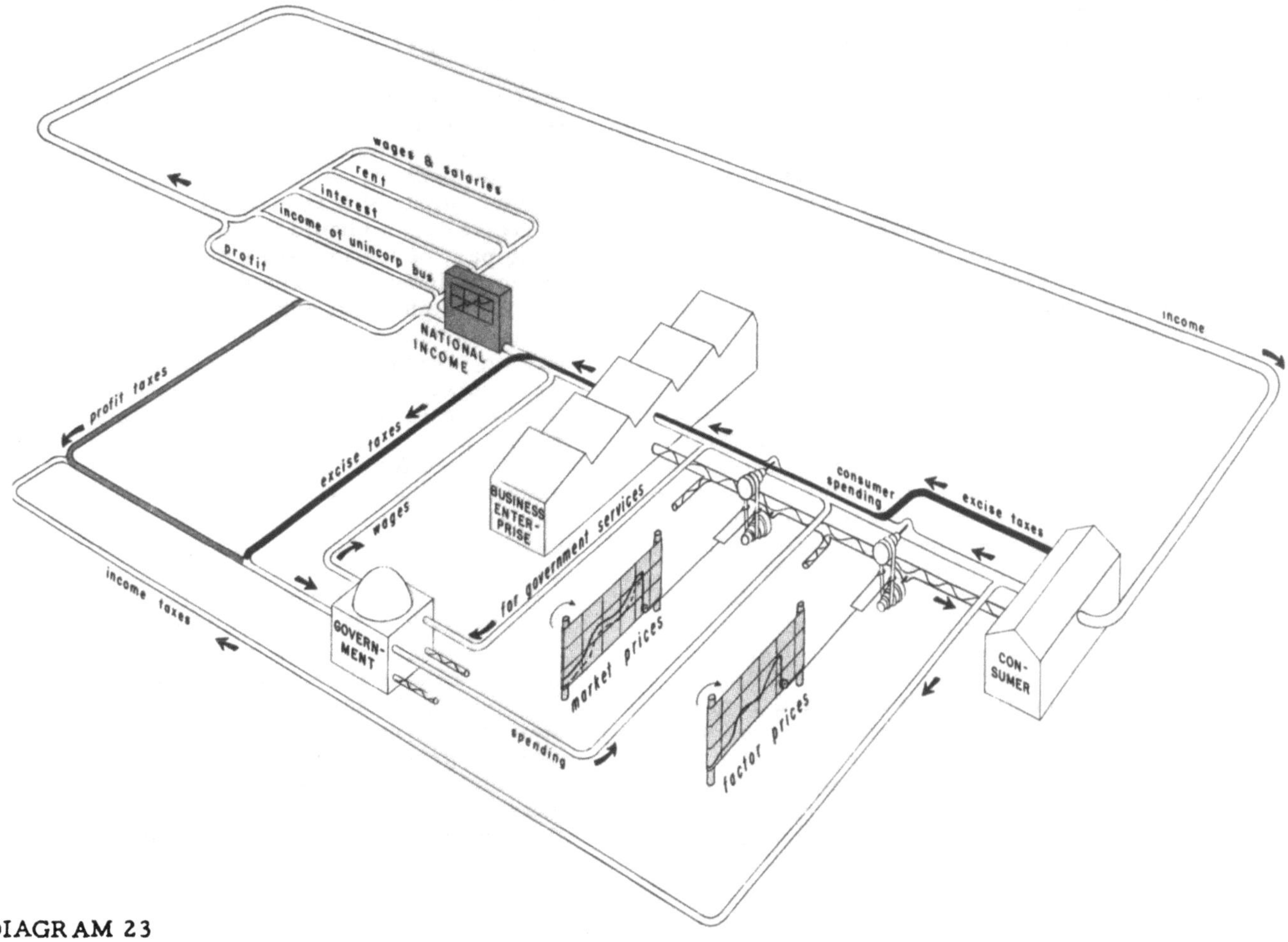

DIAGRAM 23

All firms have charges over and above their outlays for wages, interest, rent, taxes, and profit. Realistically they must also charge the consumer for both the wear-out of the plant and equipment consumed in the process of producing the goods and for the excise taxes which the government imposes on their products. These extra costs are an over-ride on the prices that manufacturers have to charge to cover merely their basic factor costs. Let us look at excise taxes first.

The federal government, besides raising revenue by means of income taxes and corporate profit taxes, obtains additional amounts by levying excise taxes on both manufacturers and consumers. Sometimes the excise taxes are levied directly upon purchases by the consumer and he pays for them directly and knowingly. For example, the excise taxes on cigarettes, liquors, gasoline, furs, jewelry, and toilet goods are added to the quoted sales prices. But the consumer also pays for other business taxes indirectly. These are taxes imposed on manufacturers who in turn usually try to pass them on to consumers by charging higher prices. Such taxes are paid by the producer or distributor on the basis of units sold. Consequently, manufacturers have to charge consumers a price in the market that provides for the excise taxes as well as for the payments to the people who contributed toward the production of the article.

These excise taxes have become a significant source of revenue since World War II. Before then excise taxes were so small that the Department of Commerce could largely ignore them as a separate charge. The sum total of dollars spent (including excise taxes) in producing goods in the market was reasonably close to all the factor payments made to produce the goods sold. But because the government greatly expanded its excise, sales, and other taxes during the war (these rose from $9.4 billion in 1939 to $28.1 billion in 1952), the difference between the total dollars (including excises) spent for goods in the market place and the dollars disbursed as "National Income" to the factors became large. The Department of Commerce could not use even as near equivalents its two main monetary measures of output: "gross national expenditures" and "national income." So it began to distinguish between "gross national product at market prices" (including excise taxes) and "national income at factor prices" (excluding excise taxes) and to emphasize that gross national expenditures—because they provide for an over-ride of government taxes—are made at market prices and not at factor prices.

Diagram 23 highlights why the Department of Commerce does not regard excise taxes as being a payment for a factor contribution to production. Excise taxes merely provide a mechanical and feasible way for the government to obtain more revenue. Because of excise taxes consumers have to inject more dollars into the spending stream for the same volume of goods. The producers in turn divert these extra amounts to the government. In contrast, as the diagram shows, Department of Commerce accounting treats the corporate profits tax as being a factor cost, that is, a payment for a contribution to production. (Government does indeed contribute to production. It renders the services of enforcing contracts and protecting property—property that private producers would have to protect with their own watchmen if the government did not protect it for them.) Corporate profits taxes thus, in contrast to excise taxes, are a part of National Income.

Students may wonder why the Department of Commerce does its accounting in such a way as implicitly to regard corporate profits taxes but not excise taxes as being factor costs. The Department of Commerce's contention is that all forms of direct business taxes—sales and excise—are usually directly transferable to the consumer via higher selling prices, but that increased profits taxes are not necessarily so transferable. This contention leads to a strange conclusion. For if the factor payment in the form of taxes is not a payment for the enforcement of contracts, and for protection, it must be—as the logic of Diagram 17 shows—a mere demand for income.

If the Department of Commerce assumes, as it has done, that excise taxes are just extra dollar amounts added to the cost of the final product without affecting the volume output of that product, then logically excise taxes should not be considered as being part of the measure of output called "national income." The diagram shows this. The physical output of goods flowing to the consumer, shown in the lower stream, remains the same regardless of excise taxes. It is only the dollar stream that becomes larger because of excise taxes.

The case for regarding corporate profits taxes as being a part of national income is not easy to justify. The implied premise that when corporate tax rates are raised the increase is not passed on by the producer to individuals through higher prices is questionable. Note how the reward to entrepreneurs, profits after taxes, has remained stable over the years in relation to gross business sales. It would appear that most of the tax load has been passed on. For undoubtedly higher tax rates on profits do eventually wind up largely in higher prices to consumers. Profits taxes today are only to a small extent a payment for the factor service that government protection renders to business. Like excise taxes, they are to a very large extent a payment for the government's greatly expanded program of defense and activity.

CHART 6

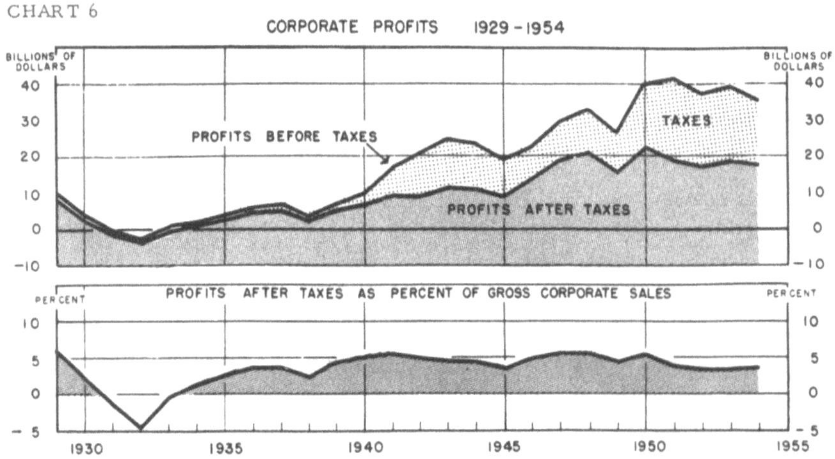

NATIONAL INCOME DOES NOT INCLUDE CHARGES FOR THE WEAR-OUT OF PLANT AND EQUIPMENT

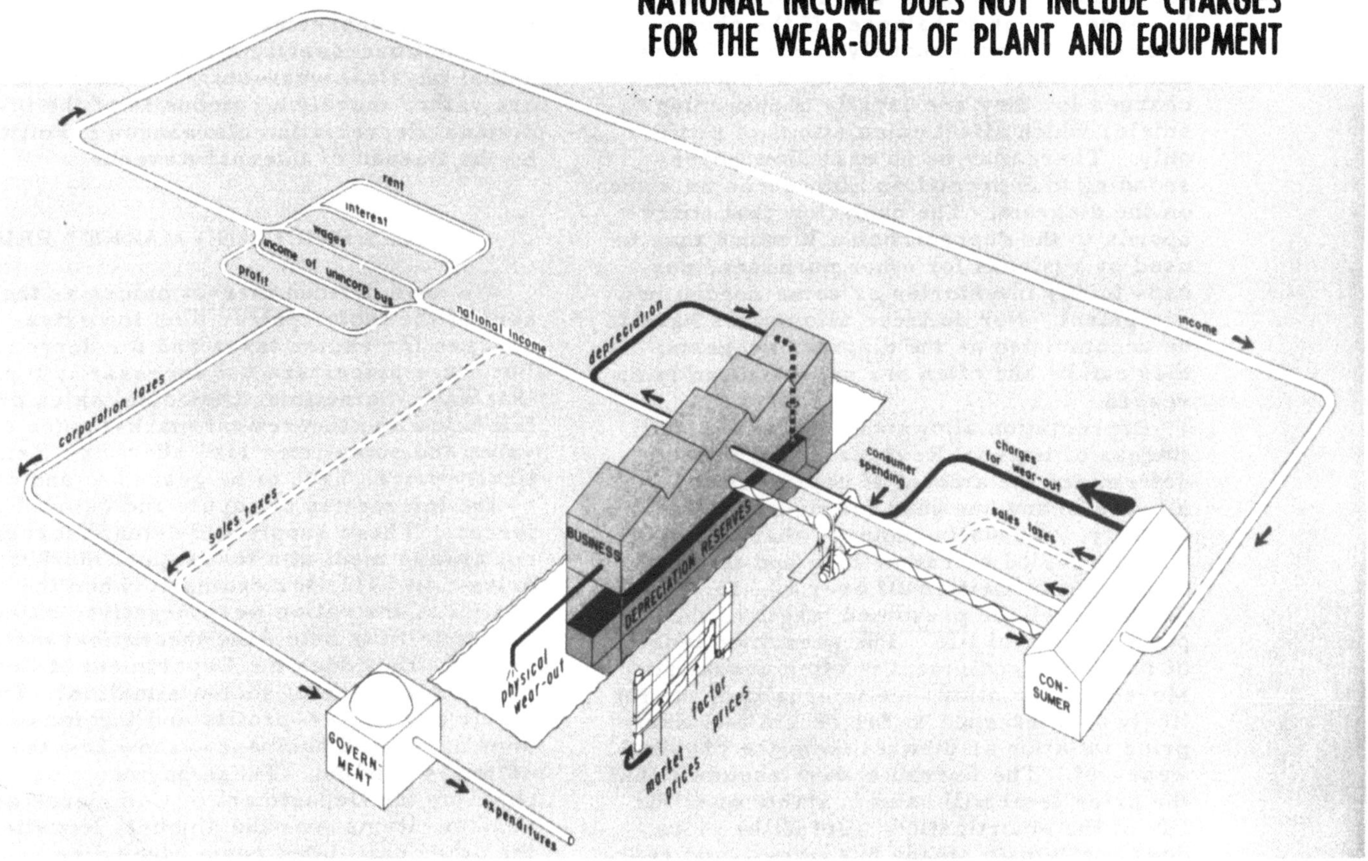

DIAGRAM 24

The nation's producers of goods and services have many factor costs to meet. A producer must pay wages in the labor market and profits taxes to the government. He must pay each of the contributing producers a fee for lending a hand. In Diagram 23 we saw how the government levies excise taxes—how it forces producers and distributors to serve to some extent as its tax collectors; also how, as a consequence, the price that sellers charge for a particular product has to be somewhat higher than just enough to cover the factor costs of production.

But there is a second reason why manufacturers over time must charge more for their goods than just enough to meet the factor cost of turning them out. Plants and equipment continually wear out, and producers must keep their sales price to the consumer high enough over a period of time to cover the wear-out costs too if they are to make a profit. In the Department of Commerce's accounting this charge is not dealt with as a factor cost to the consumer—even though in the long run the consumer is the only one who can pay it

Diagram 24 illustrates how the extra wear-out charge over the long pull is included in consumer expenditures just as excise taxes are included, and how the charge tends to operate to raise the final cost of the manufactured goods delivered to consumers. If companies did not allow for costs, the prices they charge could logically be lower or profits higher. Only a "factor price" would then need be charged. But, as first Sales Taxes and then Charges for Wear-Out are added, the Factor Price goes up to the higher Market Price. The expenditures of consuming Households at these higher market prices flow into Business. But the volume of output that flows back to Consumers remains the same. Out of their receipts from Consumer Spending producers earn a profit. The Internal Revenue Bureau allows them to exempt a portion of their annual earnings from taxation on the theory that the producers will use the exempted sums to replace the worn out plant and equipment. The exemption is presumed to be large enough to balance off the physical wear-out that continuously occurs. These allowances are referred to as nonmonetary charges for they are usually bookkeeping entries which affect calculations of profit only. There may be no cash flow corresponding to depreciation allowances as shown on the diagram. The cash flow that corresponds to the depreciation allowance may be used by business for other purposes, perhaps to buy inventories or some needed new equipment. Nor do these allowances have to be accumulated as the diagram suggests; they can be and often are spent currently as needed.

Depreciation allowances are set by the Bureau of Internal Revenue. The Bureau determines the amount of depreciation allowed in any one year for figuring tax liability. It usually requires that the amortization period be rather long and that the equipment be written off over 10, 15, or 20 years—over the presumed length of the plant's physical life. The presumed length of life of the equipment is often unrealistic. Moreover, no allowance is usually made for likely obsolescence or for recent and likely price inflation as distinct from the physical wear-out. The Bureau always assumes that the price level will remain stable over the life of the amortization. But if the price does not remain steady but rises—and realistically prices have been in an upward secular trend for twenty years—then prevailing depreciation allowances tend to be inadequate to provide for full replacement.

Because the Department of Commerce uses the Treasury's depreciation allowances to large businesses as a source of its estimates, the depreciation allowances used by it are not necessarily a realistic measure of actual physical wear-out. The allowances are rather merely a composite of the individual depreciation allowances permitted by the Bureau of Internal Revenue.

SALES PRICE AND MARKET PRICE

We have defined market prices as the sum of the factor prices plus the extra charges for excise taxes and for depreciatio But sales prices are not necessarily figured that way. Sometimes the actual sales prices fall below the theoretical market price or value and sometimes rise above it. Realistically prices have to be geared to and set by the interaction of supply and demand forces. These supply and demand forces do not always meet at a theoretical market price. In 1932, for example, when the profits of the nation were negative, sales prices fell far below the theoretical market prices. How does the Department of Commerce take care of such a situation? Two factor payments—profits and income of unincorporated business—show how the situation is handled. These payments are computed by the Department of Commerce as residual items—as the amounts left after al the other calculated costs, including depreciation, are first deducted. Because of this method of computation, profits can be and actually have been negative. The factor price for profits in that case is negative and operates to make the sales price equal to th market price.

DEPRECIATION ACCUMULATIONS PROVIDE FUNDS FOR RE-INVESTMENT

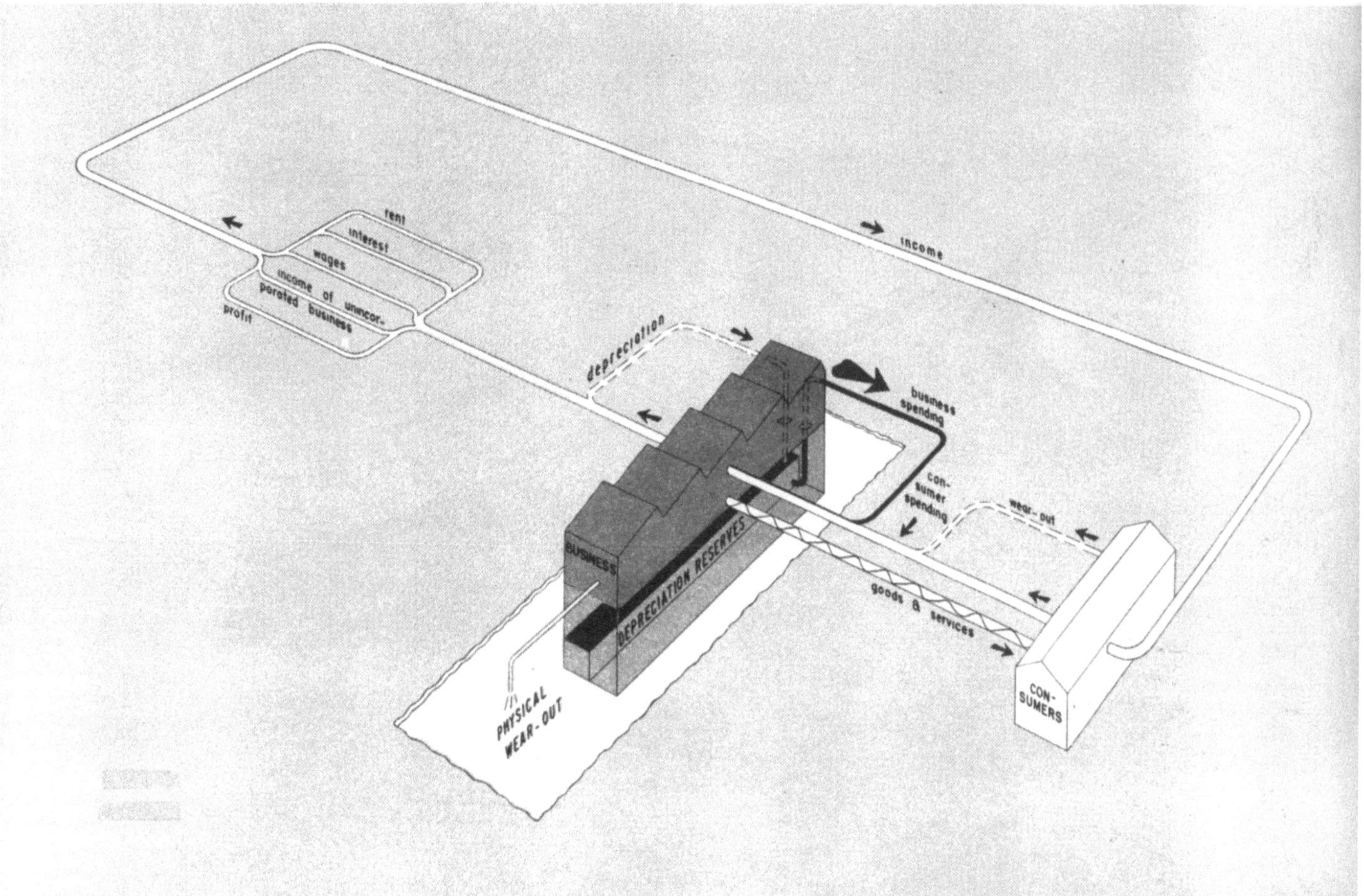

DIAGRAM 25

Over the long pull producers must—if they are both to replace their worn-out plant and equipment and make a profit—charge prices that provide for wear-out. In Diagram 25 we show how this process works in theory. In this diagram the charges for wear-out are theoretically accumulated in a fund (shown in the basement of the business building) over a period of time. When the worn-out plant and equipment have to be replaced, these funds are then supposedly pulled up from the basement and poured into the spending streams as part of business spending.

In practice it may not and usually does not work that way. The time span between accumulation and spending for replacement may not be large. For the process of investment is a continuous one. The single firm does not wait until the piece of equipment being written off is worn out before spending its accumulated depreciation allowances for replacement. It may use these allowances currently and by supplementing them with funds obtained from other sources be able to buy needed plant and equipment, either for replacement or even for expansion. Or the depreciation allowance may not be followed by any diversion of funds into investment at all, because the firm's receipts may not have been large enough to permit it to use its past depreciation allowances for new investment; the firm may have been operating with revenues very close to cost and may be forced into using all of its cash receipts to meet current payroll and other operating expenses. In such a case, the company shows a loss, and the depreciation allowance on the books is purely a bookkeeping entry.

In the Department of Commerce's accounting—which deals with the composite of spending and investment for the plant and equipment of all firms—the investment process is presumed to be a continuous one. Depreciation funds as an aggregate do tend to be spent for capital goods about as rapidly as they are deducted. And they do provide an important source of funds for the current business spending for equipment.

HOW THE TWO MAJOR MEASURES OF OUTPUT ARE RELATED TO ONE ANOTHER

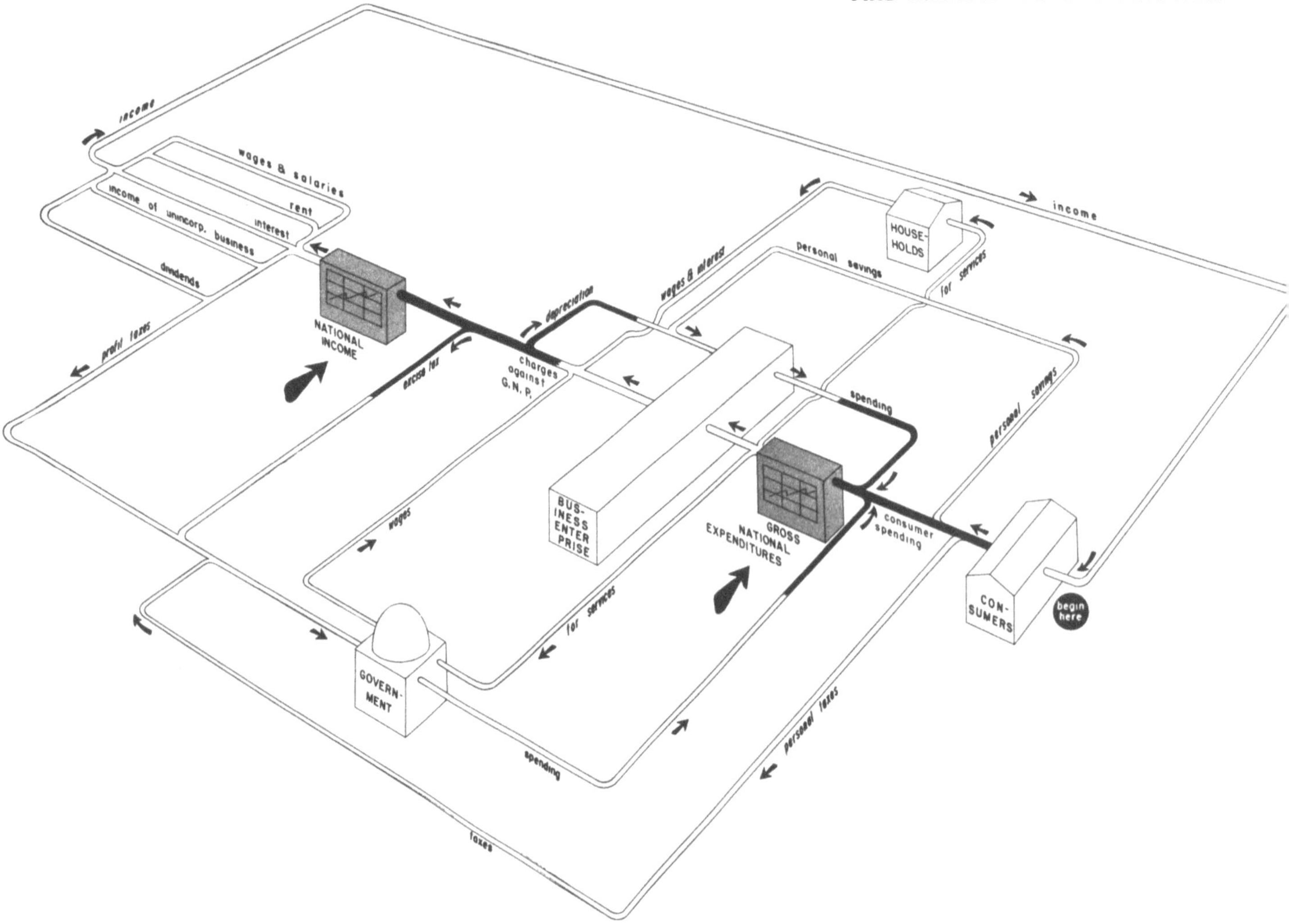

DIAGRAM 26

Here in juxtaposition we show how the Department of Commerce's two big monetary measures of output are related to one another.

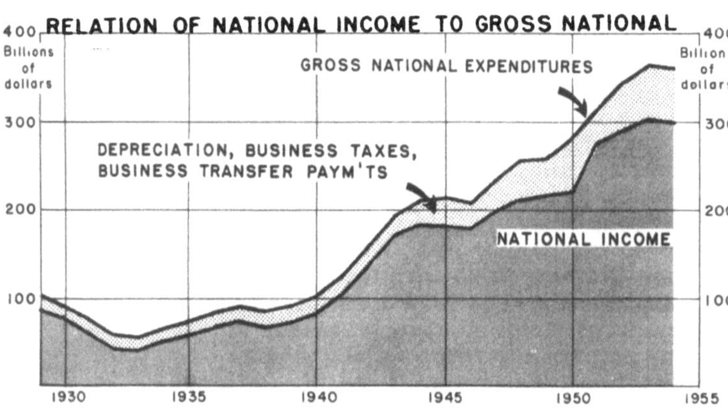

This diagram shows how the sum total of all spending for goods and services—business spending for plant and equipment and consumer spending for goods and services—is related to the income currently paid out to all those who contributed to the production of the nation's goods and services.

It has become clear by now that the Department of Commerce makes a distinction between factor costs and other costs in measuring production on the outpayments side, that is, on the left-hand side of the buildings in our diagrams. For two big sums—Excise Taxes and Depreciation Charges—are deducted from the total Charges against Production before a net is left for payment to the factors of production. The amount that is left is called "National Income." This income represents the charges against the output turned out—the payments made to factors for turning out the goods and services produced by Business Enterprise, Government, and producing Households.

HOW PERSONAL INCOME IS RELATED TO NATIONAL INCOME

billions of dollars
1950 figures

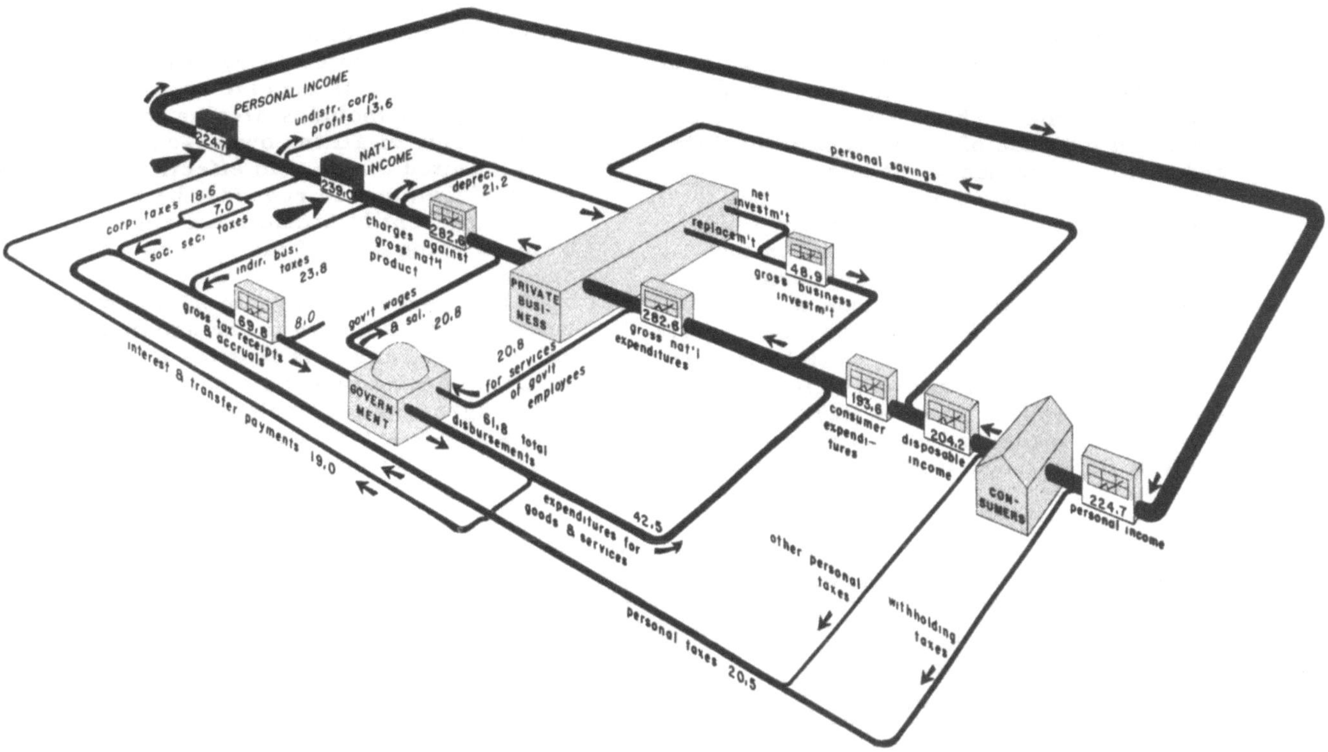

DIAGRAM 27

Besides the two major monetary meas-res of output—Gross National Expenditures nd National Income—the Department has a hird measure, namely, Personal Income.

Personal income can best be thought of as eing related to national income because it as its main source in the stream of pay-nents made by producers for help in turning ut the current production. It differs from ational income in three ways:

1. It excludes social security taxes. These taxes, although paid out by producers s income, are diverted directly into gov-rnment receipts and are not received by ndividuals as personal income.

2. It includes only part of corporate rofits. One part is diverted directly into he government receipt stream as corporate rofits taxes, and another part is retained by orporations for use in their spending. The emaining part, dividends, flows on to in-ividuals directly and becomes part of Per-onal Income.

3. In addition, Personal Income includes two items which do not have their source in the measure of current production called "national income." All the factor payments in national income and personal income are regarded as being generated in the market place through the process of production. In contrast some income is disbursed which is merely a pocket-to-pocket transfer of gov-ernment receipts to citizens whom the gov-ernment officially regards as worthy of special aid. Such pocket-to-pocket diver-sions are called transfer payments. In-cluded in them are such items as veterans' benefits, old age insurance, unemployment insurance, relief, and the like. The other stream of personal income which does not flow from the outpayments for current pro-duction is government interest.

Whether or not to count government in-terest as part of national income is not yet resolved to everyone's satisfaction. In pre-1947 accounting, the Department of

Commerce in its national income accounting regarded the interest payments which government made for borrowed sums as a factor payment and did include them in national income. However, since 1947 government income analysts have taken the position that government payments of interest to those who supply savings to government—even to state and local governments—are not factor payments. So they now exclude them from national income. This view is not easy to justify in the case of interest paid by state and local governments. It is hard to understand why the savers who supply funds to state and local governments do not render the same kind of factor services as the savers who supply funds to corporations.

Income imputations are also a part of personal income. Prior to 1947 the Department of Commerce did not publish its present series "Personal Income." It had a similar one called "Income Payments." That series measured exclusively the real tangible dollars received through payrolls, through dividends, through rent receipts, and so forth. But in 1947 the Department of Commerce broadened its concept of the income that persons receive to include non-monetary income and so added to the actual dollars received the imputed value of, for example, the food which farmers raise and themselves consume. Personal income also includes the imputed value of the food which domestic servants receive as part of their daily pay. It includes also as income the rental value of all the owner-occupied homes in the United States. In effect, the Department of Commerce regards the home-owner as paying rent to himself and regards this rent as being part of the owner's personal income.

The figures in Diagram 27 do not correspond to those shown in the accompanying table. The reason is that the Department of Commerce revised its data for 1950 after our diagram was completed. The figures in the table show the latest data that the Department of Commerce has published.

TABLE H. —*Relation of national income and personal income, 1929–55*

[Billions of dollars]

Period	National income	Less:			Plus:				Equals:
		Corporate profits and inventory valuation adjustment	Contributions for social insurance	Excess of wage accruals over disbursements	Government transfer payments	Net interest paid by government	Dividends	Business transfer payments	Personal income
1929	87.8	10.1	0.2	....	0.9	1.0	5.8	0.6	85.8
1930	75.7	6.6	.3	....	1.0	1.0	5.5	.5	76.9
1931	59.7	1.6	.3	....	2.1	1.1	4.1	.6	65.7
1932	42.5	−2.0	.3	....	1.4	1.1	2.6	.7	50.1
1933	40.2	−2.0	.3	....	1.5	1.2	2.1	.7	47.2
1934	49.0	1.1	.3	....	1.6	1.2	2.6	.6	53.6
1935	57.1	2.9	.3	....	1.8	1.1	2.9	.6	60.2
1936	64.9	5.0	.6	....	2.9	1.1	4.5	.6	68.5
1937	73.6	6.2	1.8	....	1.9	1.2	4.7	.6	73.9
1938	67.6	4.3	2.0	....	2.4	1.2	3.2	.4	68.6
1939	72.8	5.7	2.1	....	2.5	1.2	3.8	.5	72.9
1940	81.6	9.1	2.3	....	2.7	1.3	4.0	.4	78.7
1941	104.7	14.5	2.8	....	2.6	1.3	4.5	.5	96.3
1942	137.7	19.7	3.5	....	2.6	1.5	4.3	.5	123.5
1943	170.3	23.8	4.5	0.2	2.5	2.1	4.5	.5	151.4
1944	182.6	23.0	5.2	−.2	3.1	2.8	4.7	.5	165.7
1945	181.2	18.4	6.1	....	5.6	3.7	4.7	.5	171.2
1946	179.6	17.3	6.0	....	10.9	4.5	5.8	.6	178.0
1947	197.2	23.6	5.7	....	11.1	4.4	6.5	.7	190.5
1948	221.6	30.6	5.2	....	10.5	4.4	7.2	.7	208.7
1949	216.2	28.1	5.7	....	11.6	4.6	7.5	.8	206.8
1950	240.0	35.1	6.9	....	14.3	4.7	9.2	.8	227.1
1951	277.0	39.9	8.2	.1	11.6	4.8	9.1	1.0	255.3
1952	289.5	36.9	8.6	....	12.0	4.9	9.0	1.2	271.1
1953	303.6	37.2	8.7	−.1	12.8	5.0	9.3	1.2	286.2
1954	299.7	33.8	9.6	....	15.0	5.2	10.0	1.2	287.6
1955	322.2	41.4	11.0	....	15.9	5.0	11.1	1.2	303.1

Source: Economic Report of the President, 1956

WHO ARE "THE PERSONS" WHO RECEIVE "PERSONAL INCOME"

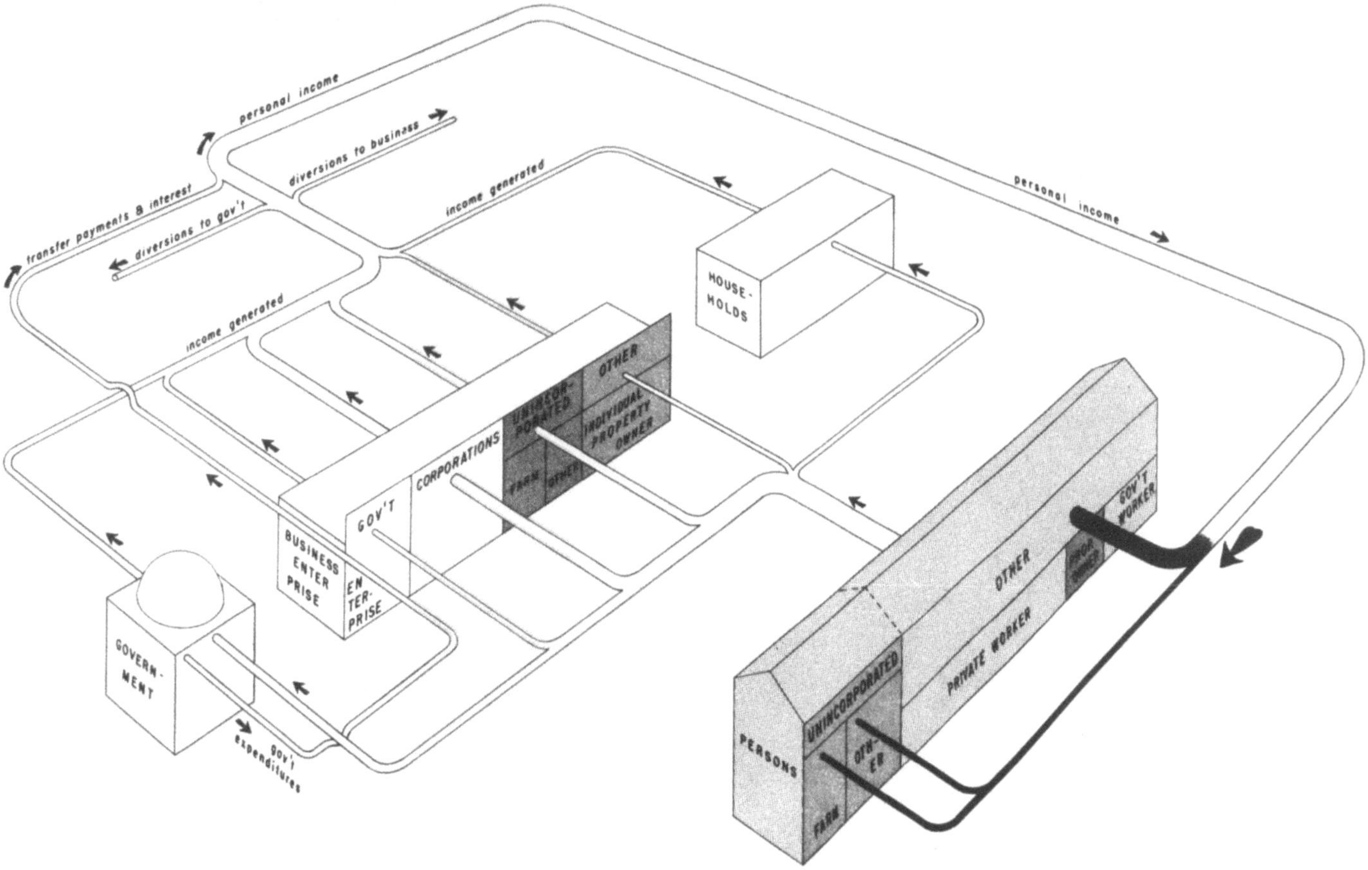

DIAGRAM 28

Diagram 28 brings out that Persons include not only workers—those who work for others, such as Private Workers and Government Workers—but also "persons" who work for themselves, such as Property Owners and Unincorporated Businessmen, of whom the Farmers are a part.

It is important to fix this coverage of Persons in one's mind thoroughly because, as we shall see in later diagrams, this definition of Persons affects concepts other than Personal Income. Most notably it affects Personal Savings. It is important to notice that many of the Persons who receive Personal Income and make consumption expenditures are also part of Business Enterprise. Unincorporated Businesses, for example, are both Persons and Business Enterprises. As enterprisers they make business expenditures which have to be included in the business spending stream—not in the consumption expenditures stream.

Take the businessman Farmer. He is classified both as a Person and as an Unincorporated Enterprise. In one role he buys consumer goods, and in the other he produces and sells goods to consumers. Because he is both a consumer and a business man, his cash expenditures are carefully reviewed by government statisticians in order to distinguish between those payments that he makes in the course of producing goods and those that he makes in the course of purchasing consumer items. When he buys a tractor the payment is considered as being a part of "business spending for equipment." When he buys a refrigerator the expenditure is regarded as being a part of consumer spending, and as such it appears in the Department of Commerce's Consumer Accounts.

INCOME DISTRIBUTION CAN BE REPORTED IN TWO WAYS:

BY FACTOR PAYMENTS
BY INCOME GROUPS

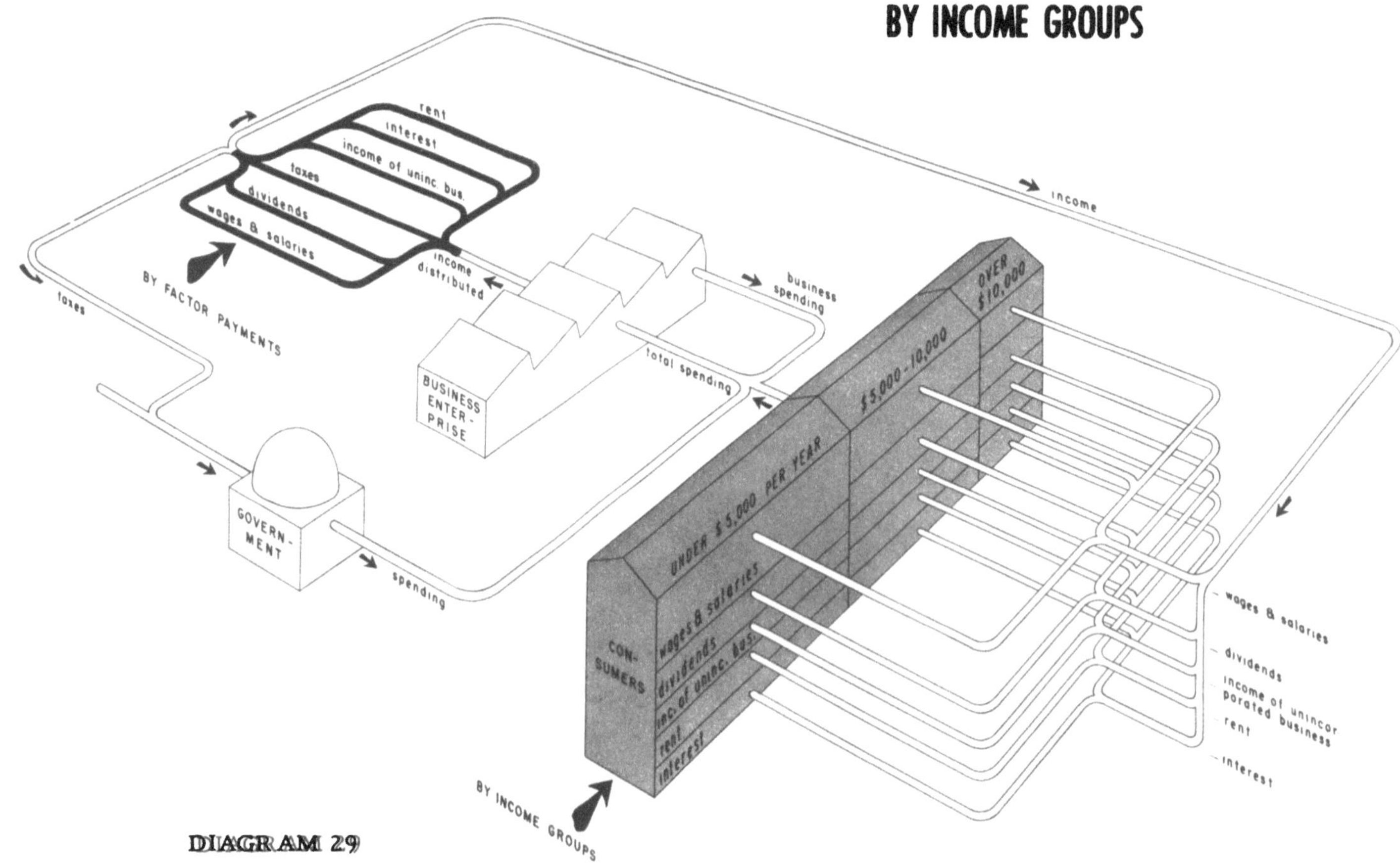

DIAGRAM 29

Diagrams 14, 15, 16, and 17 presented a breakdown of the factor payments that constitute national income. This Diagram 29 presents another possible breakdown, one by income groups.

The Department of Commerce, in measuring the income produced by the nation, proceeds in the classical tradition of measuring income in terms of factor shares: wages, interest, rent, profit, and so forth. It makes a detailed effort to do this and calls attention to the relative size of the rewards for each kind of factor contribution.

Historically, economists have always focused their attention on "production, exchange, and distribution." But the "distribution" that statisticians have reported on most fully is the distribution of the nation's income between the factors of production, not between real people. They have reported far more fully on the distribution between such functional factors as wages, interest, rent, and profit than on the distribution between flesh and blood citizens such as Joe Doakes and John D. Rockefeller. Their concern was largely with process. When in their national income accounting they necessarily became highly statistical, they also had to modify—either from necessity or choice—the classical definitions of various factor payments, such as profits and interest. The meaning and computations of factor payments in national income accounting have now become so non-classical that in dealing today with the issue of income distribution between factors, one should keep an eye on their changed meanings. In national income accounting, profit is not a factor payment for risk taking, for example, but a residual item; interest is not a factor payment for saving and waiting but (even in the state and local government sector) an arbitrary transfer payment.

In recent decades, public interest in the distribution of income between income groups has grown steadily. For society is naturally interested in knowing how the income it produces is split among income groups—how much goes to the rich, the poor, and the middle class. More and more research effort is now being devoted to discovering this breakdown of the nation's income by income groups. Recently, for example, Simon Kuznets published a book in which he showed how the percentage of personal income going to the richest 7 percent of the population has varied since 1919. And now the Department of Commerce has begun to prepare periodic releases on the distribution of income by groups, even though it does not include such information as yet in its regular national income accounting reports.

AN INTEGRATION OF NATIONAL INCOME ACCOUNTING DEFINITIONS

billions of dollars
1950 figures

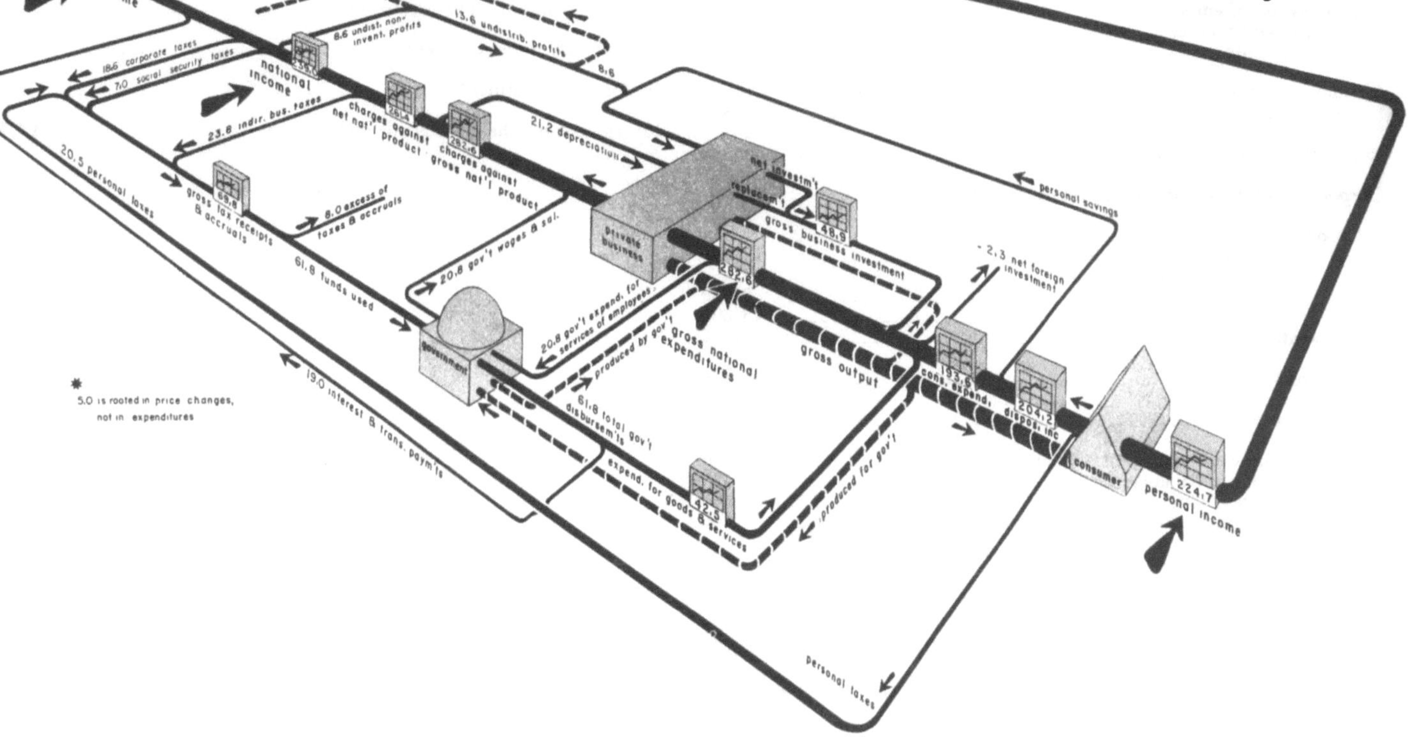

DIAGRAM 30

This diagram provides a frame of reference for all the major national income measures used by the Department of Commerce. It shows the differences in meaning of the terms used and how each term is related to every other.

The ringed pipes on the diagram represent the streams of real output that the Department of Commerce would really like to measure in unit terms but for technical reasons can not. Instead, the Department of Commerce limits itself to dealing with the monetary streams shown in solid black on the diagram.

As brought out before, the Department of Commerce decided that one way to measure the value of the output was to collect data on the spending carried out by each major spending group in payment for the output. The sum of these expenditures is shown on the right-hand side of the Private Business building and is marked by the meter Gross National Expenditures.

Because in producing the output of the nation business firms and governments have to make certain outpayments, it is also possible to measure the value of the nation's output in a second way, namely, by measuring total payments made or the charges incurred in producing the goods and services. On the diagram, the costs incurred in producing the goods and services are on the left-hand side of the Private Business building and are designated as Charges against Gross National Product. A meter shows the sum of these charges to be numerically equivalent to Gross National Expenditures. It is here on the cost side that the Department of Commerce has two other monetary measures of output. One is called Charges against Net National Product; the other is National Income. Each of these measures is related to the other because of the addition or subtraction of certain flows as shown in the diagram. Thus the Charges against Net National Product are obtained from Charges against Gross National Product by subtracting Depreciation. Thus, too, National Income is obtained from Net National Product by subtracting Indirect Business Taxes.

From the measure National Income the Department of Commerce then derives Personal Income, as shown. This series is derived from National Income by subtracting both Corporate and Social Security Taxes and then adding in government Interest Payments and certain Transfer Payments.

To help explain how the key definitions used in national income accounting are related to one another, dollar values are placed on each of the major monetary flows. The dollar values also indicate the magnitudes involved.

THE DEPARTMENT OF COMMERCE'S SIX NATIONAL INCOME AND PRODUCT ACCOUNTS, 1950

TABLE I.

Table I.—National Income and Product Account, 1950
[Millions of dollars]

Compensation of employees:		Personal consumption expenditures	193,568
Wages and salaries	145,844	Gross private domestic investment	48,867
Supplements	7,489	Net foreign investment	−2,304
Income of unincorporated enterprises and inventory valuation adjustment	35,964	Government purchases of goods and services	42,499
Rental income of persons	8,039		
Corporate profits and inventory valuation adjustment:			
Corporate profits before tax:			
Corporate profits tax liability	18,593		
Corporate profits after tax:			
Dividends	9,169		
Undistributed profits	13,605		
Inventory valuation adjustment	−5,126		
Net interest	5,386		
National income	*238,963*		
Indirect business tax and nontax liability	23,798		
Business transfer payments	752		
Statistical discrepancy	−1,800		
Less: Subsidies minus current surplus of government enterprises	260		
Charges against net national product	*261,453*		
Capital consumption allowances	21,177		
CHARGES AGAINST GROSS NATIONAL PRODUCT	282,630	GROSS NATIONAL PRODUCT	282,630

Table II.—Consolidated Business Income and Product Account, 1950 [1]
[Millions of dollars]

Compensation of employees:		Consolidated net sales:	
Wages and salaries:		To consumers	184,547
Disbursements	120,062	To government	18,129
Excess of accruals over disbursements	0	To business on capital account	44,529
		To abroad	1,111
Supplements:			
Employer contributions for social insurance	3,185	Change in inventories	4,338
Other labor income	3,136		
Income of unincorporated enterprises and inventory valuation adjustment	35,964		
Rental income of persons	8,039		
Corporate profits and inventory valuation adjustment:			
Corporate profits before tax:			
Corporate profits tax liability	18,593		
Corporate profits after tax:			
Dividends	8,782		
Undistributed profits	12,901		
Inventory valuation adjustment	−5,126		
Net interest	3,451		
Income originating	*208,987*		
Indirect business tax and nontax liability	23,798		
Business transfer payments	752		
Statistical discrepancy	−1,800		
Less: Subsidies minus current surplus of government enterprises	260		
Charges against net product	*231,477*		
Capital consumption allowances	21,177		
CHARGES AGAINST BUSINESS GROSS PRODUCT	252,654	BUSINESS GROSS PRODUCT	252,654

The Department of Commerce had the problem of showing statistically the performance of our big, intricate economy. But first the economists had to formulate some mental pictures of the design of that economy. They drew up a conceptual framework, proceeded to measure systematically every major part of the economy's performance, and then showed how its movements were statistically interlaced. They did this in six "tables of accounts," which are reproduced here for the year 1950. Although necessarily condensed, these tables are the best means that the Department of Commerce possesses

THE DEPARTMENT OF COMMERCE'S SIX NATIONAL INCOME AND PRODUCT ACCOUNTS, 1950

Table III.—Personal Income and Expenditure Account, 1950

[Millions of dollars]

Personal consumption expenditures:		Wage and salary receipts:	
Purchases of direct services:		Disbursements by:	
Compensation of employees:		Business	120,062
Wages and salaries paid	5,945	Government	19,820
Supplements paid:		Households and institutions	5,945
Employer contributions for social insurance	41	Rest of the world	17
Other labor income	21	Less: Employee contributions for social insurance	2,945
Interest paid	1,720	Other labor income:	
Income originating in and net and gross product of households and institutions	*7,727*	Business	3,136
		Government	315
Net purchases from business	184,547	Households and institutions	21
Net purchases from abroad	1,294	Income of unincorporated enterprises and inventory valuation adjustment	35,964
Personal tax and nontax payments	20,460		
Personal saving	10,693	Rental income of persons	8,039
		Dividends	9,169
		Personal interest income	10,096
		Government transfer payments	14,330
		Business transfer payments	752
PERSONAL OUTLAY AND SAVING	224,721	PERSONAL INCOME	224,721

Table IV.—Consolidated Government Receipts and Expenditures Account, 1950

[Millions of dollars]

Purchases of goods and services:		Personal tax and nontax receipts	20,460
Purchases of direct services:		Corporate profits tax accruals	18,593
Compensation of employees:		Indirect business tax and nontax accruals	23,798
Wages and salaries	19,820	Contributions for social insurance:	
Supplements:		Employee contributions	2,945
Employer contributions for social insurance	791	Employer contributions:	
Other labor income	315	Business	3,185
Income originating and net and gross product	*20,926*	Government	791
Net purchases from business	18,129	Households and institutions	41
Net purchases from abroad	3,444	Deficit (+) or surplus (−) on income and product transactions	−8,014
Transfer payments	14,330		
Net interest paid	4,710		
Subsidies minus current surplus of government enterprises	260		
GOVERNMENT EXPENDITURES	61,799	GOVERNMENT RECEIPTS AND DEFICIT	61,799

Table V.—Rest of the World Account, 1950

[Millions of dollars]

Net payments of factor income to the United States:		Net disinvestment in the United States	−2,304
Wages and salaries	17		
Interest	215		
Dividends	387		
Branch profits	704		
Income originating and net and gross product	*1,323*		
Net purchases from the United States:			
From business	1,111		
From government	−3,444		
From persons	−1,294		
NET CURRENT PAYMENTS TO THE UNITED STATES	−2,304	NET DISINVESTMENT IN THE UNITED STATES	−2,304

Table VI.—Gross Saving and Investment Account, 1950

[Millions of dollars]

Business purchases on capital account	44,529	Excess of wage accruals over disbursements	0
Change in business inventories	4,338	Undistributed corporate profits (domestic)	12,901
Net disinvestment in the United States by rest of world	−2,304	Corporate inventory valuation adjustment	−5,126
Government deficit (+) or surplus (−) on income and product transactions	−8,014	Statistical discrepancy	−1,800
		Capital consumption allowances by private business	21,177
		Foreign branch profits (net)	704
		Personal saving	10,693
GROSS INVESTMENT AND GOVERNMENT DEFICIT	38,549	GROSS PRIVATE SAVING	38,549

for describing how the major transactions are interrelated.

In order to relate these transactions one to another, the Department of Commerce reports numerical values for many of the major transfers involved in production and distribution. It thus had to relate flows representing such payments as rent, interest, profit, savings, and personal income to national income measures. Some of this will be portrayed in the pages that follow.

The major entries of the six tables shown here were summarized in Diagram 30.

HOW THE MAJOR ENTRIES IN AN INCOME STATEMENT ARE INTERRELATED

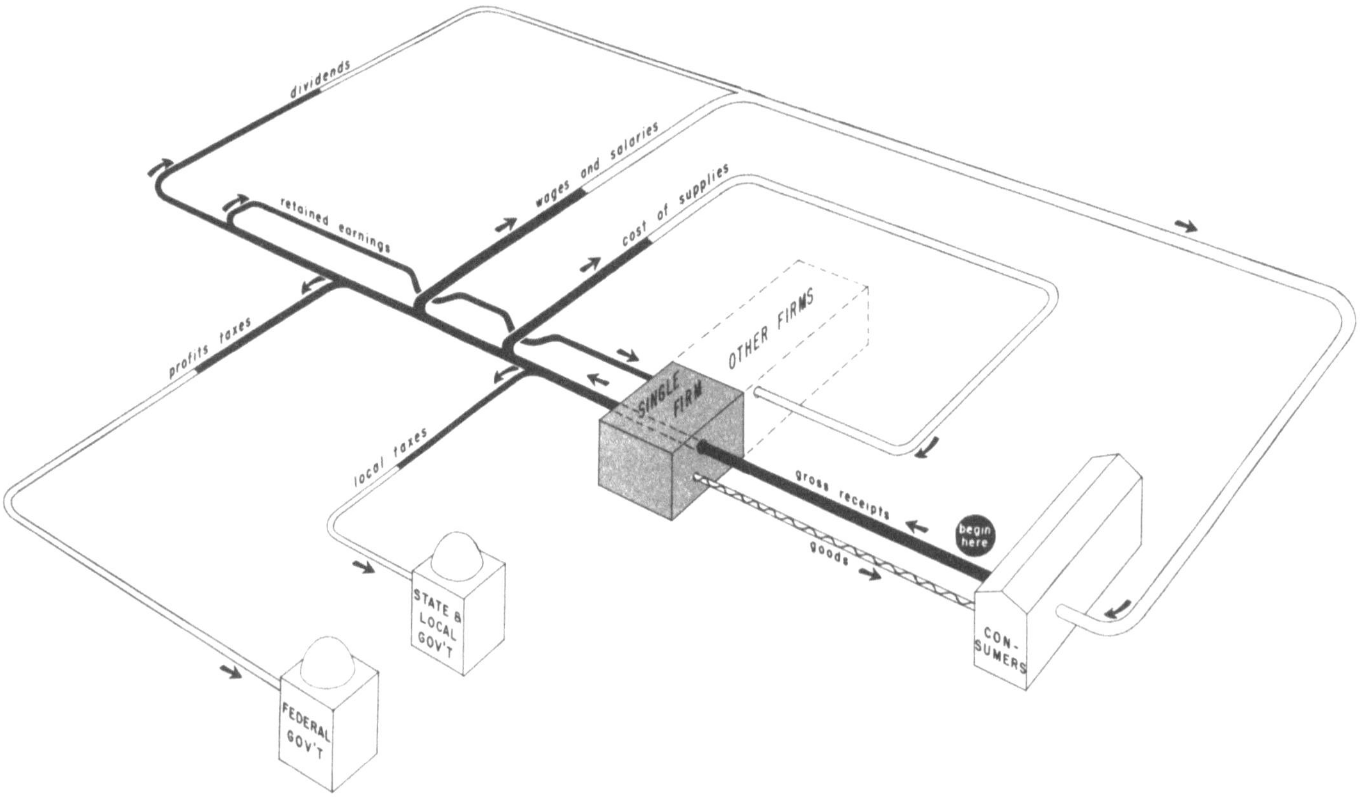

DIAGRAM 31

The principal purpose of the government's "Tables of Accounts," shown on the preceding page, is to tell us where the money of each major spending group comes from and where it goes. Those accounts present a receipts and expenditures picture for each of the major spending groups. By following the account for Persons, for example, we can see where the consumers' income came from, how much was spent, and how much was saved; by following the account for the Government we can see whether it ran a surplus or a deficit; by following it for Business we can see how all business receipts were distributed.

Since the Government's tables are essentially accounting ones, it is probably advisable to take time out to review the general aims of accounting, which Diagrams 31 and 32 illustrate.

Business firms in keeping books on their operations use widely accepted accounting conventions. Every firm has two problems: (1) to indicate from where its money comes and to where it is disbursed and (2) to show simultaneously its assets and liabilities. It is a common business practice for a firm to summarize regularly where its money came from and where it went in what is called an "income statement" or "profit and loss account." Firms also report regularly on their assets and liabilities in the "balance sheet." Diagram 31 illustrates the first of these accounting records, a simple income statement or profit and loss account. Because a firm is usually questioned by its stockholders more about its expenditures than about its receipts, it usually reports more fully on outpayments. A breakdown of a firm's income statement greatly simplified looks like this:

INCOME STATEMENT

Receipts		
Gross Revenue		
(from operations and investment)		$100,000
Expenditures		
Cost of Goods Sold		
Local taxes	1,000	
Materials and supplies	50.000	
Wages and salaries	40,000	
		91,000
Gross Profit		9,000
Profit taxes		5,000
Net Profit		4,000
Dividends		3,000
Earnings retained		1,000

HOW THE BALANCE SHEET IS RELATED TO THE INCOME STATEMENT

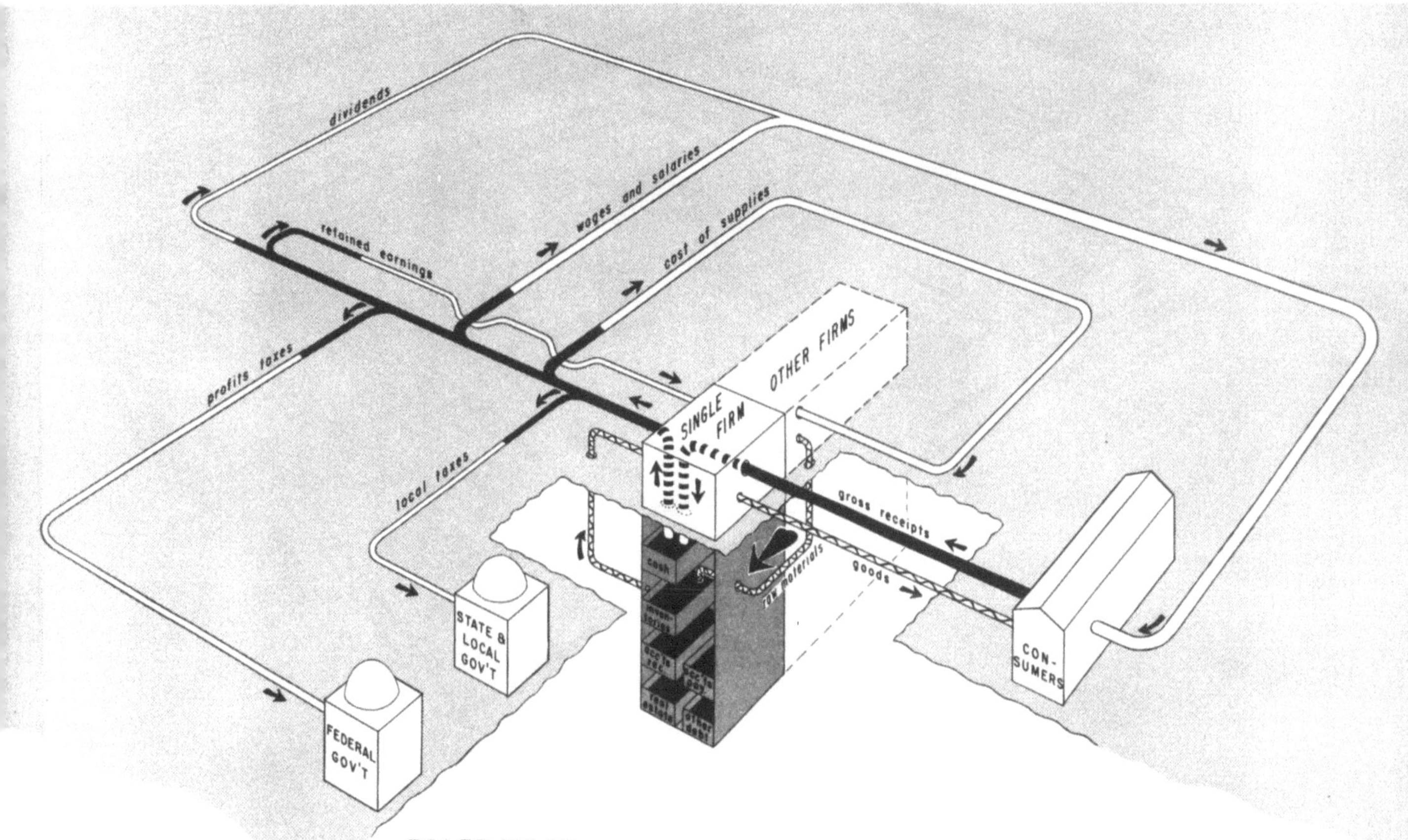

DIAGRAM 32

Besides preparing an income statement, every firm makes a second table, the Balance Sheet, to show how its assets and liabilities balance off as of certain selected dates—usually at the end of the month, quarter, or year. Thus published annual reports of a corporation always present two tables which summarize its annual performance and its changing financial strength: (1) an income statement (often called a profit and loss account) which shows for a period of time where the firm's money came from and where it went (to highlight how much profit or loss was made during the period) and (2) a balance sheet which shows how the firm's assets compare with its liabilities on certain selected dates. The two tabular statements are closely related to each other—assets and liabilities are affected and changed by the operations reported on in the income statement—but the two separate tabular presentations themselves can not show their integration.

Diagram 32 reveals how it is feasible by means of our new perspective technique to show concurrently and in an integrated way both the income statement and the balance sheet of a business firm. True, the diagram shows this for only a very simple situation, but very elaborate statements are amenable to the same kind of depiction.

In Diagram 32 we illustrate how a firm's Receipts go initially into its Cash bin and how its expenditure payments are made from that bin. Naturally, because the inflow and outflow streams are never exactly equal, the balance in the cash bin is ever-changing and always different at the end of each month, quarter, or year. This shows how the asset, cash, reported in the balance sheet is changed by the current operations of the corporation as reported on in the income statement. Similarly we show in the diagram how the raw materials which the firm puts into finished products are initially purchased from Other Firms and then flow into the firm's supply, or Inventory, bin, and how the materials are then gradually drawn on as goods are fabricated and sold. Obviously again, as production proceeds, the level in the inventory bin also always changes.

In like manner we could draw inflow and outflow streams in relation to all the other asset and liability bins to indicate that their contents too have an ever-changing level and also that this level is related to the operations of the firm. The value of the assets and liabilities reported on in the balance sheet of a firm has to be appraised from time to time along with the operating profit and loss statement to give a true and realistic picture of a firm's financial position.

NATIONAL INCOME ACCOUNTS "CLEAR" IN BOTH 1950 AND 1951 BUT AT DIFFERENT LEVELS. WHY?

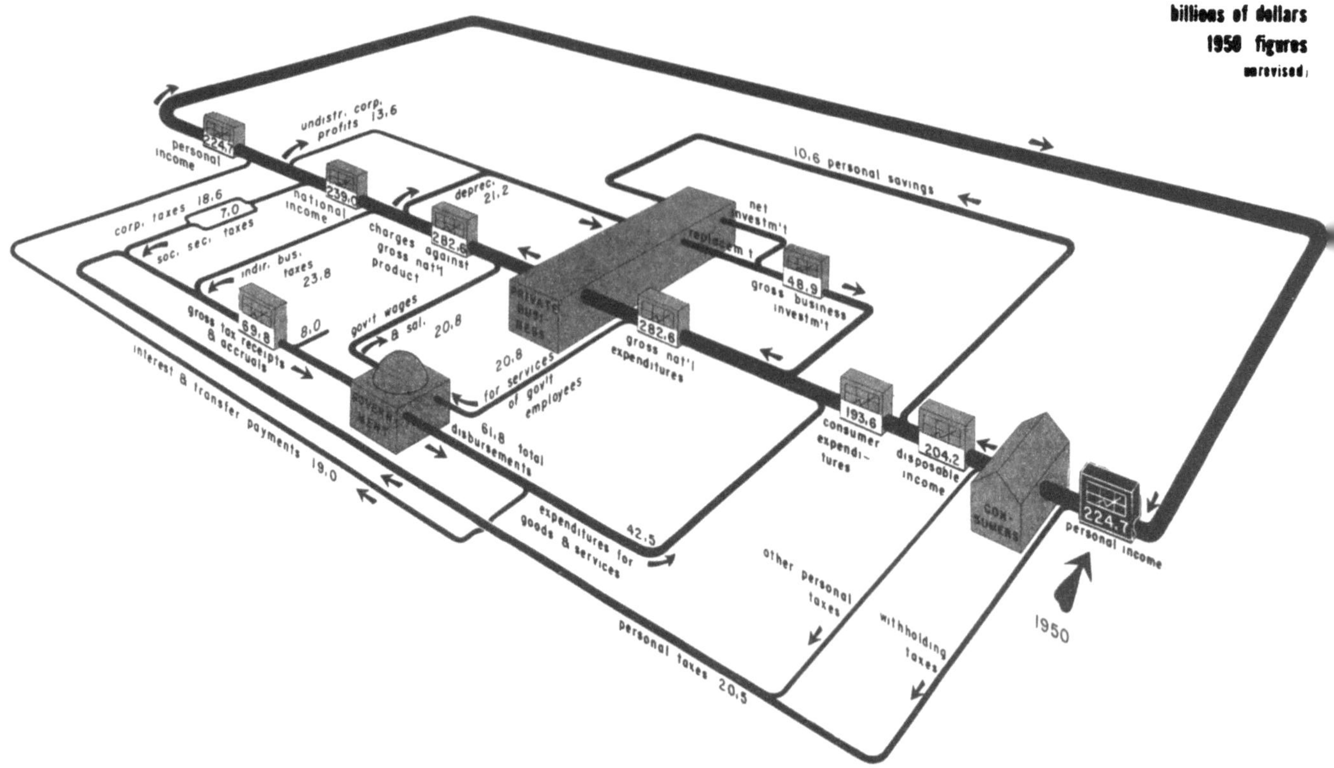

DIAGRAM 33

The purpose of the double-spread Diagrams 33 and 34 is to show that it is not statistically possible to discover how or why U. S. national income moves from one dollar level to another simply by analyzing and examining the streams of receipts and expenditures or income statements alone. For example, Diagram 33 shows that in 1950 the amount of total spending by all three major spending groups resulted in a "Personal Income" of $224. 7 billion. It also shows that there was a complete clearance or balance of receipts and expenditures in that year. Diagram 34 shows that for 1951 "Personal Income" was $254. 1 billion one year later, and that at that higher level there was also a complete clearance or balance of receipts and expenditures for that year. But what made the level rise about $30 billion during that one year period? One will never find the answer by examining the Department of Commerce's income accounting data alone. But then its accounts were not set up to throw light on that matter.

NATIONAL INCOME ACCOUNTS "CLEAR" IN BOTH 1950 AND 1951 BUT AT DIFFERENT LEVELS. WHY?

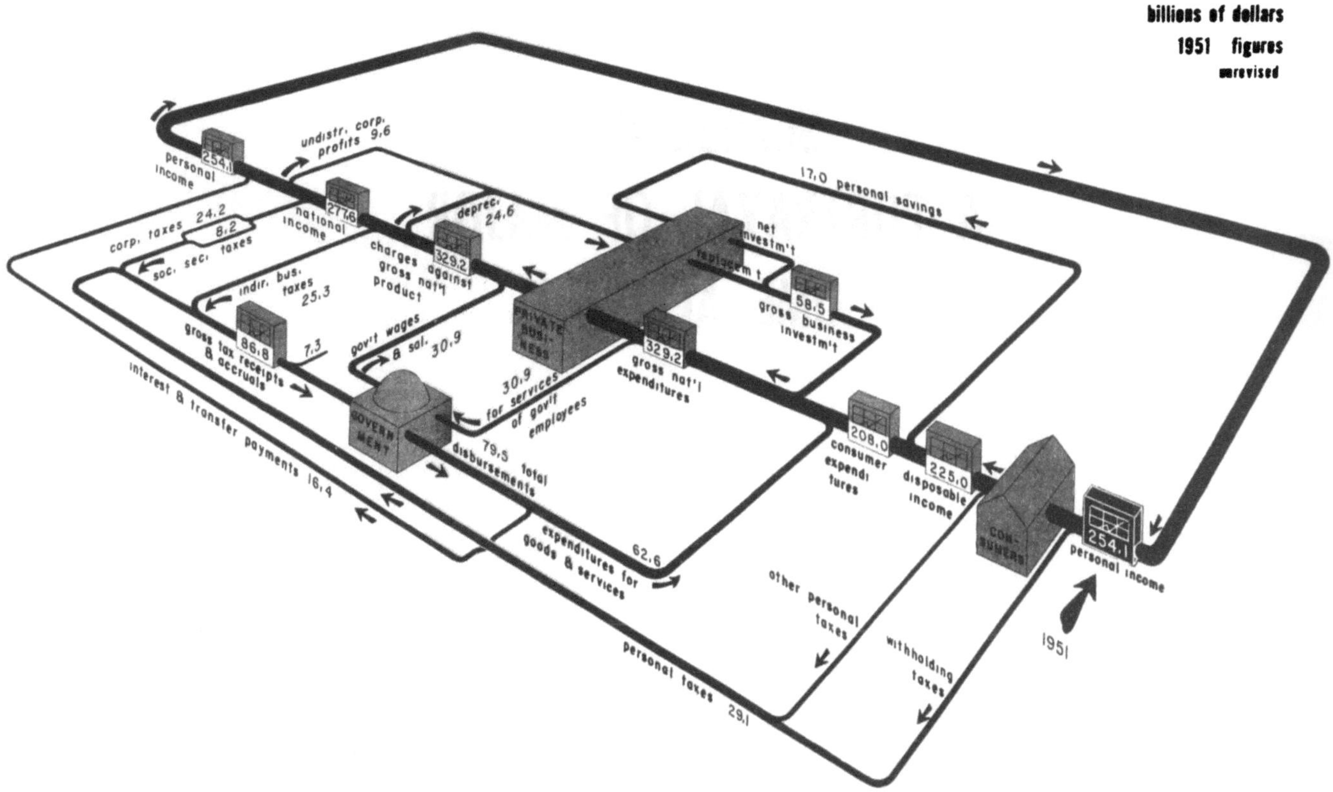

DIAGRAM 34

To understand why such changes in personal income occur, it is necessary, among other things, to keep an eagle eye on the ever-changing levels of the assets and liabilities of each of the major spending groups. (Diagram 32 illustrated how the changing assets and liabilities of a single firm influence and are influenced by its operations at the expenditure level.)

The double-spread of Diagrams 33 and 34 highlights the fact that the system of national income accounting, which we are now reviewing, is a sort of one-legged system of accounting. For it provides no systematic balance sheet data on the various spending groups. Absence of such information reduces much of the potential value of the government data as they stand for market research and business forecasting purposes.

Section III

A PORTRAYAL OF MAJOR INCOME ACCOUNTS

A PORTRAYAL OF "TABLE 1-NATIONAL INCOME AND PRODUCT ACCOUNT, 1950"

BILLIONS OF DOLLARS

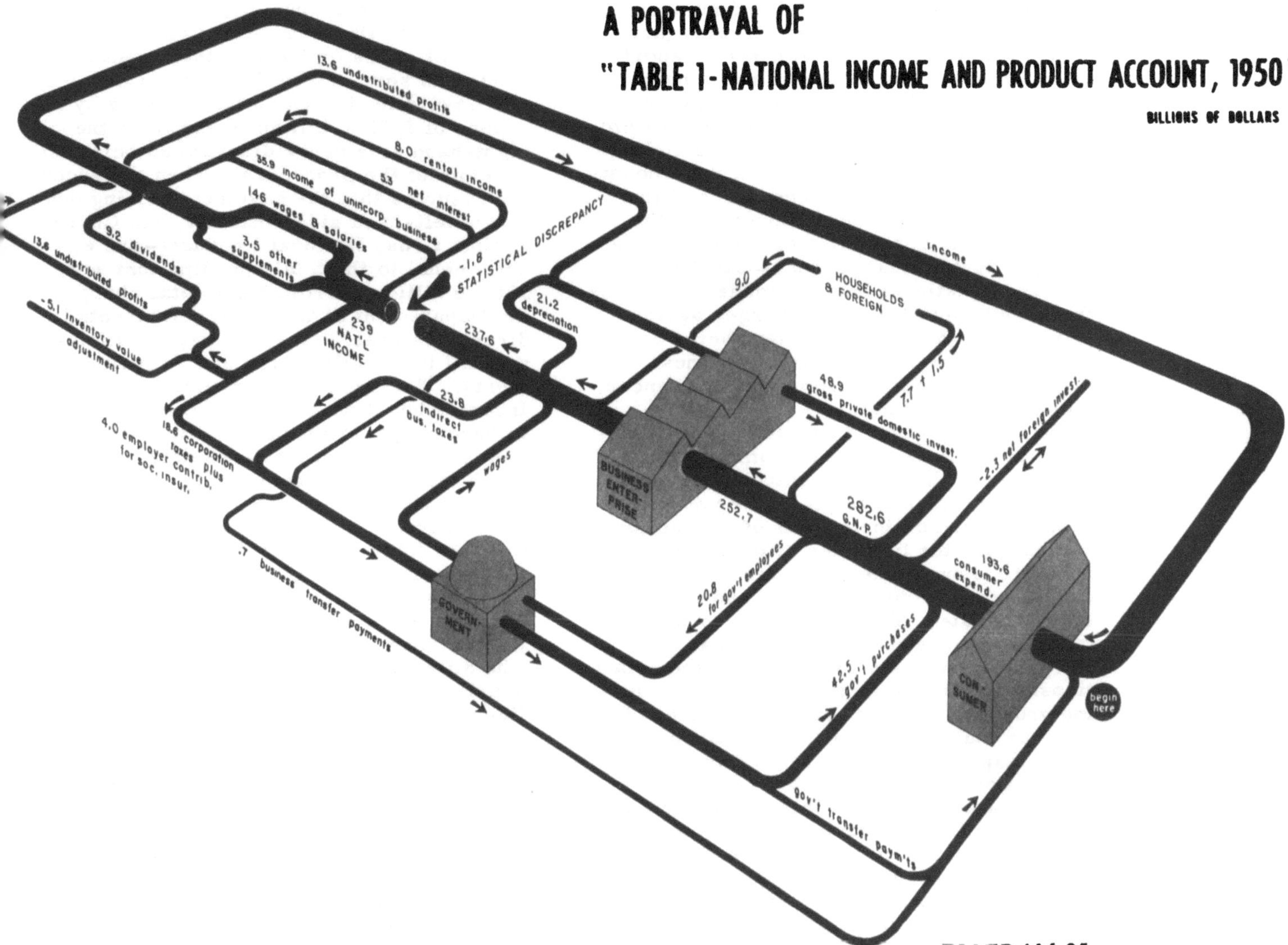

DIAGRAM 35

Table 1.—*National Income and Product Account, 1950*

[Millions of dollars]

Compensation of employees:		Personal consumption expenditures	194, 026
Wages and salaries	146, 526	Gross private domestic investment	51, 219
Supplements	7, 799	Net foreign investment	−2, 201
Income of unincorporated enterprises and inventory valuation adjustment	36, 140	Government purchases of goods and services	42, 023
Rental income of persons	8, 473		
Corporate profits and inventory valuation adjustment:			
Corporate profits before tax:			
Corporate profits tax liability	17, 829		
Corporate profits after tax:			
Dividends	9, 207		
Undistributed profits	12, 934		
Inventory valuation adjustment	−4, 864		
Net interest	5, 912		
National income	*239, 956*		
Indirect business tax and nontax liability	23, 741		
Business transfer payments	843		
Statistical discrepancy	215		
Less: Subsidies minus current surplus of government enterprises	204		
Charges against net national product	*264, 551*		
Capital consumption allowances	20, 516		
CHARGES AGAINST GROSS NATIONAL PRODUCT	285, 067	GROSS NATIONAL PRODUCT	285, 067

Diagram 35 is a pictorial and numerical integration of all the money streams (and nonmonetary accounting transfers) reported on in Table I. The table itself is a numerical summary of the four major measures of production on which the Department of Commerce regularly keeps tab. On the right-hand side of the table are shown the amounts spent by the four major consumers of the nation's Gross National Product. On the left-hand side of the table are listed all the charges against that product—all the factor payments (National Income) made to produce the output, plus the other charges against production, the most important being depreciation, excise taxes (indirect business taxes), and capital consumption allowances, including depreciation.

So far as it goes, Table I is a good summary of the Department of Commerce's measures of the nation's output—measures built on the sales receipts of the nation's producers and on their costs of production. But how are the two sides of the accounts related? How do the quantities move from one spending group to another and where do they originate? The single entries in the table cannot answer such questions. The integrating Diagram 35 does show the relationship between the consuming and producing groups. It shows how expenditures of the four major spending groups (Gross National Expenditures) are related to the several major streams of factor payments which make up National Income and how the other two charges against production, depreciation and indirect business taxes, are handled. (In Diagram 31 we pictured how the income statement of a single business firm describes a large part of the firm's operations. Diagram 35 is a similar composite income statement for all the producers of the nation.

This diagram also brings to light the bothersome item of Statistical Discrepancy. Statistical discrepancy grows out of an operating difficulty. In collecting monetary data on how the economy is currently performing, the Department of Commerce collects figures on the amounts spent for goods and services by Business, Consumers, and Government. The total spending by all groups of $282.6 billion is shown on the right-hand side of the diagram as being the receipts of the producers. Then the accounting assumes that the payments coming out on the left-hand side—namely, the Charges against Gross National Product—are exactly equal to the total spending that went in: $282.6 billion. From these total charges the Department of Commerce subtracts Indirect Business Taxes and Depreciation and a small item called Business Transfer Payments. The result should equal National Income, but it never does—exactly. This is because government statisticians concurrently collect in great detail data on how much the Business community, the Government, and the producing Households hand out in payroll, rent, interest, and profits to cover their factor costs. The sum of all these factor costs is of course National Income and is never equal to the amount obtained by subtracting Depreciation and Excise Taxes from Gross National Product. The difference is not large as a rule; it usually runs between $1 billion and $4 billion per year and is called the Statistical Discrepancy.

Because the Statistical Discrepancy is entered on the left-hand side, that is, on the outpayments side, there is a tabular implication that the sum of the expenditures entered on the right-hand side is the more correct or control figure, and that it is the sum of all outpayments plus the indirect business taxes and depreciation allowances that is regarded as the less reliable figure. This is not necessarily true. The Department of Commerce merely placed the entry in a convenient spot and specifically states that no inferences as to relative accuracy should be drawn from the choice it made.

PART A: THE GOVERNMENT ACCOUNT

A PORTRAYAL OF "TABLE IV-CONSOLIDATED GOVERNMENT RECEIPTS AND EXPENDITURES ACCOUNT, 1950"

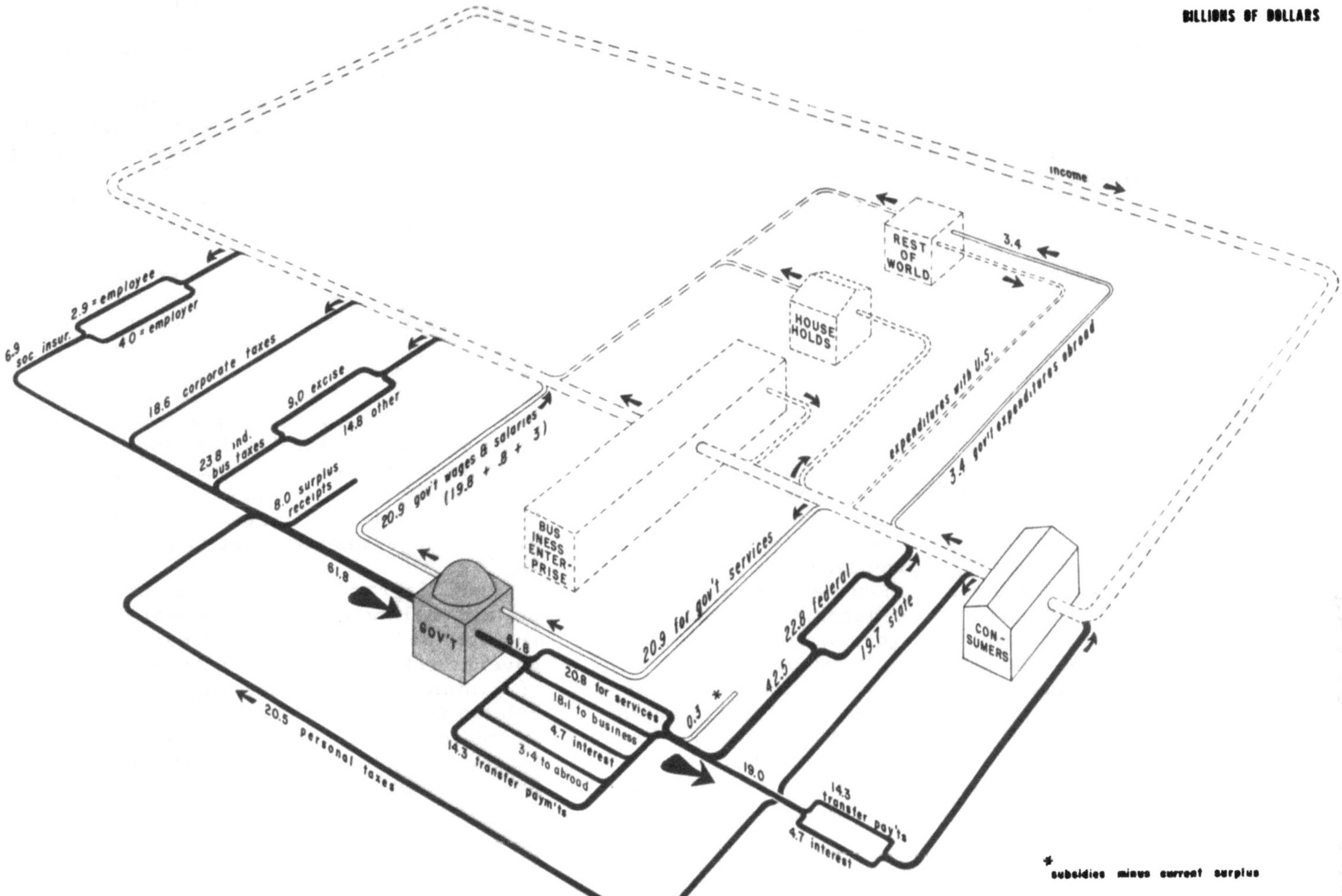

DIAGRAM 36

Table IV.—*Consolidated Government Receipts and Expenditures Account, 1950*

[Millions of dollars]

Purchases of goods and services:		Personal tax and nontax receipts	20, 920
Purchases of direct services:		Corporate profits tax accruals	17, 829
Compensation of employees:		Indirect business tax and nontax accruals	23, 741
Wages and salaries	19, 631	Contributions for social insurance:	
Supplements:		Personal contributions	2, 894
Employer contributions for social insurance	812	Employer contributions:	
Other labor income	330	Business	3, 146
		Government	812
Income originating and net and gross product	*20, 773*	Households and institutions	18
Net purchases from business	17, 828		
Net purchases from abroad	3, 422		
Transfer payments	14, 304		
Net interest paid	4, 716		
Subsidies minus current surplus of government enterprises	204		
Surplus (+) or deficit (−) on income and product transactions	8, 113		
GOVERNMENT EXPENDITURES AND SURPLUS	69, 360	GOVERNMENT RECEIPTS	69, 360

This table, the "Consolidated Government Receipts and Expenditures Account," is pictured in Diagram 36. The diagram attempts not only to show the government's major receipts and expenditures streams, but also to weave these government streams in with other major money and account flows of the economy. Accounting tables by themselves (such as the one reproduced above) do not show much integration. Table IV, like Table I, by reporting on only the receipts and expenditures streams and ignoring changes in assets and liabilities, provides only a partial accounting portrait of the government's 1950 operation. The four diagrams that follow provide additional material that will help to show some of the processes by which changes in the government's balance sheet affect national income.

Diagram 36 is a picture of how government receipts and expenditures were balanced off in 1950. Take a look at the list of expenditures on the right-hand side of the government building. The diagram shows five major classifications of expenditures. These in turn converge into two major kinds: (1) expenditures for goods and services that pour into the major spending, or GNP, stream, and (2) expenditures for pocket-to-pocket transfers of money and interest payments to deserving citizens. Note that the money spend by the government for goods and services ($42.5 billion) was spent partly in buying goods and services from business ($18.1 billion), and partly in disbursements to the Rest of the World ($3.4 billion). Expenditures with the Rest of the World consist almost exclusively of foreign economic and military aid. Such disbursements do not really constitute purchases from abroad because no goods or services flow back to the United States in return for the money poured into foreign countries. (In dealing with this item the Department of Commerce carries on some very unorthodox bookkeeping.)

On the left-hand side of the government building the major kinds of government receipts are shown. Because the volume of receipts and expenditures never exactly balance one another, there is always a dangling item—either a surplus or a deficit. In 1950 there was a surplus of $8 billion on income and product transactions, as shown in the diagram. The implication of this entry is that an $8 billion stream of current income flowed into an asset bin of the government and operated to modify its asset and liability position vis-a-vis its creditors. Because the Department of Commerce does not (as yet) keep records on the assets and liabilities of the major spending groups, it has to do something with this dangling item, and so it includes it—with perhaps questionable logic—as either a savings or investment item in its catch-all table, Table VI: Savings and Investments, sketched in Diagram 48.

This Diagram 36 is thus a summary—for national income purposes—of the major receipts and expenditures streams of the government as reported by the Department of Commerce. How these figures are related to the more widely known and publicized series on budget receipts, expenditures, and deficits compiled by the Treasury Department will be shown in the next four diagrams.

HOW THE DEPARTMENT OF COMMERCE CLASSIFIES THE CASH EXPENDITURES OF THE FEDERAL GOVERNMENT- FISCAL 1950

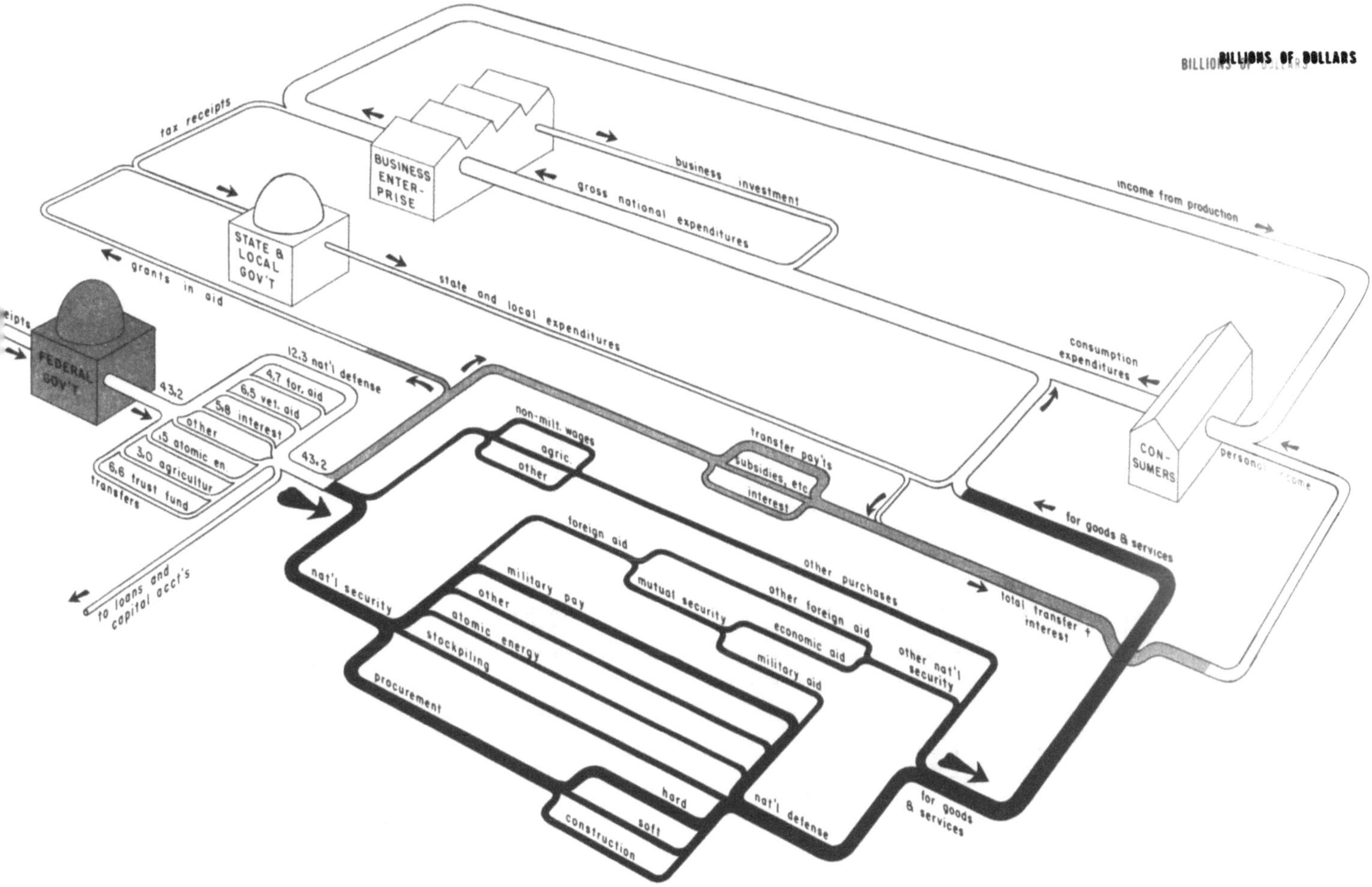

DIAGRAM 37

This diagram shows that the Department of Commerce classifies federal expenditures in a slightly different way than does the Treasury and the Bureau of the Budget. As a rule the Department of Commerce's accounting follows rather closely the breakdown pattern of the Treasury and the Bureau of the Budget. But it does differ in a few ways. And for a reason: the Department of Commerce is interested in isolating from the total those expenditures that are payments for the goods and services produced for government. It strives to separate these from that part of the total which represents merely pocket-to-pocket transfers. But in doing so the Department of Commerce makes some very arbitrary decisions. For example, until 1947 the Department of Commerce regarded interest payments made by government as a factor payment and included them in national income, but since then it has implicitly regarded all government interest payments—even those made by state and local governments—as being not payments for services rendered by savers, but as grants made to deserving citizens. Interest payments are now excluded both from Gross National Expenditures and National Income.

The diagram illustrates too the distinction between the government's payments for goods and services produced and its pocket-to-pocket transfers to deserving citizens. The expenditures for goods and services are shown as solid black flows, the pocket-to-pocket transfers as gray ones. The expenditures made by the government for goods and services become part of the receipts of the nation's producers from which they pay all the costs involved in producing the goods and services. The money disbursed as transfer payments includes old age assistance relief, veterans' aid, and unemployment benefits. Together with interest payments they flow to individuals directly from the government and are regarded as being outside of the production process.

TABLE J. *—Government Expenditures*

[Millions of dollars]

Line		1950
1	**Total expenditures**	**61,247**
2	**Federal**	**40,948**
3	Purchases of goods and services	22,138
4	Compensation of employees	10,649
5	Net purchases from business	8,067
6	New construction	1,625
7	Other	6,488
8	Less: Domestic sales of surplus consumption goods	46
9	Net purchases from abroad	3,422
10	Purchases from abroad	3,631
11	Less: Sales to abroad	209
12	Transfer payments	10,884
13	Grants-in-aid to State and local governments	2,339
14	Net interest paid	4,431
15	Interest paid	5,804
16	Less: Interest received	1,373
17	Subsidies less current surplus of government enterprises	1,156
18	**State and local**	**22,638**
19	Purchases of goods and services	19,885
20	Compensation of employees	10,124
21	Purchases from business	9,761
22	New construction	5,375
23	Other	4,386
24	Transfer payments	3,420
25	Net interest paid	285
26	Interest paid	624
27	Less: Interest received	339
28	Less: Current surplus of government enterprises	952

Source: National Income, 1954

TAXES ARE THE MAJOR SOURCE OF GOVERNMENT RECEIPTS

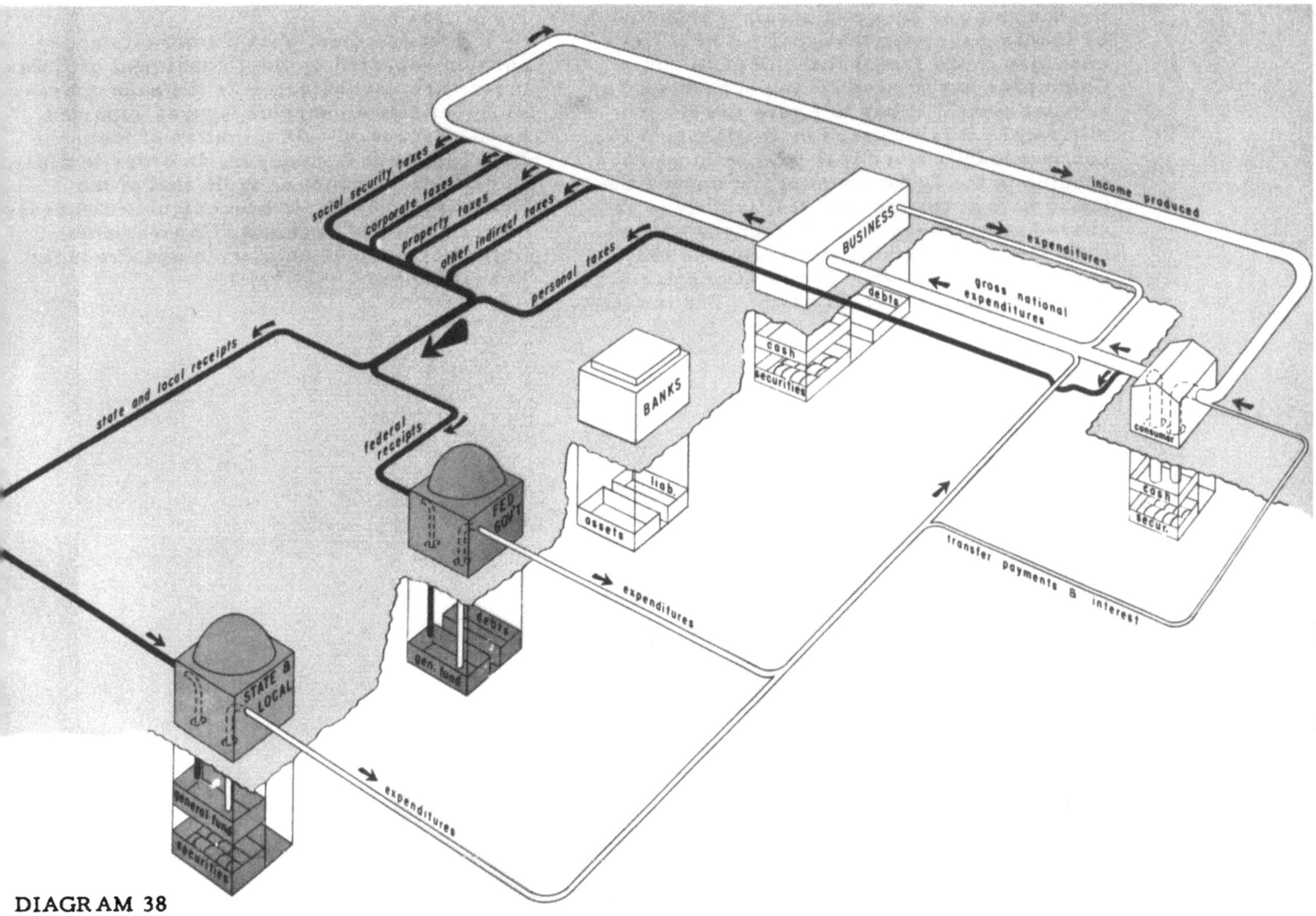

DIAGRAM 38

All governments have the sovereign power to levy taxes. Throughout history they have taken advantage of that power. In undeveloped societies they even collect taxes in kind. But usually, ever since money was invented, taxes have been levied against the recipients and possessors of money.

The federal government of the United States was originally one of limited powers. Because the Constitution sought to preserve considerable strength at the state and local levels, the federal government was not allowed by the Constitution to tax the revenue receipts of state and local governments, lest it weaken or destroy them. However, since the adoption of the income tax amendment to the Constitution, the federal government has been able to hurdle this barrier by taxing the state and local voter directly and heavily.

The Department of Commerce classifies all government tax revenues into five main categories:

1. Personal taxes, including income, estate and gift taxes, fines, penalties, and business and property taxes other than on owner-occupied dwellings.
2. Corporate profit taxes.
3. Property taxes on dwellings.
4. Other indirect business taxes (consisting mainly of such items as sales taxes, and excise taxes.
5. Social security taxes paid by both employers and employees on earnings.

In 1950, according to the Department of Commerce, personal taxes totaled \$20.5 billion, corporate profit taxes \$18.6 billion, property taxes on owner-occupied dwellings \$7.3 billion, other indirect business taxes \$16.5 billion, and social security taxes \$7.0 billion. Total taxes for the year were \$69.8 billion. In recent years state and local governments in combination have obtained only about one third of the total tax receipts and the federal government about two thirds.

State and local receipts consist of contributions for unemployment insurance, corporate profit tax accruals, property taxes, motor vehicle taxes, and excise taxes on such items as gasoline, liquor, and tobacco. The federal government's grants-in-aid to state and local governments (for highways and certain other kinds of construction) are the only other state and local receipts of consequence.

The federal tax receipts compiled by the Department of Commerce for any year are not the same as the cash receipts reported by the Treasury for that year. The difference lies in the fact that the Department of Commerce has to keep its tax accounts on an accrual basis. It has to figure the tax liability when it is incurred by the taxpayer, not necessarily when it is paid by him. According to the Department of Commerce the tax is paid at the moment the liability is incurred even though no cash changes hands until later. A striking illustration is the corporate profits tax. Corporations are not fully on a pay-as-you-go basis. The tax liability incurred in 1950 is usually paid in 1951. Because of this time lag the Department of Commerce has to adjust the Treasury's records of cash tax receipts to allow for accruals.

It follows, then, that the deficits and surplus reported by the Department of Commerce are not the same as the cash operating deficits or surplus figures reported by the Treasury. As a matter of fact, the Department of Commerce, in order to distinguish its accounting from that of the Treasury's, calls its own calculated excess or deficiency of receipts "Government Deficit or Surplus on Income and Product Transactions."

BORROWING IS A SECOND SOURCE OF GOVERNMENT RECEIPTS

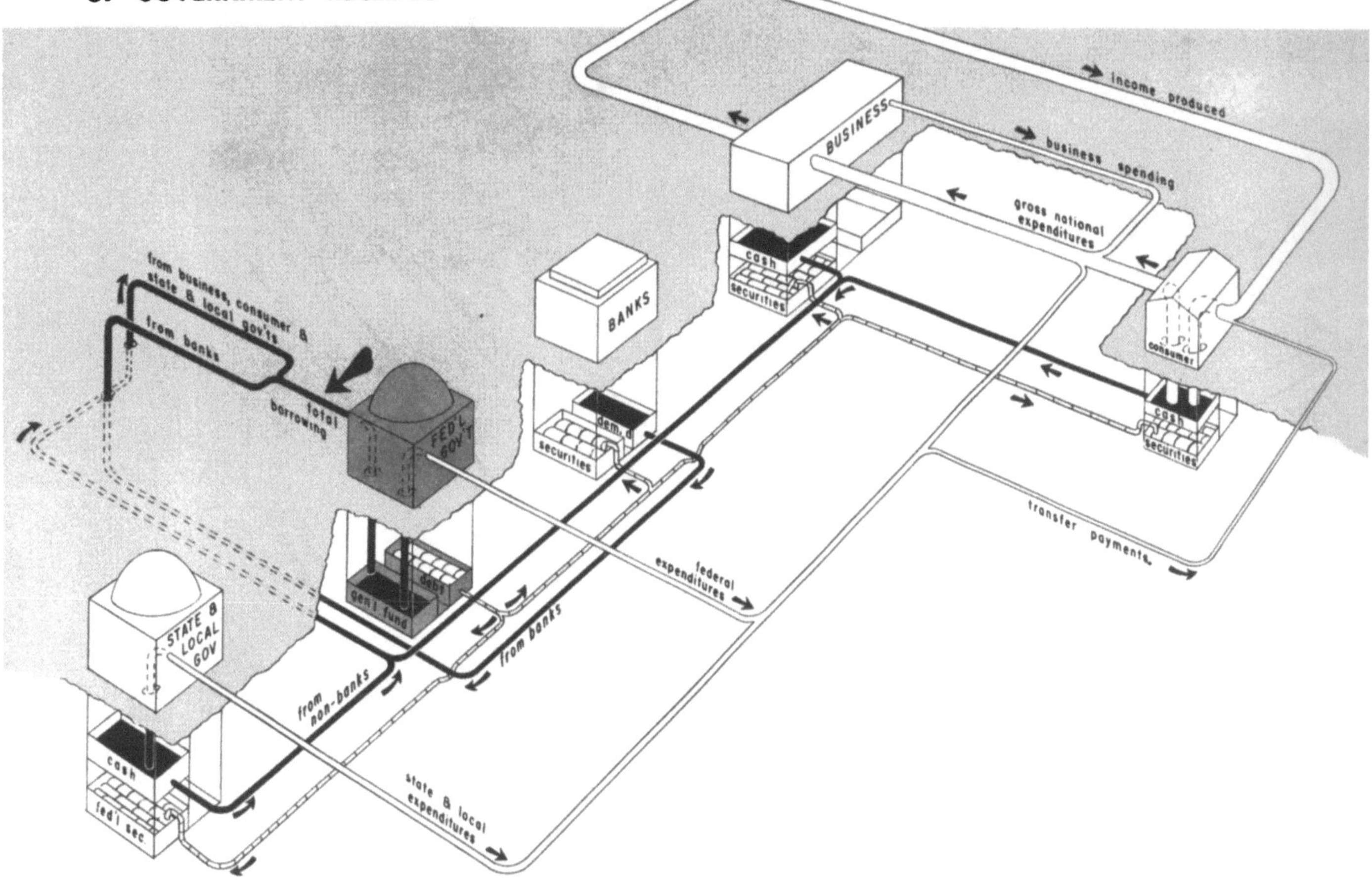

DIAGRAM 39

When a government's tax revenues do not meet its expenditures a government can always resort to borrowing. The federal government in particular has so many economic controls that it can as a practical matter always obtain funds. No sovereign government with control over its banking system, for example, ever went broke in the sense of finding itself unable to obtain legal tender—currency and bank deposits. A government can usually do two things:

1. It can tap the stream of current savings of individuals, businesses, and state and local governments. It can even force its citizens to save money and make the supply of money relatively more plentiful for the government to borrow. For it can influence in many ways the extent to which consumers and businessmen save money out of their current income. During World War II, for example, the federal government restricted supply by prohibiting the production of houses, automobiles, refrigerators, and the like, and it restricted demand through rationing and other means. These restrictions made it much more difficult for consumers to obtain goods. The result was that consumer savings increased enormously (as is shown in Diagram 44: "Where Consumer Buying Power Comes From"). So a federal government can usually arrange that its citizens have large sums of current savings available for borrowing as an exchange for the government's own debt obligations—bills, notes, certificates, and bonds. Or, if the federal government does not wish to exchange its securities for the current savings of its citizens, it has a second recourse:

2. It can sell its securities for new demand deposits created by the bank. It can always obtain more deposits for the Treasury's account by monetizing its government securities at the banks, that is, by creating the money it needs.

Thus a federal government is always in a position either to borrow the current savings which its citizens retain out of current income or, as an alternative, to monetize its debt obligations at the bank through an exchange of federal securities for the demand deposits of banks. In contrast, a state or local government can borrow money that has already been created through the monetization of private or federal government debt, but it can not always monetize its own debt by exchanging its securities for the new demand deposits of banks.

WHO OWNS THE FEDERAL DEBT?

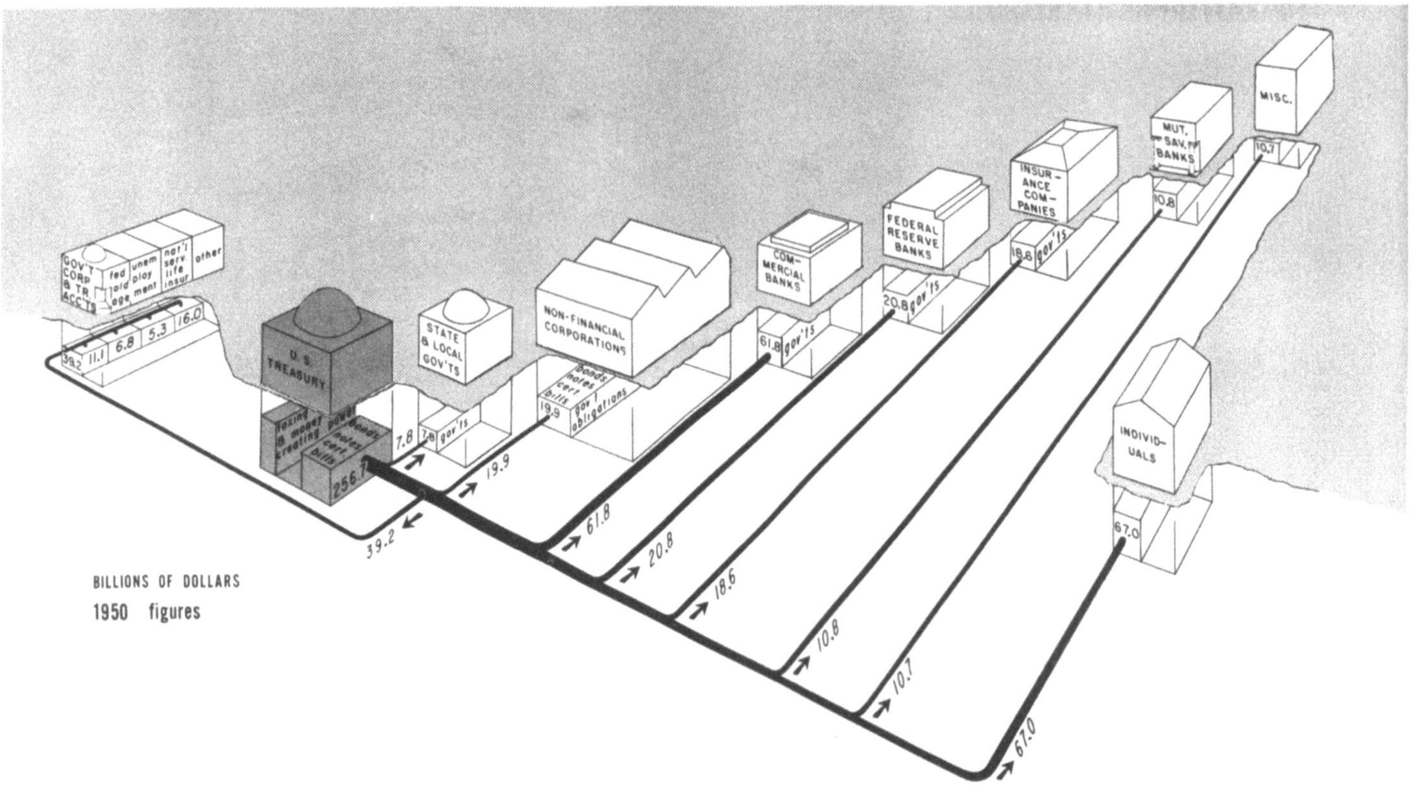

DIAGRAM 40

In Diagrams 38 and 39 we saw two major sources of government revenue. Government borrowing was one of these. Particularly since the beginning of World War II has the federal government been obtaining revenues by exchanging its securities both for current savings and for new money from the banks.

Diagram 40 shows, as of December 31, 1950, who owned the then outstanding federal government securities of $256 7 billion. The two largest groups holding government bonds were individuals and commercial banks Note that another very large holder of Treasury securities was an agency of the government itself, the Government Corporations and Trust Accounts These government corporations and trust accounts acquire securities continually because the tax money which they obtain from the nation's workers through payroll deductions for old age insurance and unemployment relief continually exceed their outpayments. They buy government bonds with the excess. These government agencies can invest in nothing else and have no other permissible outlet for their funds when their receipts exceed their outpayments.

The federal debt is issued in four major forms: bonds, notes, certificates, and bills. In Diagram 40 this breakdown of the debt i shown illustratively only in the liability bir of the U. S. Treasury and in the asset bin the Non-financial Corporations. The detai for other holders of government securities has been omitted.

The Treasury issues short-term, intermediate, and long-term securities. Short-term paper carries very low interest rates and long-term paper relatively high ones. Both because the Federal Reserve Board i its open market operation has discretion in buying and selling bills, and because U. S. Treasury officials have discretion over refunding one kind of paper with another, the two agencies working together have the means by which they can vary the length an complexion of the debt, and, by so doing, can exert a powerful influence on interest rates, on private borrowing, and on the ge eral availability of funds. For example, they insure that the Federal Reserve with ease can be the buffer-buyer of governmen securities during Treasury funding and refunding operations. If the public sale of securities by the Treasury goes poorly, th Federal Reserve can buffer the situation b buying bills.

TABLE K. OWNERSHIP OF UNITED STATES GOVERNMENT SECURITIES, DIRECT AND FULLY GUARANTEED

[Par value in billions of dollars]

End of month	Total gross debt (including guaranteed securities)	Held by U. S. Govt. agencies and trust funds[1]		Held by the public										
		Special issues	Public issues	Total	Federal Reserve Banks	Commercial banks[2]	Mutual savings banks	Insurance companies	Other corporations	State and local govts.	Individuals: Savings bonds	Individuals: Other securities	Misc. investors[3]
1941—Dec.	64.3	7.0	2.6	54.7	2.3	21.4	3.7	8.2	4.0	.7	5.4	8.2	.9
1945—Dec.	278.7	20.0	7.0	251.6	24.3	90.8	10.7	24.0	22.2	6.5	42.9	21.2	9.1
1947—Dec.	257.0	29.0	5.4	222.6	22.6	68.7	12.0	23.9	14.1	7.3	46.2	19.4	8.4
1950—Dec.	256.7	33.7	5.5	217.5	20.8	61.8	10.9	18.7	19.7	8.8	49.6	16.7	10.5
1951—Dec.	259.5	35.9	6.4	217.2	23.8	61.6	9.8	16.5	20.7	9.6	49.1	15.5	10.6
1952—Dec.	267.4	39.2	6.7	221.6	24.7	63.4	9.5	16.1	19.9	11.1	49.2	16.0	11.7
1953—Dec.	275.2	41.2	7.1	226.9	25.9	63.7	9.2	15.8	21.0	[r]12.7	49.4	[r]16.0	13.2
1954—June	271.3	42.2	7.1	222.0	25.0	63.6	9.1	15.3	16.4	[r]13.9	49.5	[r]15.5	13.7
1954—Oct.	278.8	42.2	7.0	229.5	24.4	70.1	8.9	15.1	18.7	[r]13.9	49.8	[r]14.7	14.0
Nov.	278.9	42.4	7.1	229.5	24.9	69.7	8.8	15.0	19.3	[r]13.8	49.9	[r]14.3	13.8
Dec.	278.8	42.6	7.0	229.2	24.9	69.2	8.8	15.0	19.3	[r]13.8	50.0	[r]14.2	13.9
1955—Jan.	278.5	42.3	7.2	229.0	23.9	68.7	8.8	15.2	20.0	[r]14.1	50.0	[r]14.5	13.9
Feb.	278.2	42.0	7.2	229.0	23.6	66.9	8.8	15.2	21.2	[r]14.3	50.1	[r]14.9	13.9
Mar.	274.1	42.1	7.3	224.7	23.6	64.2	8.8	15.0	19.0	[r]14.5	50.2	[r]15.3	14.2
Apr.	276.7	41.7	7.2	227.8	23.6	[r]65.8	8.8	15.0	20.1	[r]14.6	50.2	[r]15.3	14.4
May	277.5	42.2	7.2	228.1	23.7	[r]64.8	8.8	14.9	21.2	[r]14.7	50.2	[r]15.3	14.4
June	274.4	43.3	7.3	223.9	23.6	[r]63.5	8.7	14.8	18.8	[r]14.7	50.2	[r]15.1	14.4
July	277.6	43.3	7.3	227.0	24.1	[r]63.8	8.8	14.9	19.9	[r]15.0	[r]50.2	[r]15.3	15.0
Aug.	278.4	44.2	7.3	226.8	23.8	[r]62.7	8.8	15.0	21.0	[r]15.1	50.3	[r]15.4	14.9
Sept.	277.5	43.9	7.3	226.3	23.8	62.1	8.7	15.0	20.9	15.1	50.2	15.6	15.0
Oct.	279.9	43.7	7.4	228.8	24.0	62.7	8.6	14.9	22.2	15.3	50.2	15.6	15.2

[r] Revised.

[1] Includes the Postal Savings System.

[2] Includes holdings by banks in territories and insular possessions, which amounted to $300 million on June 30, 1955.

[3] Includes savings and loan associations, dealers and brokers, foreign accounts, corporate pension funds, and nonprofit institutions.

NOTE.—Holdings of Federal Reserve Banks and U. S. Govt. agencies and trust funds are reported figures; holdings of other investor groups are estimated by the Treasury Department.

Source: Federal Reserve Bulletin, 1956

A PORTRAYAL OF "TABLE 111-THE PERSONAL INCOME AND EXPENDITURES ACCOUNT, 1950"

BILLIONS OF DOLLARS

WHERE INDIVIDUALS GET THEIR INCOME AND HOW THEY DISPOSE OF IT

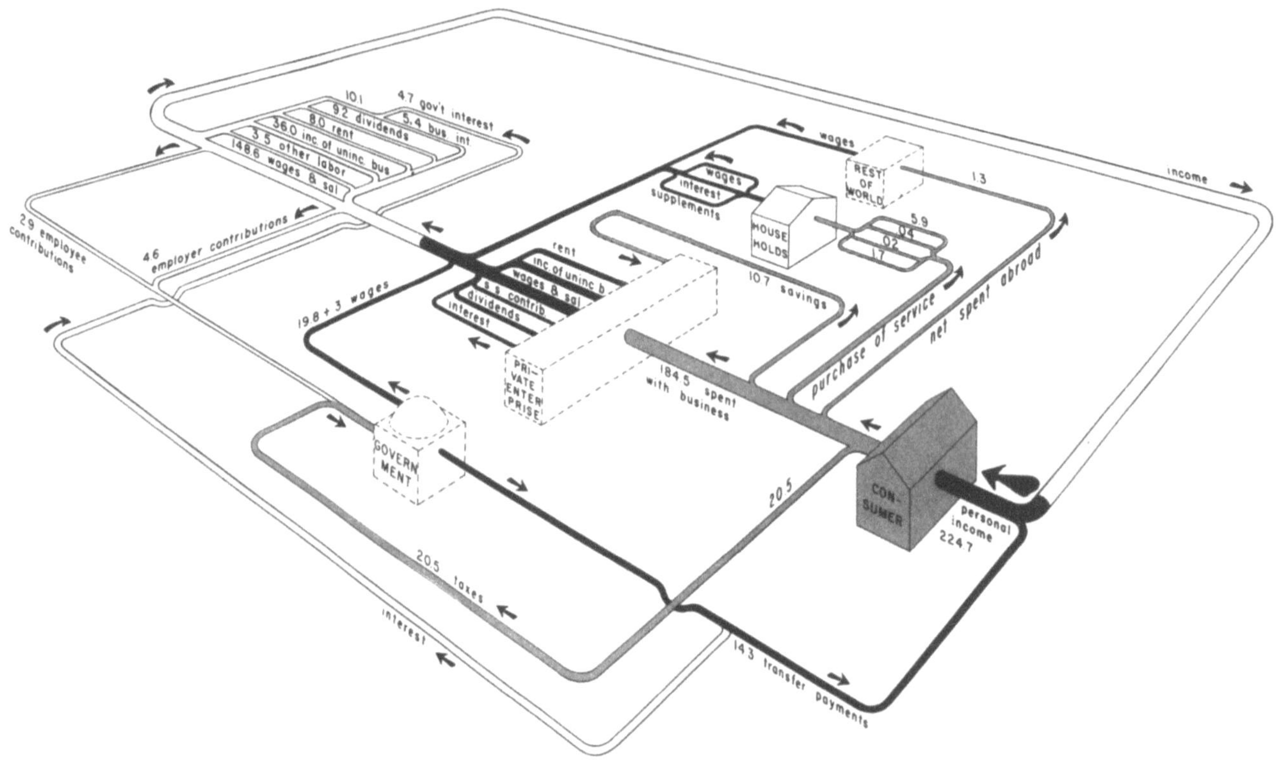

DIAGRAM 41

Table III.—*Personal Income and Expenditure Account, 1950*

[Millions of dollars]

Personal consumption expenditures:	
Purchases of direct services:	
Compensation of employees:	
Wages and salaries paid	6, 312
Supplements paid:	
Employer contributions for social insurance	18
Other labor income	53
Interest paid	1, 956
Income originating in and net and gross product of households and institutions	*8, 339*
Net purchases from business	184, 340
Net purchases from abroad	1, 347
Personal tax and nontax payments	20, 920
Personal saving	12, 104
PERSONAL OUTLAY AND SAVING	227, 050

Wage and salary disbursements:	
Business	120, 565
Government	19, 631
Households and institutions	6, 312
Rest of the world	18
Other labor income:	
Business	3, 440
Government	330
Households and institutions	53
Income of unincorporated enterprises and inventory valuation adjustment	36, 140
Rental income of persons	8, 473
Dividends	9, 207
Personal interest income	10, 628
Government transfer payments	14, 304
Business transfer payments	843
Less: Personal contributions for social insurance	2, 894
PERSONAL INCOME	227, 050

A major portion of the income of the household consumer has its source in the current production of the nation. The table of accounts shown above lists that fact; Diagram 41 highlights it. The factor payments of business, government, and producing households make up the major part of personal income, as was shown in many of the preceding diagrams.

This diagram shows that the big fountainhead of personal income is the business organization which annually pours out billions of dollars of factor payments, as wages, interest, rent, dividends, and so forth. In 1950, for example, business paid out $123 billion in wages and salaries and other labor income, $5.4 billion in interest payments, $8.0 billion in rents, and $8.8 billion in dividends, and $36.0 billion as income of unincorporated enterprise—a contribution to Personal Income of $178 billion in that year.

Government also contributes to personal income—in two ways. Government, like business, pays out wages which are a factor cost and are counted by the Department of Commerce as part of National Income. These wages, amounting to $20.1 billion in 1950, are shown in the diagram flowing out of the back door of government to join the factor payments of business. But the consumer also receives some government income in the form of transfer payments and government interest. These payments are outside of the stream of payments for current production and are shown in our diagram coming out of the front of the government building and joining up with the stream of current income produced flowing to the consumer. The transfer payments are outside of the production stream partly as a matter of logic and partly as a matter of choice by the Department of Commerce.

Households are another producing unit which contributes to the income of individuals. Households make two main kinds of factor payments: wages and interest. The interest payments are those made by individuals on their consumer installment credit. These were as high as $1.7 billion in 1950. The wages are in the main those paid to domestic help both in the form of money payments and in kind, such as in the form of food and lodging. There are other workers included in the producing households too, and the next diagram shows in more detail who they are.

The diagram completes the circuit of personal account by showing how consumers disburse their receipts (gray areas), as well as where the receipts originate. In 1950, as shown, consumers paid $20.5 billion in taxes, saved $10.7 billion, and spent $193.5 billion for consumption goods and services, mostly with business. A part of the expenditures, $5.9 billion, was made to purchase the services of household workers, and about $1.7 billion went for interest payments on consumer installment credit. In 1950 consumers also purchased about $1.3 billion of goods and services from the Rest of the World.

WHO ARE THE PRODUCERS INCLUDED IN "HOUSEHOLDS"

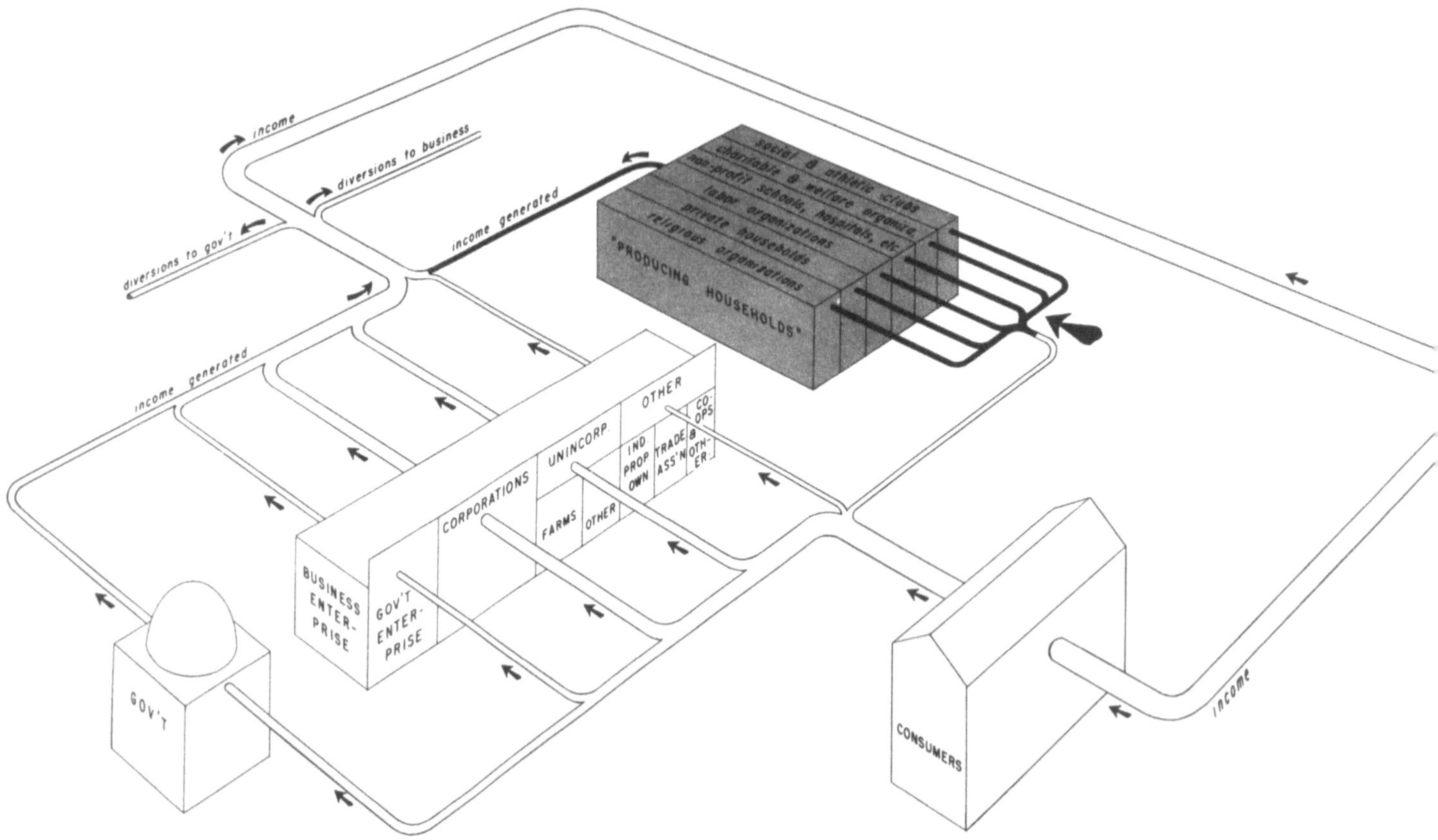

DIAGRAM 42

We have seen in several diagrams that the Department of Commerce deals with a producing group in the economy named Households, in addition to the other producing groups: Business Enterprise, Rest of the World, and Government.

This diagram shows the groups that make up Producing Households. One producing unit is obviously the Private Household. But there are others too. There are charitable, labor, religious, athletic, and other nonprofit organizations. The wages paid to the workers of these nonprofit organizations are regarded as the value of their output. Diagram 42 shows conceptually how the nonprofit producing group, Producing Households, fits into the Department of Commerce's accounting. Its role as a producer is significant. In 1950 Producing Households generated a total income of $7.7 billion.

The output of Private Households relates only to that output that is turned out by paid workers. As was explained in Diagram 3, for practical reasons the Department of Commerce has to exclude the contribution of housewives to the nation's real output.

The income generated by Producing Households is mostly in the form of wage payments, but some of it is also disbursed as interest payments. The payments that persons make on their installment and other short-term debts are included here.

KINDS OF SAVINGS BY KINDS OF PERSONS

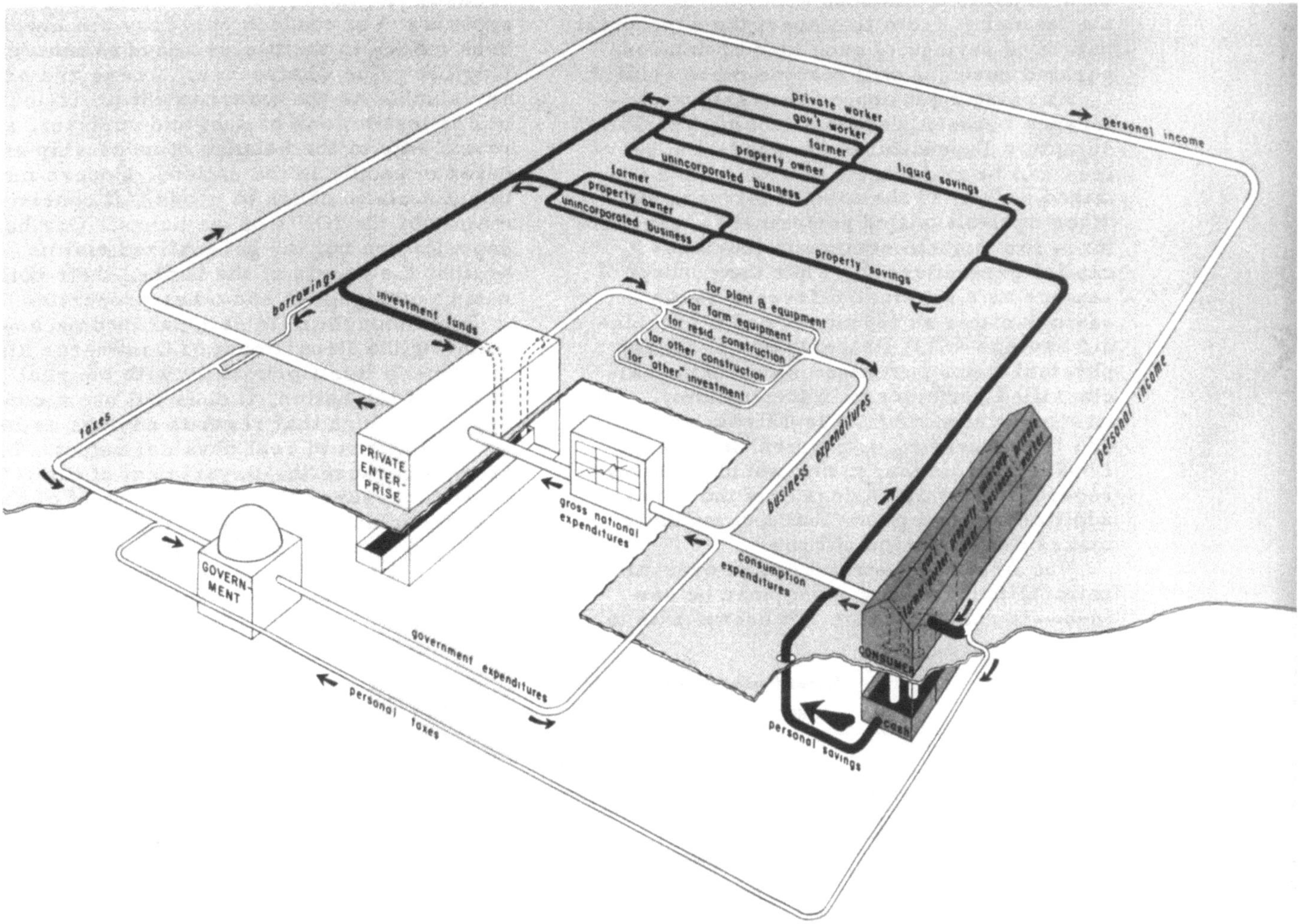

DIAGRAM 43

Personal Savings, according to the Department of Commerce, equal Disposable Income minus Consumption Expenditures. Because Personal Savings are thus defined as a residual item, that is, as the amount remaining after the purchase of goods and services and the payment of taxes to the government, they are a conglomerate of many items thrown together only because of the definitions used by the Department of Commerce. To understand fully what the composition of the residual savings is, we must fix in our minds again what makes up Personal Income, who the Persons are who receive Personal Income, who the spenders are, and who the savers are.

Diagram 43 deals with those matters. It shows that the recipients of Personal Income include Farmers, small Unincorporated Businesses, and individual Property Owners as well as wage earners. Because the income of Unincorporated Business is included with that of individuals in the Personal Income tabulation, it follows that the savings of unincorporated business are also a part of Personal Savings, as shown in the diagram. Thus all the income of unincorporated businessmen is included in the personal account. The amounts which unincorporated businessmen do not spend for consumer goods or services are saved, according to the Department of Commerce's definitions. But what about the spending for equipment by these businessmen?

Unincorporated businessmen make business capital expenditures as well as expenditures for consumer goods and services. Because the Department of Commerce distinguishes between these two kinds of expenditures, we show the Business Expenditures for capital items separately in our diagram. When unincorporated businessmen buy tractors, new store fronts, small trucks, or new houses out of their income, their expenditures are classified as business capital expenditures in contrast to consumption expenditures. Clearly the concept of savings as being the difference between total Disposable Income and Consumption Expenditures forces one to include the business expenditures for capital goods items by unincorporated businessmen as a part of Personal Savings. Confusing? Yes, but necessitated by the Department of Commerce's definitions. In the next diagram we will analyze the "savings" of one of the unincorporated business accounts: that of the farmer. From that chart the conceptual nature of savings of each kind of unincorporated business will become more evident.

As pointed out above, the residual difference between Personal Income and Consumption Expenditures for goods and services can be in the form of either cash retained or—as in the case of farmers and other dual-classified performers—expenditures for tangible equipment (business capital expenditures). Thus the concept of savings as a residual difference views savings either as (1) money and other Liquid Savings or (2) Property Savings—the physical items purchased by certain dual-classified performers in the economy. The first view of savings is legalistic, the second is engineering or physical in concept. Looked at from Mars, one would probably regard as earthly savings only those net additions to real goods that a community makes over a period of time.

The first view—that from an over-all national point of view money can be savings—is really strange. It seems akin to the eighteenth-century view of the mercantilists that a country got richer as it increased its money stock as a result of exports. For modern currency and checkbook money in themselves have no inherent tangible value whatsoever. These are only as valuable as the enforcement provisions of our institutions of debt and contract, and relate only to the balance of ownership as between people in the nation. Modern money is but a claim check to goods. It consists mainly of the IOU's of the banks. Our bank deposits are but the generalized claims against the assets of the banks, their bonds, notes, mortgages, and other properties.

Even though in its national income accounting the Department of Commerce aims to concern itself primarily with the real output of the nation, it does not use a concept of savings that regards savings as being accumulations of real physical output. Instead—because the Department of Commerce measures the physical output of the nation exclusively in monetary terms—it was forced to measure savings too in monetary, not physical, terms. Considerable popular confusion has resulted from that dilemma.

TABLE L. —*Financial saving by individuals, 1939–55*

[Billions of dollars]

Period	Total	Currency and bank deposits	Savings and loan associations	Insurance and pension reserves: Total	Insurance and pension reserves: Private	Insurance and pension reserves: Government	Securities: Total	Securities: U. S. savings bonds	Securities: Other government	Securities: Corporate and other	Liquidation of mortgage debt (1)	Liquidation of debt not elsewhere classified (1)
1939	4.25	3.00	0.04	3.01	1.72	1.30	−0.53	0.66	−0.83	−0.36	−0.50	−0.78
1940	4.24	2.88	.20	3.14	1.85	1.30	−.17	.86	−.81	−.22	−.84	−.97
1941	10.52	4.80	.36	4.01	2.14	1.86	2.83	2.75	.44	−.36	−.82	−.66
1942	29.30	10.95	.26	5.04	2.49	2.55	10.25	7.98	2.17	.09	−.09	2.89
1943	38.71	16.18	.55	6.77	2.85	3.92	13.83	11.14	2.88	−.20	.38	1.01
1944	41.41	17.55	.81	8.17	3.21	4.96	14.96	11.80	3.89	−.73	.06	−.14
1945	37.39	19.06	1.06	8.59	3.46	5.14	9.36	6.85	3.43	−.92	−.20	−.48
1946	13.74	10.56	1.18	6.97	3.42	3.55	.89	.90	−.65	.65	−3.60	−2.28
1947	6.67	2.01	1.20	7.13	3.64	3.49	3.51	1.78	.89	.84	−4.46	−2.73
1948	2.99	−1.84	1.21	7.32	3.75	3.57	3.22	2.13	−.43	1.52	−4.61	−2.31
1949	2.86	−1.46	1.51	6.05	3.71	2.34	3.03	1.53	.52	.98	−3.87	−2.40
1950	1.80	3.62	1.51	5.01	3.92	1.09	2.04	.55	.12	1.36	−7.16	−3.22
1951	11.34	5.96	2.10	8.28	4.07	4.21	2.06	−.52	.01	2.57	−6.53	−.54
1952	12.98	6.84	3.07	9.22	4.92	4.29	3.96	.08	.82	3.06	−6.26	−3.85
1953	11.76	4.80	3.64	8.46	5.17	3.29	5.10	.33	2.29	2.48	−7.01	−3.24
1954	11.85	6.84	4.48	7.92	5.30	2.62	1.56	.76	−1.80	2.60	−8.58	−.37

Source: Economic Report of the President, 1956

(1) The liquidation of debt is counted as an addition to liquid savings; conversely, the incurrence of new debt is a subtraction from liquid savings. In this accompanying table the figures with a minus sign relate to the years when new debt was incurred.

WHERE CONSUMER BUYING POWER COMES FROM

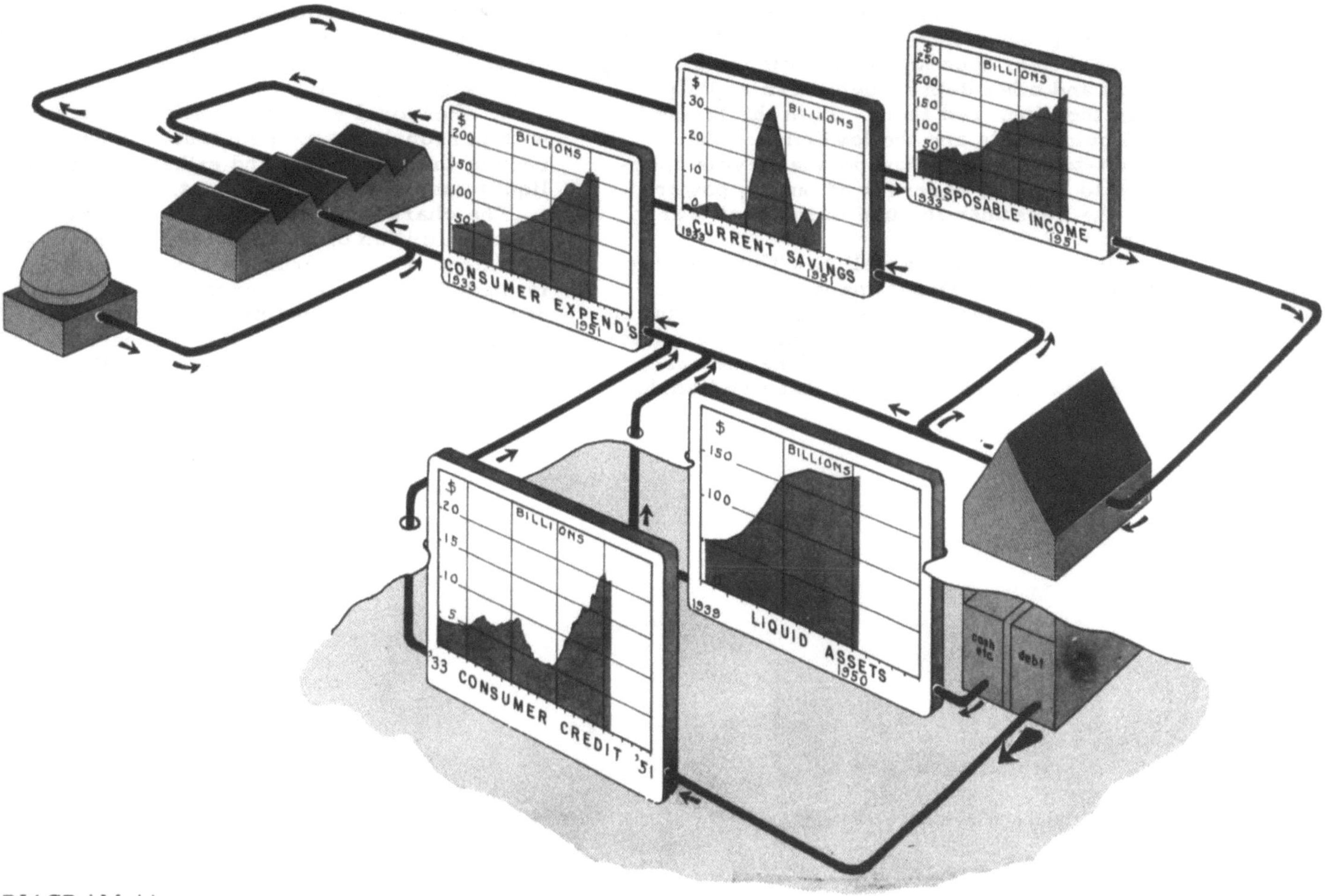

DIAGRAM 44

In an exchange economy such as ours where almost everyone is a specialist and lives by exchanging his own specialized product for the thousands of items produced by others, practically all buying power has its source in the current contributions that individuals make to the world of production. But because of our institutions of money and debt, people can store buying power that results from past production or obtain buying power before it is earned by incurring debt. Diagram 44 shows how some buying power is rooted in the incurrence of debt and some in the past liquid savings of individuals. At any moment in time the buying power of the consumer comes from and has its roots in his current disposable income, in his past accumulation of liquid assets, and in his incurrable debt.

When societies evolve to where their institutions of property and contract are well established and operate smoothly, consumers can either spend more than their current income or spend less and accumulate liquid assets such as bank deposits; they can then spend their past savings or their pledged future income. Under good contract enforcement, tradesmen are willing to accept several kinds of short-term debt—such as book credit, charge accounts, and installment debt—in the same way as they accept cash.

A striking illustration of how buying power is affected by both the accumulation of liquid assets and the incurrability of debt can be found in the experience of World War II. Diagram 44 illustrates how the consumer during World War II deferred using some of his income as it came in and, instead, accumulated it both as a liquid asset (currency, deposits, and Series E bonds) and as a borrowing potential (established by repaying debt). The diagram pictures the extent to which the Consumers' Disposable Income rose (in dollars during the war years). Because the government curbed consumer spending both by means of rationing and by making certain kinds of goods unavailable, it caused Current Savings (which is defined as income not spent) to rise precipitously. Thus huge sums of money were made available to financial institutions and to the government during those years. In return consumers obtained such liquid assets as deposits, currency, and Series E bonds. Naturally these assets rose precipitously in volume too, as the meter in the basement shows. Simultaneously, because our regulations prohibited the production of durable goods, items like refrigerators and automobiles, consumers paid off installment and other debts much more rapidly than they incurred them. Both the laying in of liquid assets and the lowering of the short-term debts below normal levels operated to build up reserves of buying power for the consumer for use in the post-war period.

Diagram 44 shows well how Current Personal Savings in Department of Commerce accounting is the residual difference between Disposable Income and Consumption Expenditures. The three billboard-like meters above the ground illustrate that relationship. The diagram also illustrates why—in order to maintain in the accounts the relationship that savings equals income minus spending—

1. Personal savings must fall when—with personal income constant—consumption expenditures are boosted by consumers' using either past liquid assets or credit to pay for goods, and

2. Personal savings must rise when—with personal income constant—consumers reduce their spending and either accumulate liquid assets or pay back debt.

The chart thus indirectly illustrates another definition of savings used by the Department of Commerce: "Personal savings is made up of the net increase in all kinds of assets in which recipients of personal income invest, offset by the net increase in the several kinds of liabilities that they incur."

THE FARMER AS PRODUCER, SPENDER, AND SAVER

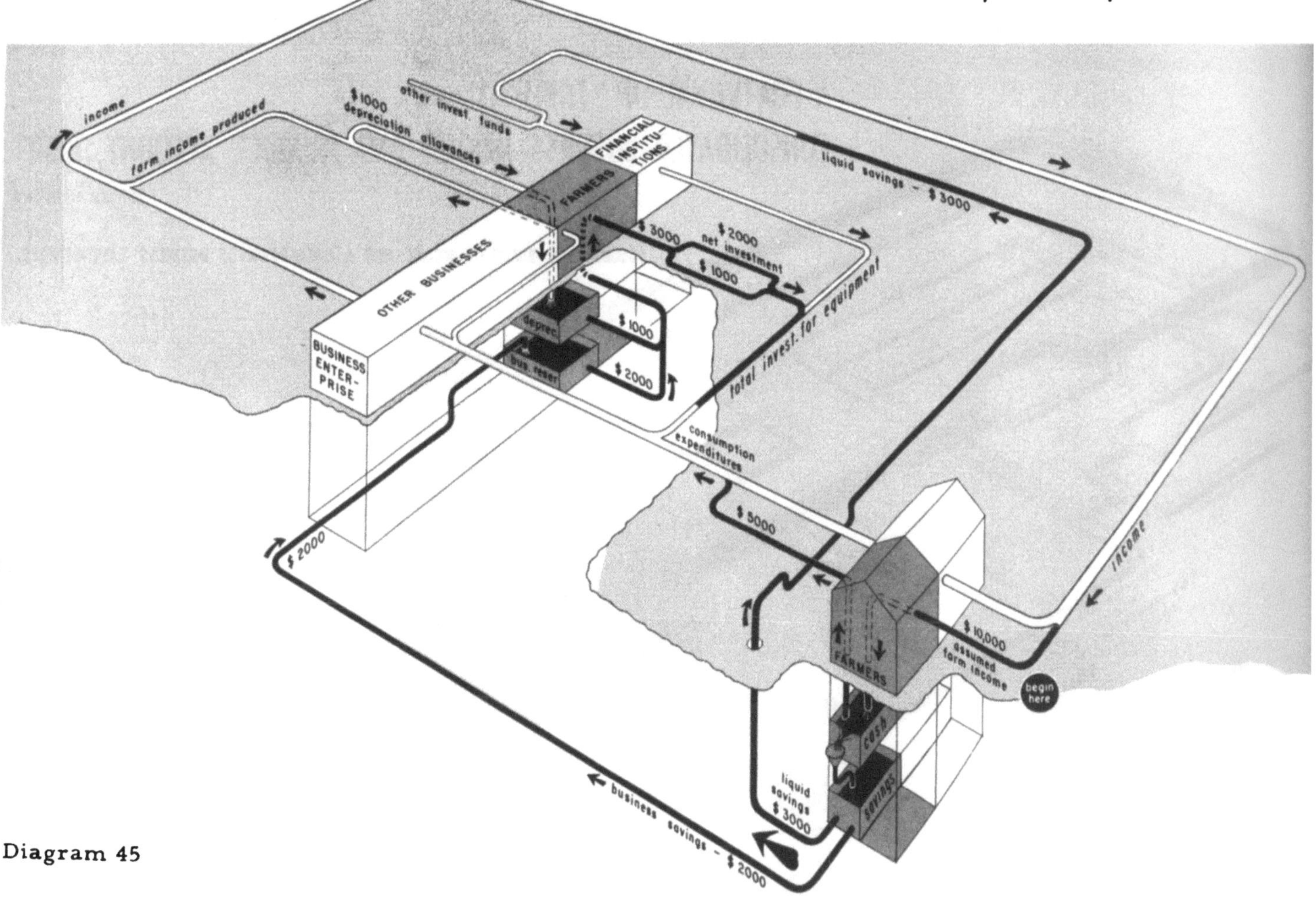

Diagram 45

Almost all people are both producers and consumers. Our first diagram pictured that fact. People go to work, receive wages, and spend the wages for goods. But when people are producers who own their own businesses, like farmers and small shopkeepers, the statistical portrayal of their role and performance becomes more complicated. The income that the farmer receives, for example, in contrast to the wages that the worker receives, has to provide not only for consumption goods but also for the machinery and equipment used in production. The farmer is thus both a Business Enterprise, turning out product and buying capital equipment, and a Person receiving Personal Income and buying consumption goods.

Diagram 45 pictures the farmer's double function as dealt with in national income accounting. He first appears in the Personal Account. There he receives Personal Income, buys consumer goods, and saves. He also appears in the Business Account. There he spends money for equipment. The source of his funds for both consumer goods and production equipment is the same income stream—it is the money he receives from the sale of his products to processors and consumers.

Because the Department of Commerce defines personal savings as the difference between personal income and consumption expenditures, the farmer's spending for business equipment—which is not a consumption expenditure—must by definition (because he is a "person") be part of his personal savings.

Diagram 45 shows the process behind this kind of accounting: The farmer's net income (i. e., his income minus his costs of production) is shown entering the back door of his home. In this case the amount is $10,000. He spends $5,000 for consumers' goods. Thus by definition he "saves" $5,000. These savings are shown flowing into the basement of his home. Of this $5,000 saved, $3,000 is in the form of liquid savings—cash, bonds, insurance reserves, and so forth. This portion is shown flowing into the nation's financial institutions. The farmer uses the remaining $2,000 of "savings" to buy capital equipment. In the diagram, the $2,000 cash asset of the "Person Farmer" is transferred to the "Businessman Farmer." There it joins the farmer's premised depreciation allowance of $1,000 and is poured out or disbursed by the farmer as business spending for farm equipment. Thus, in the accounts, the farmer's spending for a tractor is a saving (because it is not a consumption expenditure), whereas his spending for a refrigerator is not.

A PORTRAYAL OF "TABLE 11 - CONSOLIDATED BUSINESS INCOME AND PRODUCT ACCOUNT, 1950"

Billions of Dollars

(SOURCES OF BUSINESS INCOME AND A BREAKDOWN OF BUSINESS EXPENDITURES)

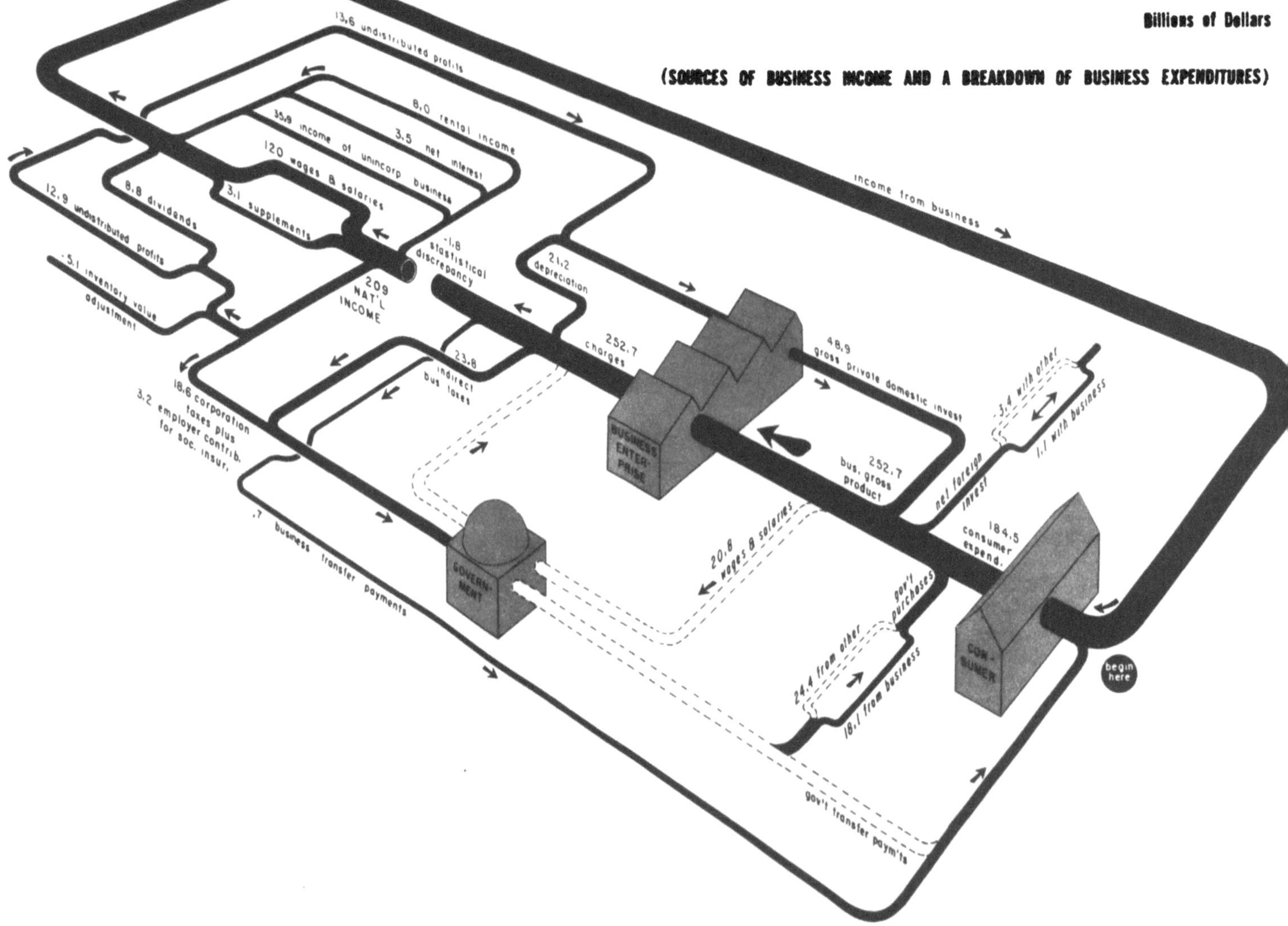

DIAGRAM 46

This diagram shows the sources of business income and a breakdown of business expenditures other than for supplies.

The business enterprise section of the economy is the heart of the industrial engine. It is in this sector that the productive energy of most of the labor force finds its outlet. The enterprise represented by this business account has four big customers for its output: consuming households; federal, state, and local government; foreign countries; and business itself. For one section of business buys goods from other sections. Auto companies, for example, buy machine tools from machine tool manufacturers, or they may contract with the construction industry for a new plant.

In the diagram the entries on the right-hand side of the business building give the 1950 magnitudes for the four main sources of business receipts. On the left-hand side are shown the factor costs incurred by the producers in manufacturing their product. The charges against the products of business consist of factor costs plus depreciation and indirect business taxes. As a routine, business promptly disburses as costs of doing business most of the receipts it takes in. What it does not so disburse is called profit. In the table shown, this residual item is called Corporate Profits Before Tax.

The term "corporate profits before tax" is an intellectually muddled one. It is like saying "earnings before bills paid." For the item "corporate profits before tax" contains a charge by the federal government against the operations of a business that precedes what is left to the business. Usually the term "profit" is used to denote the residual reward to the risk taker; but in national income and U. S Treasury accounting "corporate profit before taxes" includes a federal charge that is prior to the owner's reward. It is perhaps best to regard the federal government as a joint owner of every corporation because of its prior claim to 52 percent of the profit—and then to regard "corporate profits before tax" as the joint profit of the owner and the government.

Table II.—*Consolidated Business Income and Product Account, 1950*

[Millions of dollars]

Compensation of employees:		Consolidated net sales:	
Wages and salaries:		To persons	184, 340
Disbursements	120, 565	To government	17, 828
Excess of accruals over disbursements	0	To abroad	1, 302
		To business on capital account	43, 868
Supplements:			
Employer contributions for social insurance	3, 146	Change in inventories	7, 351
Other labor income	3, 440		
Income of unincorporated enterprises and inventory valuation adjustment	36, 140		
Rental income of persons	8, 473		
Corporate profits and inventory valuation adjustment:			
Corporate profits before tax:			
Corporate profits tax liability	17, 829		
Corporate profits after tax:			
Dividends	8, 781		
Undistributed profits	12, 360		
Inventory valuation adjustment	−4, 864		
Net interest	3, 708		
Income originating	*209, 578*		
Indirect business tax and nontax liability	23, 741		
Business transfer payments	843		
Statistical discrepancy	215		
Less: Subsidies minus current surplus of government enterprises	204		
Charges against net product	*234, 173*		
Capital consumption allowances	20, 516		
CHARGES AGAINST BUSINESS GROSS PRODUCT	254, 689	BUSINESS GROSS PRODUCT	254, 689

A PORTRAYAL OF "TABLE V-REST OF THE WORLD ACCOUNT, 1950"

Millions of Dollars

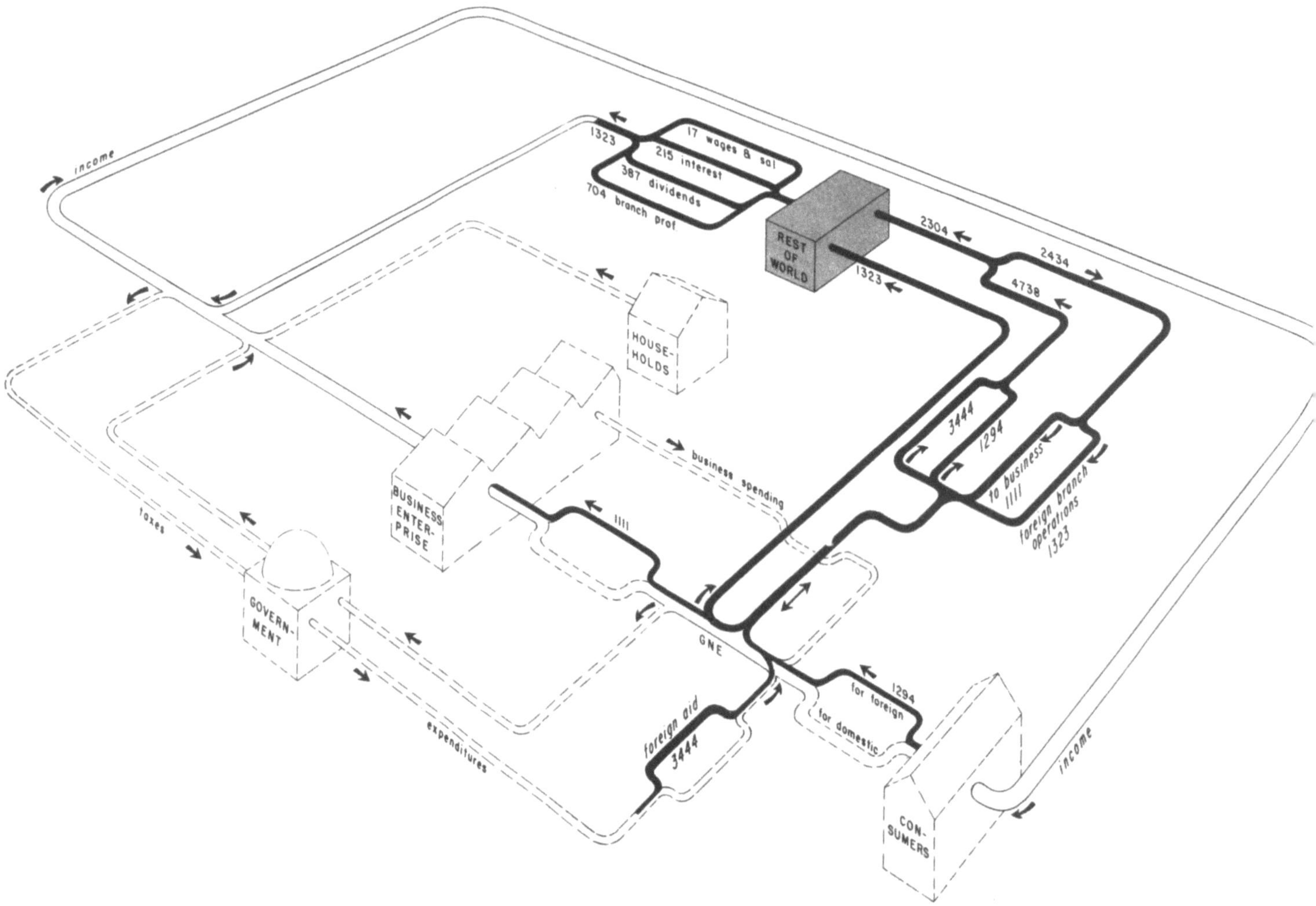

DIAGRAM 47

Table V.—*Rest of the World Account, 1950*

[Millions of dollars]

Net purchases of goods and services:		Net disinvestment in the United States	−2, 201
Net purchases of direct services:			
Wages and salaries	18		
Interest	248		
Dividends	426		
Branch profits	574		
Income originating and net and gross product	*1, 266*		
Net purchases from business	1, 302		
Net purchases from government	−3, 422		
Net purchases from persons	−1, 347		
NET CURRENT PAYMENTS TO THE UNITED STATES	−2, 201	NET DISINVESTMENT IN THE UNITED STATES	−2, 201

There are two important things to remember about the coverage of national income accounts. One is that the data pertain to the production in the continental United States only; the production in territories and possessions is excluded. A second matter is that the income, when measured by payments to the factors of production, refers only to the income of residents and factors located in the United States. Because of the continuous exchange of goods, money, and employment between the U. S. and other nations, and because domestic corporations have foreign branch offices abroad, the Department of Commerce has had to make adjustments in its national income accounting, both to exclude the personal income of foreigners and to include the income earned abroad by U. S. citizens. Hence the need for the Rest of the World account. It is shown in the accompanying table and also portrayed in Diagram 47.

The combination of Table V and Diagram 47 shows that in 1950 about $2, 304 million flowed out of the U. S. into foreign accounts. Although foreign countries bought on net $1, 111 million of goods from U. S. business and contributed another $1, 323 million because of foreign branch operations, the U. S. government and individuals together disbursed $4, 738 million to foreign countries, as shown. The difference of $2, 304 million represents the net outflow of funds from the country.

To portray the breakdowns in detail, to show how they were derived, and to show the many accounting decisions made would require several additional diagrams. Still, Diagram 47 is an integrated picture of the many types of payments involved in the rather limited summary of figures presented in Table V. These payments are of two major types.

First, there are the factor incomes that are paid to residents of the United States by the Rest of the World. These include Wages and Salaries, Interest, Dividends, and Branch Profits. They are shown as contributing a total of $1, 323 million to Gross National Expenditures and National Income.

Secondly, there are the payments for transactions which involve U. S. production and other net purchases by the Rest of the World. These payments include:

1. Merchandise purchases—the estimates of the Department of Commerce equal U. S. exports minus U. S. imports.
2. Transportation costs—included here are the sums paid for ocean traffic and air travel for both passengers and freight.
3. Unilateral transfers—these sums include cash gifts to foreign countries both by U. S. citizens and by the U. S. government. Net purchases from the U. S. government shown in the table include foreign aid programs—both military and economic aid—less transfers from abroad. These transfers from abroad include cash lend-lease settlements and special currency supplied to U. S. government agencies by occupied countries without cost to the U. S.

The table and diagram highlight the large sums paid by the U. S. government to foreign countries. These sums have since World War II dwarfed the net contribution of merchandise transfers—exports minus imports—which had been dominant in pre-war days.

A PORTRAYAL OF "TABLE VI-GROSS SAVING AND INVESTMENT ACCOUNT, 1950"

Millions of Dollars

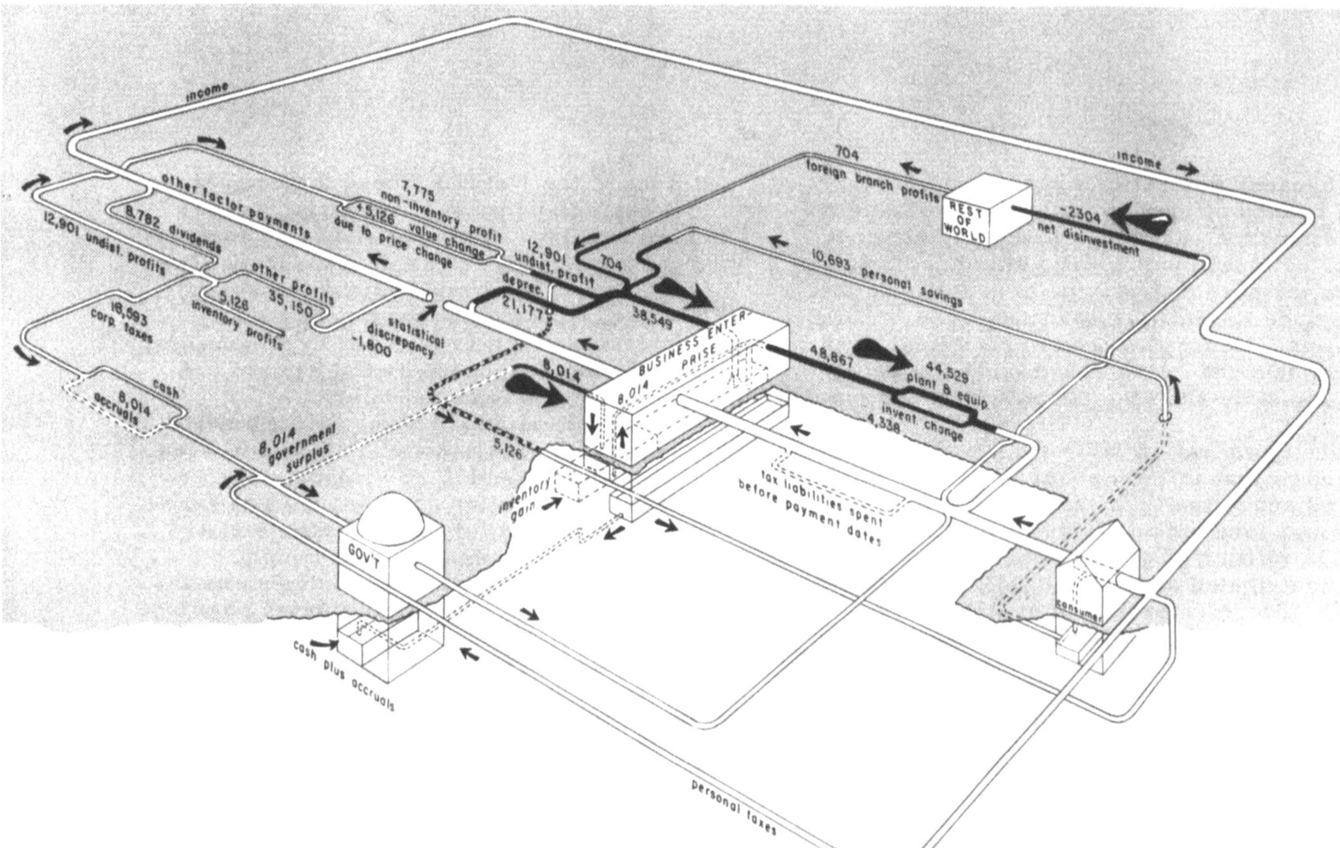

DIAGRAM 48

Table VI.—*Gross Saving and Investment Account, 1950*

[Millions of dollars]

Business purchases on capital account	43, 868	Excess of wage accruals over disbursements	
Change in business inventories	7, 351	Undistributed corporate profits (domestic)	12, 36
Net disinvestment in the United States by rest of world	—2, 201	Corporate inventory valuation adjustment	—4, 86
		Capital consumption allowances by private business	20, 51
		Foreign branch profits (net)	57
		Personal saving	12, 10
		Government surplus (+) or deficit (—) on income and product transactions	8, 11
		Statistical discrepancy	21
GROSS INVESTMENT	49, 018	GROSS SAVING AND STATISTICAL DISCREPANCY	49, 01

In the process of receiving money and distributing it, recipients are at any moment likely to hold on to a part of their current income after taxes. They are privileged to respend it, to hold it idle, or to entrust it to savings institutions, business institutions, or government institutions to respend it for them. As explained in previous diagrams, the amounts not respent by the "persons" directly are called "personal savings."

Thus at any particular time, each of the major spending groups is either saving (spending less than the current income) or dis-saving (spending more than current income), a fact that can have great significance for the future levels of total business operations. It would be helpful and useful if national income accounting indicated directly the detailed figures on the savings (or dis-savings) of each of the major spending groups of the nation. This it does not do. Instead, the Department of Commerce in its sixth table of accounts shows a summary of the savings of all the spending groups combined. Diagram 48 is a picture of this account.

But a picture of savings all by itself tells only half the story because it leaves open the question of what happens to the savings. For savings have to be injected into the stream of total payments somehow or the total flow of payment shrinks. Take consumer spending and savings as an example. If the consumer were the only purchaser of the nation's output and if he did not spend all his income but instead withheld part of it, then the sales, output, and resultant income of the nation would be reduced. His reduced spending would eventually reduce his income. But because there are two other consumers of the nation's output, namely, government and business, ready to receive or avail themselves of the money which individuals do not themselves spend for consumption goods, it is possible for the flow of funds to be a continuous one and to be maintained. The accounting conventions of national income accounting are such that for a given period of time the savings of one group are shown as always being respent by another. But such an accounting balance really tells us little about real spending or hoarding behavior. Business activity can go up 10 percent and the balance remains undisturbed—savings are always respent by others even at times when the interval between transactions gets longer and longer. The disrupters of the equilibrium cannot be found by examining national income accounting data alone.

How the savings of one group is spent for that group by another was schematically shown in Diagram 9, where Business was portrayed as a substitute spender of the personal savings of Consumers. In that Diagram we showed Business using the savings of individuals to buy plant and equipment. But Business also has its own savings which it can use for investment in plant and equipment. For the Unincorporated Business group these savings are part of "personal savings" because the income is calculated as a part of personal income. (See Diagrams 43 and 45 for clarification of this point.) For corporations the savings are the profits retained by the corporation and not paid out as dividends.

Government too can have savings to a certain extent. But in the case of government the amount of receipts in excess of government expenditures is called a "surplus." If the expenditures are greater than the receipts, then the difference is called a "deficit."

By now we are familiar with the fact that the Department of Commerce in all its accounts concerns itself only with actual and imputed money flows and that all its money payments are part of a circuit, that is, that payments by one sector of the economy are receipts for another. It therefore follows that in the Department of Commerce's accounting for any accounting period the savings of all groups (including the excess or deficit of the government) becomes the receipts of some other group, which in turn invests them.

This identity is often referred to as follows: Total Savings plus Government Deficit (or Surplus) Equals Investment. In the diagram the savings are highlighted by the black streams shown to the left of the Business Enterprise building. They can be summarized as follows:

	(Millions of dollars)
Undistributed non-inventory corporate profits	$7,775
Depreciation charges	21,177
Foreign branch profits	704
Personal savings	10,693
Sub total	40,349
Less statistical discrepancy	1,800
Gross private saving	38,549
Plus government surplus	8,014
Gross saving	46,563

The investment of the U. S. is shown on the right-hand side of the building and can be summarized as follows:

	(Millions of dollars)
Net investment by business	$48,867
Net investment by foreigners	-2,304
Gross investment	46,563

Diagram 48, which portrays this identity of savings and investment, brings into relief some of the arbitrariness of the Department of Commerce in forcing this relationship.

A large question is posed by the government deficit or surplus figure. How are these funds used? While it is easy to figure out what happens when the government runs a deficit (it simply borrows money from the savings of individuals and business by exchanging government securities for cash), it is not so easy to trace the reverse process. What happens, for example, when the government runs a surplus as it did in 1950?

When the government actually receives money in excess of its expenditures, it uses the surplus either to retire debt or to increase cash assets. Thus a net change occurs in its balance sheet. But at the same time one must remember that in the Department of Commerce's accounting, it is possible for the government to run a surplus which is not a cash surplus at all. This is because government receipts in national income accounting are partly on an accrual and partly on a cash basis, that is, some taxes are figured as part of government receipts at the time the liability is incurred, not necessarily when the taxes are paid. Corporations, for example, always pay their taxes in the calendar year following that in which the liability is incurred. Even though, for example, the Department of Commerce calculates—as we show—corporate taxes at $18.6 billion in 1950, corporations actually paid out only $12.5 billion in that year according to the record of the Bureau of Internal Revenue. So $6.1 billion represented accruals owed by corporations to the government. The taxes as reported by the Department of Commerce were not all cash.

To highlight this fact in the diagram, and to simplify the portrayal, we have assumed that all the $8 billion government surplus reported in the income accounting for 1950 represented business accruals. (This was not true—some of it may have been cash or some of it may have been other accruals.) Under our assumption that the surplus consisted entirely of business accruals, the $8 billion—although owed to the government—was still in the hands of business and was still available for the payment of business expenses. In our diagram we show the $8 billion tax accrual stream as being a theoretical one (represented by the broken lines) moving toward the Government building but diverted back to the corporations. In return the government received an asset, namely, tax accruals, as shown in the basement of the Treasury building. (We have assumed that all of the surplus was an accrual.)

Inventory profits are also highlighted in the diagram. Corporate profits include inventory profits. There have been years when this component of profits became a large and significant part of the total. The year 1950, the year used in the illustration, was such a time.

After the start of the Korean War in July, 1950, prices rose so rapidly that the cost of the stocks of goods used up in production was far below the cost of replacement. Therefore profits, because they were figured by subtracting costs that were based on lower prices than those prevailing later, were unrealistically high. In measuring U. S. output the Department of Commerce isolates and subtracts the above inventory profit (or loss) from total profit. It does this because it wants to measure only the current value of goods used in current production. Changes in the value of inventories resulting merely from price swings are not counted as being part of the value of current production.

The inventory valuation adjustment is a very complicated one. The accountants and national income technicians have still not come to a final conclusion as to how best to handle it.

The flows of Diagram 48 when traced through in relation to the balance sheet asset and liability positions of spending groups—and that is what a tabular review of savings and investment implies—tell a far more integrated story than Table VI alone with its terse tabulations can convey. However, Table VI contains no entries that reveal how in any year the monetization of private and government debt at the banks affects the savings and investment relationship. Diagram 48 does not show this either. Several additional diagrams would have to be drawn to show the role of the banks in the economy.

GROSS NATIONAL EXPENDITURES CAN BE ACCURATELY FORECAST

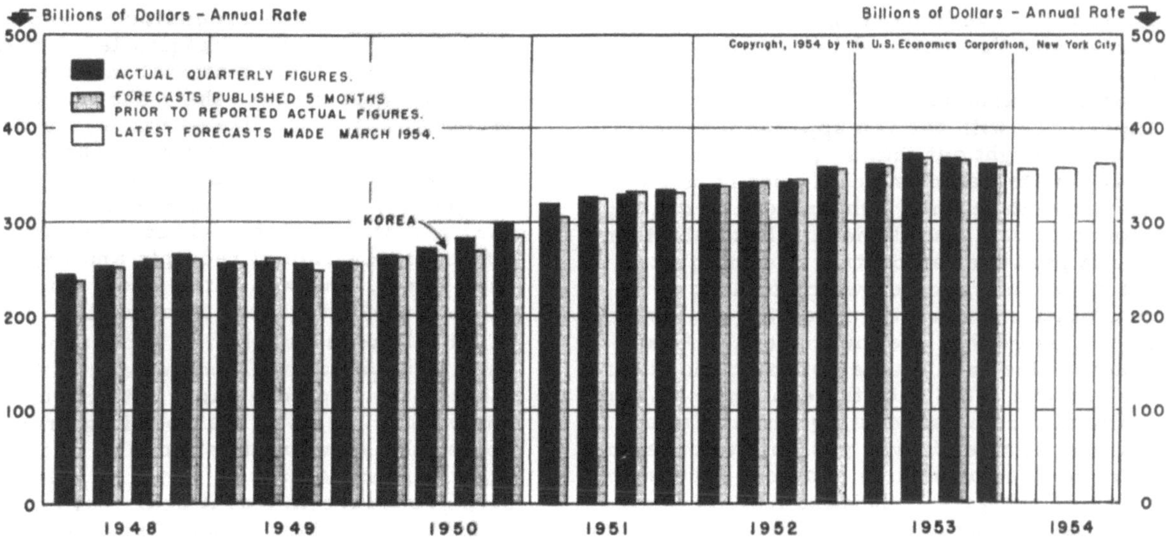

DIAGRAM 49

The innovation of national income accounting, despite its imperfections and omissions, has strikingly improved the feasibility of making forecasts of business activity. Helping business to gauge its markets better was one of the Department of Commerce's announced reasons for compiling its national income data. For it said: "Even when the active influencing of economic events is not the aim, it is desirable to have some knowledge of these events so that the best possible adjustments to them can be made. For example, the businessman wants to gauge a probable market for his output so as to obtain a more rational basis for determining his policies; and the tax administrator must estimate what government revenues are likely to be so that intelligent decisions can be made about matters relating to the expenditures and revenue policies of the various levels of government." On the score of providing a helpful tool, national income accounting has been a huge success. Diagram 49 shows the degree of accuracy to which Gross National Expenditures was forecast when heavy reliance was placed on the rationale and data of national income accounting.

Until national income accounting was instituted, accurate business forecasting was extremely difficult. Historically there have been several approaches toward making business projections, but all were limited and unintegrated because national income accounting had not yet been invented as an over-all statistical frame of reference and of course had not yet been made available regularly in quarterly government reports.

Back in the 1920's, the practice prevailed of looking for pilot series—early turning indexes—which would precede the ups and downs of the economy as a whole. Colonel Leonard Ayres and the Cleveland Trust Company, for example, developed a blast furnace activity indicator, Dun and Bradstreet an index of business failures. Professor Wesley Mitchell and the National Bureau of Economic Research examined hundreds of business indexes in an effort to find statistical series that would consistently lead the rest. They found some, but the search for early turning indexes has not been too rewarding. Moreover, the leads of these indexes are relatively short; usually they are too short for practical purposes. Today, most large companies systematically budget a year ahead and make commitments six or more months ahead. As a result, business indexes having only two or three months lead—and there are not many of them—have little practical value.

During the 1930's, a second major development in business forecasting occurred. A studied effort was made to discover and measure the maladjustments in the economy. Efforts were made to find unbalances and distortions as they developed. For example, indexes were built of the rates at which distributors placed commitments with manufacturers in order to ascertain whether over-ordering or under-ordering was occurring in the economy. The distortions were then used as a major clue toward predicting future business change. Several such successful efforts to discover and measure unbalances and distortions have been made. But again the lead time was often relatively short and the evidence unintegrated in a quantitative way.

Helpful and suggestive as the two approaches above have been, it is not necessary—now that national income accounting is here—to rely on either of the above approaches exclusively. The writer's own experience with the two approaches mentioned brought out that as procedures they were unintegrated and could not be used to best advantage until a means of integrating economic data was devised. Not until then was it possible to construct an integrated frame of reference on which to hang in a quantitative and additive way the multitude of estimates that one must prepare from special clues and studies of the outlook for the various sectors of the economy. When national income accounting finally did become available, it was possible to develop a third method of making business forecasts: "circuit analysis." It leans heavily upon national income accounting and would be impossible without it.

When the Department of Commerce began to organize U. S. business data in relation to the three major spending groups—consumers, business, and government—and to report systematically both on each group's expenditures for major purposes and on their disbursements by kinds of business cost, it became feasible to develop this new and integrated method of forecasting national income.

Recognizing the far-reaching impact and significance of fluctuations in the spending of money by each of the economy's spending groups, a few of us made an effort to uncover those situations that normally bear on each group to cause each to modify its future rates of spending. Those pressures, unbalances, incentives, and relationships which signaled how each of the major spending groups would probably behave down each channel of spending were sought out. This approach has brought demonstrably good results.

It was while proceeding with this approach that we discovered that the Department of Commerce's data on national income accounting, being confined exclusively to receipts and expenditures, had inadequate coverage for forecasting business activity and national income. For the data failed to throw continuous light on the changing asset and liability positions of the major spending groups. (The Department of Commerce calls attention to the limited coverage of its data. For it says—on page 21 of its Supplement—"The construction of balance sheet accounts showing the structure of the assets and liabilities of various sectors likewise would expand the scope and usefulness of the national economic accounting system.") Research work of our own had made clear that the inclination of both consumers and business firms to make expenditures was heavily influenced by the changing level of their liquid assets, their material inventories, their finished stocks, their short and long term debt, and the like—that is, by the changing level of their balance sheet items. In time we were able to combine in a weighted manner our consideration of monetary and other balance sheet influences with our consideration of receipts and expenditure items, and weave the whole into a systematic and integrated treatment.

This "circuit analysis" approach, built as it is upon national income accounting as a base, has big advantages It provides an analysis in terms of the spending pressures on and the spending intentions of each of the major spending groups. It is an all-inclusive procedure in that it deals not only with a few selected barometers but also with a host of spending rivulets that contribute to and make up total gross national expenditures. It is a procedure that leads one to assign a statistical weight in the total figures to the influence of every constituent force or situation. It is a method, too, which forces one at all times to consider the asset and liability position of each spending group along with each group's receipts and expenditures. Then, too, it provides a frame of reference that enables one—because of the very requirements of the circuit—to set up an accurate system of reconciliation and, by so doing, to maintain internal consistency and realism in one's component projections.

Diagram 49 evidences the accuracy that was obtained over the past six years in forecasting the government's Gross National Expenditures series by using the "circuit analysis" approach described. The diagram is a published record—a running comparison—of what came up against what had been forecast several months before. The accuracy obtained suggests that it would be desirable for the Department of Commerce, besides reporting on changing receipts and expenditures, also to organize and systematically report business data that highlight the changing balance sheet situations of all those spending groups which have discretion about spending more or less of their income. Today, people interested in projecting the over-all levels of business must themselves compile that kind of information from miscellaneous sources as best they can.

GROSS NATIONAL PRODUCT REFLECTS PRICE CHANGES AS WELL AS CHANGES IN OUTPUT

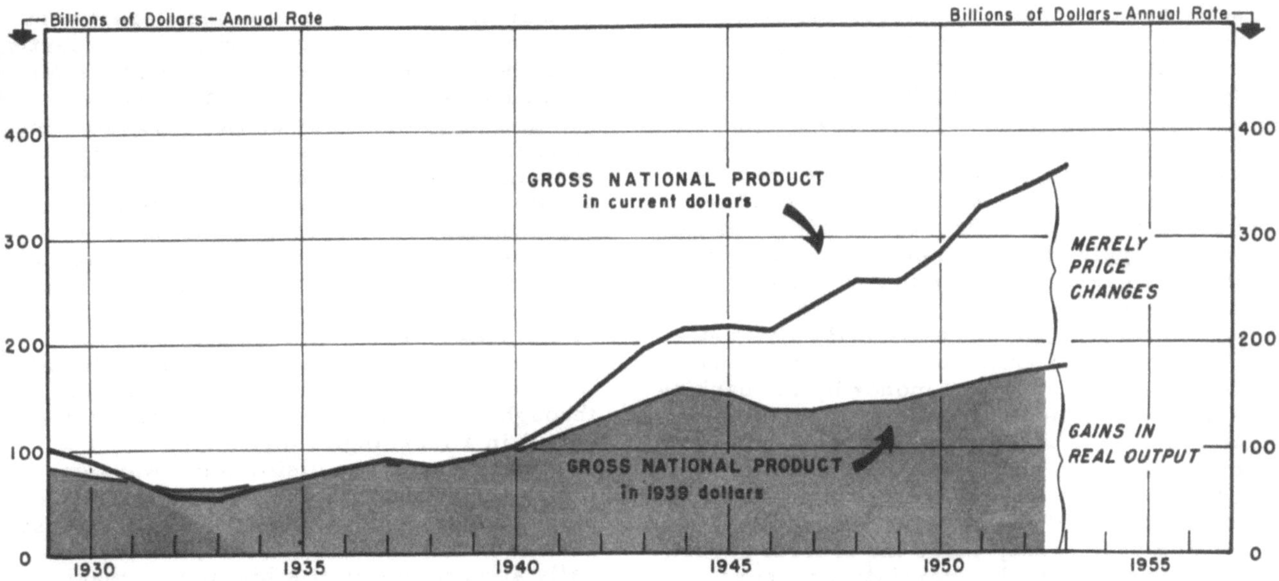

DIAGRAM 50

While national income accounting is a way of measuring economic activity, it is necessarily to a high degree an improvisation—a good one, but an improvisation nonetheless. All activity is equated through the money spent for it—or imputedly spent for it One should consequently be careful not to attribute more significance to the total figures than the component figures possess. Because of its limited goal, the rationale of national income accounting does not concern itself with two basic considerations.

For one thing, it does not deal with the changing financial and political strengths of the major spending groups but deals only with the cash and imputed flow of receipts and expenditures of these groups. On the financial side this will probably soon be supplemented by another source. Based on a study by Morris Copeland into major money flows and the changing balance sheets of major spending groups, the Federal Reserve Board will shortly be reporting annually on the changing assets and liabilities of the spending groups. But as of today, national income accounting does not of itself show the social cost—in expanded debt and growth of centralized spending power, for example—that society often pays for maintaining or lifting the level of gross national expenditures.

Then, too, national income accounting regards the value of the output of government workers—which to a high degree is indirectly on the tens of billions of dollars spent. While UNRRA functioned, for example, federal spending for aid to Britain, not subject to the test of the market place—as being on the same plane of value as the output of private producers. Government spending for goods and services is assumed to have just as much meaning as a measure of output as have consumer spending and business spending.

Federal spending for goods and services and the income generated by it was relatively minor in World War II days when total government spending constituted only 7 to 10 percent of the total and federal spending constituted only 2 to 5 percent. But it is another matter when total government spending constitutes about 22 percent of the total and federal outlays about 16 percent.

In the case of state and local spending, citizens vote specific taxes for, say, roads, schools, and hospitals. So the spending is usually in response to a very genuine consumer demand. But in the case of federal spending, "emergencies" must first be declared. Then Congress may rather uncritically grant to the executive and his agencies, as it did for several years after 1933, 1941, and 1950, a blank check of spending power running into the tens of billions of dollars. In the first case, people in their local voting cautiously appraise, as it were, the relative value of highways and groceries. In the second case, they pass judgment only very

Russia, Yugoslavia, India, etc., appeared in Gross National Expenditures as the equivalent of domestic private spending for U. S. groceries.

Gross National Expenditures, or Gross National Product, is, as mentioned above, a monetary measure of performance. But, because the physical output of the nation sells at ever-changing prices, the gross expenditures made for the output obviously do not reflect exclusively the changes in the real, physical, and tangible output exclusively. Output is always related to expenditures or—vice versa—expenditures are always related to output through the mechanism of price, as shown in Diagram 13. Prices of course reflect the relative changes in the supply of and demand for goods, but they also reflect—other things being equal—changes in the nation's supply of money.

In practice, prices are constantly modified through an artificial management and control of the supply of money by the banking system. Particularly since the beginning of World War II have prices reflected not only changes in the supply of and demand for goods but also the managed changes in the nation's supply of money.

For over twenty years the federal government has been rather persistently spending more money than it has taken in through taxes and has been raising its additional needed revenue by monetizing government debt. This practice has lowered the value of money. Since the beginning of World War II particularly, this dilution has been pronounced and has operated to raise the price level. (Private business too has been monetizing private debt. But because its monetization of debt has been more often tied in with genuine increases in the output of goods, prices were affected much less by its actions.) Consequently only by adjusting the monetary measures of output for price changes can one get a fairly true picture of the real output of the nation. Without adequate adjustment for price changes and changes in the historic value of the dollar, the Gross National Expenditure series shown in Diagram 50 for 1929 through 1953 does not provide a good measure of the real output during that period. Both the Gross National Expenditure series and the National Income series are dollar series, and necessarily measure output in rubber dollars. Conscious of this situation, the Department of Commerce worked out and rather recently published a price deflator for the Gross National Expenditure series so that the series can now be plotted—as on the accompanying diagram—both in constant dollars and in current dollars. When adjusted for price and converted into constant dollars the two big monetary measures do become very meaningful as measures of the changing output of the nation. Unfortunately the common practice is to report and discuss the output of the nation always in terms of current dollars without qualification. Still national income figures simply have to be viewed through a price filter if they are to reflect output in a meaningful way.

Awareness of the distortion always contained in national income figures because of price changes brings one up sharply against the realization that our society has continually at work within it a big money-making and money-destroying machine. As our country's industrial engine churns away at turning out ever more real goods, an auxiliary mechanism within it—under very fallible human manipulation—is always altering the money supply and thereby distorting the monetary measurement of the machine's output. One should therefore thoroughly understand this money-making mechanism—and the very nature of money and banking—if one is to interpret correctly the full meaning of currently reported Gross National Expenditure figures.

The Visual Economics Laboratory as one of its future projects hopes soon to portray visually society's big money-making machine and the nature of money and banking too.

CONCLUSION

This book has now presented a new teaching procedure. It has shown how a new set of simple symbols has been able—with relatively few accompanying words—to make an involved economic theme easier to understand.

The symbolism has certain characteristics and a certain logical construction. It is not random. It is orderly and could be taught to others just as engineering drawing is taught. We proceeded to use it in this book to picture the rationale of national income accounting without first describing the symbolism in detail. But now—that a practical application of the symbolism has been given—comment about the technique itself is probably in order.

As a graphic language the technique deliberately aimed to meet certain requirements that any visual portrayal of economics should logically possess.

Because economics deals with transactions between groups, the technique had to possess specific symbols for designating each of the major economic groups. This the symbolism did with the houses, factories, and domed government buildings.

Then it had to symbolize the process of exchange between economic groups. This the symbolism did through a system of flows through pipes. Thus the buildings and the pipes together were used to symbolize both the economic groups involved in transactions and the exchanges between them.

The technique's portrayals also had to be made easy for laymen to understand. This requirement was met by using perspective drawings exclusively. In the main, engineering drawing uses only two dimensions; our symbolism uses three. A symbolism to be helpful must be easy for everyone to follow and relatively self-explanatory. Perspective drawings meet that test.

Where statistics are available, as is the case in national income accounting, graphic portrayals should be subject to statistical check, just as engineering drawings are in their way. Unless this requirement is met, the portrayals would soon become arbitrary and in time become as unintegrated as are cartoons.

A symbolism to be rigorous from an accounting point of view must also be able to present both rates and levels simultaneously. For national income specifically, it must be able to show concurrently both the rate at which each participant receives and disburses income and the changing level of assets and liabilities of each of the economic participants. It should be able to present simultaneously the two tabular devices of accounting: the income statement and the balance sheet. Our symbolism does this, as was illustrated particularly in Diagrams 31 and 32.

Economics deals with two major aspects of social organization. It deals concurrently both with the engineering world of physical production and distribution and the financial world of ownership and debt. Consequently, an adequate symbolism must portray simultaneously the physical circuits of the engineering world and the financial circuits of the economic world and keep the two related. This, too, our symbolism does.

Again, in logic, a symbolism should—where statistics are available—be able to show the relative importance of the component circuits. Our symbolism did this by making the cross-sectional area of each pipe correspond roughly to the magnitudes carried by each pipe. There is, however, a practical limit to the degree that this can be done; in particular, there is a lower limit to the diameter or dimension that can be given to the smaller pipes in the diagrams. For that reason the technique used an auxiliary means—the flow meter—for showing the varying quantities carried by the several pipes. Just as engineers, in portraying water flows in a boiler room use larger or smaller pipes depending on the average load carried by each pipe and then use flow meters to record the wider ranges of variation, so we too have used pipes and meters in our portrayals.

A still further requirement for an adequate symbolism is that it be able to portray those exchange ratios between flows which represent the various kinds of prices: wage rates, rent, interest, and so forth. This our symbolism does by means of step-pulleys, like those shown in Diagrams 13, 17, 22, and 24.

Satisfactory graphic portrayal also requires that the contents of each portrayal be expansible or contractible at the portrayer's discretion. Sometimes one wishes to highlight the details of a situation, at other times only the over-all picture. The methodology should be like the Dewey Decimal System in that it be infinitely expansible or contractible at the user's will and still retain integration of the material shown. Then, too, because it is not always feasible to present in books of normal size, charts that portray large portions of the economic process at one time, good graphic portrayal requires that one be able to drop one portion of a sketch while adding another and still retain the frame of reference. One should be able to go from simple component sketches to larger integrations by adding a bit here and dropping a bit there. This our technique permits.

Besides dealing with the world of physical production and distribution and the world of ownership and finance, economics is related to the world of government and legislation. In logic therefore an adequate symbolism for economics should ideally be able to interlace the structures and actions of government with the two major concerns of economics just mentioned. In Diagrams 36 and 39 this book showed just a little of what can be done in that connection. With adequate time and effort all the three major concerns of economics could be interlaced vividly and helpfully.

In the past, visual presentations in economics have consisted largely of portraying by means of line graphs those fluctuations which have been measurable. But this procedure is analogous to what the behavior of engineers would be if they went down into the boiler rooms and merely recorded the readings on their gauges—the temperatures, the pressures, and the flows—but neglected to describe in anything but words the "hook-up" of the boiler to the engines and other devices. Heretofore our economic engine has been described mainly in words. Now it is possible to portray its structure and operation in pictures—and make it dynamically alive for television and motion pictures if one so desires.

Today social scientists badly need some easy simplifying and integrating means for bringing their complex material out from the world of specialists and for making their findings so obvious and compelling that all people who want to know will understand the important social situations that constitute the "facts" of social sciences—the substance from which they necessarily project their every day behavior.

The effort currently being made to use mathematical symbols to portray economic process is not too promising. Mathematics as a symbolism is probably too limited for the purpose. Even though economic institutions are the structures to which those variables relate that mathematical economics considers, mathematical symbols cannot delineate such institutional frameworks. Mathematical formulae can no more portray structure in economics than they can in engineering. For this reason, whenever mathematics is applied to problems involving physical or institutional frames of reference, one is apt thoughtlessly to assume or imply that the institutional model premised—but often left undescribed—is satisfactory or inviolable for the time being. At least it is not under inspection while the mathematical computations are being made. Mathematics is able to portray symbolically to the initiated the interdependence of several fluctuating variables, but it cannot describe the structural institutional arrangements under which the variables operate. In contrast our diagrammatic technique does this. It holds before us the institutional frame of reference underlying the mathematical economists' computations.

An integrated visualization of economics may even induce a change in our student attitudes. For when one sees economic structure and process integrated it is easy to think less as a learner and more as a problem-solver. The technique itself makes it easier to conceive of knowing as being something active and operative instead of as being something self-sufficing and self-enclosed; it makes it easier to view knowledge as the faculty of knowing how best to act instead of merely the possession of fixed truths. It inclines one to express knowledge in relatives and indisposes one to express it in absolutes. The visualizing technique illustrated induces one to see that his ideas are philosophically complete. It necessarily outlines problems and reveals relations and data that test hypotheses for their solution. It also makes it more difficult to claim or premise without danger of graphic contradiction that abstract cliches and personified concepts constitute something definite in themselves apart from the portrayable relationships associated with the terms.

Over the centuries men strive to equip themselves with orderly aids for thought: hieroglyphics, alphabets, number systems, chemical symbols, drawing conventions, Cartesian Coordinates. For men ever seek quick and vivid means for organizing their knowledge and for communicating with one another. But even so, today after centuries of advance, we are still handicapped in the complex fields of government and economics by inadequate tools of communication. Even though movies and television now offer us unparalleled opportunity for effective mass communication, we have no appropriate visual tools for taking advantage of the situation. Mainly verbal means are still exclusively relied upon to convey our complex economic problems to the limitless seekers of understanding.

It is hoped that the pictorial technique described and illustrated in this book will make this conveyance easier and perhaps in time be accepted in our schools, in television, and in the channels of communication generally.

APPENDIX

Statistical Tables from NATIONAL INCOME, 1954 Edition

Table 1.—*National Income by Distributive Shares, 1929–38*

[Millions of dollars]

Line		1929	1930	1931	1932	1933	1934	1935	1936	1937	1938
1	**National income**	87,814	75,729	59,708	42,547	40,159	48,959	57,057	64,911	73,618	67,581
2	**Compensation of employees**	51,085	46,844	39,740	31,054	29,539	34,296	37,340	42,910	47,934	44,994
3	Wages and salaries	50,423	46,187	39,119	30,477	28,997	33,705	36,690	41,920	46,107	42,976
4	Private	45,485	41,033	33,861	25,511	23,855	27,629	30,189	34,054	38,614	34,752
5	Military	308	311	304	292	267	258	303	334	354	365
6	Government civilian [1]	4,630	4,843	4,954	4,674	4,875	5,808	6,198	7,532	7,139	7,859
7	Supplements to wages and salaries	662	657	621	577	542	590	650	900	1,827	2,018
8	Employer contributions for social insurance	101	106	111	126	133	147	171	418	1,234	1,423
9	Other labor income	561	551	510	451	409	443	479	572	593	595
10	**Income of unincorporated enterprises and inventory valuation adjustment**	14,759	11,540	8,734	5,316	5,599	7,010	10,387	10,482	12,691	11,128
11	Business and professional	8,791	7,410	5,581	3,384	3,166	4,564	5,351	6,530	7,073	6,793
12	Income of unincorporated enterprises	8,649	6,655	4,970	3,089	3,691	4,618	5,401	6,650	7,102	6,572
13	Inventory valuation adjustment	142	755	611	295	−525	−54	−50	−120	−29	221
14	Farm	5,968	4,130	3,153	1,932	2,433	2,446	5,036	3,952	5,618	4,335
15	**Rental income of persons**	5,425	4,778	3,761	2,713	1,971	1,694	1,661	1,776	2,081	2,560
16	**Corporate profits and inventory valuation adjustment**	10,100	6,582	1,634	−1,970	−1,992	1,091	2,918	5,002	6,204	4,263
17	Corporate profits before tax	9,628	3,322	−780	−3,017	151	1,716	3,145	5,740	6,235	3,300
18	Corporate profits tax liability	1,369	842	498	385	521	744	951	1,409	1,502	1,029
19	Corporate profits after tax	8,259	2,480	−1,278	−3,402	−370	972	2,194	4,331	4,733	2,271
20	Dividends	5,813	5,490	4,088	2,565	2,056	2,587	2,863	4,548	4,685	3,187
21	Undistributed profits	2,446	−3,010	−5,366	−5,967	−2,425	−1,615	−669	−217	48	−916
22	Inventory valuation adjustment	472	3,260	2,414	1,047	−2,143	−625	−227	−738	−31	963
23	**Net interest**	6,445	5,985	5,839	5,434	5,042	4,869	4,751	4,741	4,708	4,636

1. Includes also the pay of employees of government enterprises and of permanent United States residents employed in the United States by foreign governments and international organizations.

Table 2.—*Gross National Product or Expenditure, 1929–38*

[Millions of dollars]

Line		1929	1930	1931	1932	1933	1934	1935	1936	1937	1938
1	**Gross national product**	104,436	91,105	76,271	58,466	55,964	64,975	72,502	82,743	90,780	85,227
2	**Personal consumption expenditures**	78,952	70,968	61,333	49,306	46,392	51,894	56,289	62,616	67,259	64,641
3	Durable goods	9,212	7,155	5,485	3,646	3,469	4,213	5,111	6,304	6,925	5,686
4	Nondurable goods	37,677	34,010	28,946	22,758	22,251	26,656	29,319	32,836	35,185	33,985
5	Services	32,063	29,803	26,902	22,902	20,672	21,025	21,859	23,476	25,149	24,970
6	**Gross private domestic investment**	16,231	10,265	5,523	913	1,391	2,888	6,277	8,404	11,747	6,661
7	New construction	8,707	6,183	3,968	1,876	1,431	1,709	2,299	3,281	4,403	3,960
8	Residential nonfarm	3,625	2,075	1,565	630	470	625	1,010	1,565	1,875	1,990
9	Other	5,082	4,108	2,403	1,246	961	1,084	1,289	1,716	2,528	1,970
10	Producers' durable equipment	5,850	4,465	2,839	1,593	1,589	2,304	3,066	4,169	5,095	3,644
11	Change in business inventories	1,674	−383	−1,284	−2,556	−1,629	−1,125	912	954	2,249	−943
12	Nonfarm	1,836	−83	−1,608	−2,590	−1,370	195	376	2,066	1,726	−1,046
13	Farm	−162	−300	324	34	−259	−1,320	536	−1,112	523	103
14	**Net foreign investment**	771	690	197	169	150	429	−54	−93	62	1,109
15	**Government purchases of goods and services**	8,482	9,182	9,218	8,078	8,031	9,764	9,990	11,816	11,712	12,816
16	Federal	1,311	1,410	1,537	1,480	2,018	2,991	2,931	4,815	4,552	5,280
17	National security (lines 17–20)	1,344	1,432	1,549	1,484	2,022	2,997	2,935	4,818	4,557	5,286
18	National defense										
19	Other national security										
20	Other										
21	Less: Government sales	33	22	12	4	4	6	4	3	5	6
22	State and local	7,171	7,772	7,681	6,598	6,013	6,773	7,059	7,001	7,160	7,536

1. Breakdown into "National defense" and "Other national security" not available.

Table 1.—*National Income by Distributive Shares, 1939–53*

[Millions of dollars]

1939	1940	1941	1942	1943	1944	1945	1946	1947	1948	1949	1950	1951	1952	1953	Line
72,753	**81,634**	**104,710**	**137,694**	**170,310**	**182,639**	**181,248**	**179,577**	**197,168**	**221,641**	**216,193**	**239,956**	**277,041**	**290,959**	**305,002**	1
48,108	**52,129**	**64,789**	**85,271**	**109,587**	**121,286**	**123,181**	**117,697**	**128,757**	**140,927**	**140,858**	**154,325**	**180,420**	**195,423**	**209,061**	2
45,941	49,818	62,086	82,109	105,828	116,823	117,577	111,836	122,858	135,172	134,334	146,526	170,881	185,039	197,980	3
37,742	41,395	51,894	66,123	79,197	83,843	82,664	91,241	105,512	116,424	113,873	124,297	142,050	152,222	164,503	4
388	563	1,866	6,168	14,133	20,033	21,819	7,818	4,067	3,970	4,248	4,999	8,684	10,465	10,207	5
7,811	7,860	8,326	9,818	12,498	12,947	13,094	12,777	13,279	14,778	16,213	17,230	20,147	22,352	23,270	6
2,167	2,311	2,703	3,162	3,759	4,463	5,604	5,861	5,899	5,755	6,524	7,799	9,539	10,394	11,081	7
1,540	1,624	1,983	2,302	2,677	2,937	3,805	3,970	3,565	3,042	3,503	3,976	4,753	4,874	4,745	8
627	687	720	860	1,082	1,526	1,799	1,891	2,334	2,713	3,021	3,823	4,786	5,510	6,336	9
11,610	**13,010**	**17,401**	**23,907**	**28,187**	**29,565**	**30,835**	**35,265**	**34,433**	**38,389**	**34,149**	**36,140**	**40,809**	**39,918**	**38,444**	10
7,293	8,442	10,897	13,899	16,823	18,040	19,011	21,321	19,948	21,649	21,431	22,855	24,791	25,727	26,215	11
7,459	8,487	11,512	14,266	16,979	18,109	19,117	23,026	21,419	22,061	20,963	23,989	25,135	25,519	26,410	12
−166	−45	−615	−367	−156	−69	−106	−1,705	−1,471	−412	468	−1,134	−314	208	−195	13
4,317	4,568	6,504	10,008	11,364	11,525	11,824	13,944	14,485	16,740	12,718	13,285	16,018	14,191	12,229	14
2,742	**2,885**	**3,465**	**4,547**	**5,097**	**5,413**	**5,634**	**6,208**	**6,510**	**7,198**	**7,874**	**8,473**	**9,129**	**10,021**	**10,596**	15
5,689	**9,120**	**14,511**	**19,678**	**23,781**	**23,033**	**18,413**	**17,288**	**23,626**	**30,619**	**28,141**	**35,106**	**39,913**	**38,165**	**38,466**	16
6,403	9,320	16,982	20,882	24,554	23,320	18,977	22,551	29,525	32,769	26,198	39,970	41,173	37,174	39,430	17
1,441	2,834	7,610	11,415	14,074	12,949	10,689	9,111	11,283	12,510	10,411	17,829	22,476	19,965	21,144	18
4,962	6,486	9,372	9,467	10,480	10,371	8,288	13,440	18,242	20,259	15,787	22,141	18,697	17,209	18,286	19
3,788	4,043	4,458	4,289	4,484	4,673	4,691	5,784	6,521	7,248	7,458	9,207	9,090	9,128	9,365	20
1,174	2,443	4,914	5,178	5,996	5,698	3,597	7,656	11,721	13,011	8,329	12,934	9,607	8,081	8,921	21
−714	−200	−2,471	−1,204	−773	−287	−564	−5,263	−5,899	−2,150	1,943	−4,864	−1,260	981	−964	22
4,604	**4,490**	**4,544**	**4,291**	**3,658**	**3,342**	**3,185**	**3,119**	**3,842**	**4,508**	**5,171**	**5,912**	**6,770**	**7,442**	**8,435**	23

Table 2.—*Gross National Product or Expenditure, 1939–53*

[Millions of dollars]

1939	1940	1941	1942	1943	1944	1945	1946	1947	1948	1949	1950	1951	1952	1953	Line
91,095	**100,618**	**125,822**	**159,133**	**192,513**	**211,393**	**213,558**	**209,246**	**232,228**	**257,325**	**257,301**	**285,067**	**328,232**	**346,095**	**364,857**	1
67,578	**71,881**	**81,875**	**89,748**	**100,541**	**109,833**	**121,699**	**146,617**	**164,973**	**177,609**	**180,598**	**194,026**	**208,342**	**218,424**	**230,080**	2
6,670	7,771	9,659	6,968	6,605	6,764	8,105	15,892	20,593	22,214	23,573	28,608	27,148	26,815	29,749	3
35,131	37,215	43,208	51,324	59,259	65,368	73,222	84,501	93,077	98,741	96,879	100,386	111,054	116,012	118,925	4
25,777	26,895	29,008	31,456	34,677	37,701	40,372	46,224	51,303	56,654	60,146	65,032	70,140	75,597	81,406	5
9,309	**13,155**	**18,072**	**9,875**	**5,600**	**7,130**	**10,430**	**27,125**	**29,705**	**41,176**	**32,549**	**51,219**	**56,864**	**50,655**	**51,408**	6
4,757	5,452	6,629	3,721	2,326	2,712	3,833	10,291	14,029	17,904	17,453	22,733	23,332	23,723	25,536	7
2,680	2,985	3,510	1,715	885	815	1,100	4,015	6,310	8,580	8,267	12,600	10,973	11,100	11,930	8
2,077	2,467	3,119	2,006	1,441	1,897	2,733	6,276	7,719	9,324	9,186	10,133	12,359	12,623	13,606	9
4,180	5,531	6,942	4,343	4,027	5,438	7,654	10,733	16,667	19,110	17,833	21,135	23,177	23,307	24,378	10
372	2,172	4,501	1,811	−753	−1,020	−1,057	6,101	−991	4,162	−2,737	7,351	10,355	3,625	1,494	11
316	1,902	4,049	652	−577	−575	−595	6,350	1,298	3,026	−1,862	6,428	8,951	2,971	2,169	12
56	270	452	1,159	−176	−445	−462	−249	−2,289	1,136	−875	923	1,404	654	−675	13
888	**1,509**	**1,124**	**−207**	**−2,245**	**−2,099**	**−1,438**	**4,586**	**8,942**	**1,956**	**534**	**−2,201**	**227**	**−164**	**−1,866**	14
13,320	**14,073**	**24,751**	**59,717**	**88,617**	**96,529**	**82,867**	**30,918**	**28,608**	**36,584**	**43,620**	**42,023**	**62,799**	**77,180**	**85,235**	15
5,157	6,170	16,923	52,027	81,223	89,006	74,796	20,934	15,776	21,019	25,445	22,138	40,995	53,951	60,105	16
[1] 1,258	[1] 2,223	[1] 13,794	[1] 49,567	[1] 80,384	[1] 88,615	[1] 75,923	[1] 21,188	13,349	15,984	19,288	18,511	37,260	48,501	52,022	17
....	....	....	....	....	....	....	....	12,254	11,578	13,570	14,257	33,864	46,096	49,993	18
....	....	....	....	....	....	....	....	1,095	4,406	5,718	4,254	3,396	2,415	2,029	19
3,908	3,956	3,173	2,664	1,480	1,552	1,031	2,469	3,751	5,570	6,570	3,882	4,154	5,805	8,485	20
9	9	44	204	641	1,161	2,158	2,723	1,324	535	413	255	419	355	402	21
8,163	7,903	7,828	7,690	7,394	7,523	8,071	9,984	12,832	15,565	18,175	19,885	21,804	23,229	25,130	22

Table 3.—*Personal Income and Disposition of Income, 1929–38*

[Millions of dollars]

Line		1929	1930	1931	1932	1933	1934	1935	1936	1937	1938
1	**Personal income**	**85,763**	**76,881**	**65,698**	**50,115**	**47,208**	**53,575**	**60,210**	**68,480**	**73,921**	**68,554**
2	Wage and salary disbursements	50,423	46,187	39,119	30,477	28,997	33,705	36,690	41,920	46,107	42,976
3	Other labor income	561	551	510	451	409	443	479	572	593	595
4	Proprietors' and rental income	20,184	16,318	12,495	8,029	7,570	8,704	12,048	12,258	14,772	13,688
5	Dividends	5,813	5,490	4,088	2,565	2,056	2,587	2,863	4,548	4,685	3,187
6	Personal interest income	7,428	6,949	6,923	6,575	6,212	6,099	5,892	5,842	5,912	5,828
7	Transfer payments	1,496	1,533	2,714	2,170	2,116	2,194	2,400	3,520	2,418	2,834
8	*Less*: Personal contributions for social insurance	142	147	151	152	152	157	162	180	566	554
9	*Less*: Personal tax and nontax payments	2,643	2,507	1,858	1,455	1,464	1,595	1,888	2,258	2,921	2,862
10	Federal	1,263	1,134	607	331	474	595	827	1,130	1,723	1,635
11	State and local	1,380	1,373	1,251	1,124	990	1,000	1,061	1,128	1,198	1,227
12	**Equals: Disposable personal income**	**83,120**	**74,374**	**63,840**	**48,660**	**45,744**	**51,980**	**58,322**	**66,222**	**71,000**	**65,692**
13	**Less: Personal consumption expenditures**	**78,952**	**70,968**	**61,333**	**49,306**	**46,392**	**51,894**	**56,289**	**62,616**	**67,259**	**64,641**
14	**Equals: Personal saving**	**4,168**	**3,406**	**2,507**	**−646**	**−648**	**86**	**2,033**	**3,606**	**3,741**	**1,051**

Table 4.—*Relation of Gross National Product, National Income, and Personal Income, 1929–38*

[Millions of dollars]

Line		1929	1930	1931	1932	1933	1934	1935	1936	1937	1938
1	**Gross national product**	**104,436**	**91,105**	**76,271**	**58,466**	**55,964**	**64,975**	**72,502**	**82,743**	**90,780**	**85,227**
2	Less: Capital consumption allowances	8,617	8,541	8,166	7,615	7,161	7,112	7,235	7,496	7,746	7,783
3	Depreciation charges	7,698	7,737	7,552	7,038	6,661	6,598	6,665	6,700	6,910	6,939
4	Accidental damage to fixed capital	413	389	351	329	275	237	236	381	304	387
5	Capital outlays charged to current expense	506	415	263	248	225	277	334	415	532	457
6	**Equals: Net national product**	**95,819**	**82,564**	**68,105**	**50,851**	**48,803**	**57,863**	**65,267**	**75,247**	**83,034**	**77,444**
7	Plus: Subsidies minus current surplus of government enterprises	−147	−123	−49	−45	18	283	403	39	60	176
8	Less: Indirect business tax and nontax liability	7,003	7,155	6,859	6,768	7,055	7,815	8,190	8,663	9,157	9,154
9	Business transfer payments	587	534	649	737	659	641	594	594	567	429
10	Statistical discrepancy	268	−977	840	754	948	731	−171	1,118	−248	456
11	**Equals: National income**	**87,814**	**75,729**	**59,708**	**42,547**	**40,159**	**48,959**	**57,057**	**64,911**	**73,618**	**67,581**
12	Less: Undistributed corporate profits	2,446	−3,010	−5,366	−5,967	−2,426	−1,615	−669	−217	48	−916
13	Corporate profits tax liability	1,369	842	498	385	521	744	951	1,409	1,502	1,029
14	Corporate inventory valuation adjustment	472	3,260	2,414	1,047	−2,143	−625	−227	−738	−31	963
15	Contributions for social insurance	243	253	262	278	285	304	333	598	1,800	1,977
16	Excess of wage accruals over disbursements	0	0	0	0	0	0	0	0	0	0
17	Plus: Net interest paid by government	983	964	1,084	1,141	1,170	1,230	1,141	1,101	1,204	1,192
18	Government transfer payments	909	999	2,065	1,433	1,457	1,553	1,806	2,926	1,851	2,405
19	Business transfer payments	587	534	649	737	659	641	594	594	567	429
20	**Equals: Personal income**	**85,763**	**76,881**	**65,698**	**50,115**	**47,208**	**53,575**	**60,210**	**68,480**	**73,921**	**68,554**

Table 5.—*Sources and Uses of Gross Saving, 1929–38* [1]

[Millions of dollars]

Line		1929	1930	1931	1932	1933	1934	1935	1936	1937	1938
1	**Gross private saving**	**15,703**	**12,197**	**7,721**	**2,049**	**1,944**	**4,958**	**8,372**	**10,147**	**11,504**	**8,881**
2	Personal saving	4,168	3,406	2,507	−646	−648	86	2,033	3,606	3,741	1,051
3	Undistributed corporate profits	2,446	−3,010	−5,366	−5,967	−2,426	−1,615	−669	−217	48	−916
4	Corporate inventory valuation adjustment	472	3,260	2,414	1,047	−2,143	−625	−227	−738	−31	963
5	Business depreciation charges	7,698	7,737	7,552	7,038	6,661	6,598	6,665	6,700	6,910	6,939
6	Accidental damage to fixed business capital	413	389	351	329	275	237	236	381	304	387
7	Capital outlays charged to current expense	506	415	263	248	225	277	334	415	532	457
8	Excess of wage accruals over disbursements	0	0	0	0	0	0	0	0	0	0
9	**Government surplus on income and product transactions**	**1,031**	**−265**	**−2,841**	**−1,721**	**−1,351**	**−2,372**	**−1,978**	**−2,954**	**553**	**−1,567**
10	Federal	1,159	281	−2,136	−1,480	−1,316	−2,853	−2,563	−3,477	−186	−1,971
11	State and local	−128	−546	−705	−241	−35	481	585	523	739	404
12	**Gross investment**	**17,002**	**10,955**	**5,720**	**1,082**	**1,541**	**3,317**	**6,223**	**8,311**	**11,809**	**7,770**
13	Gross private domestic investment	16,231	10,265	5,523	913	1,391	2,888	6,277	8,404	11,747	6,661
14	Net foreign investment	771	690	197	169	150	429	−54	−93	62	1,109
15	**Statistical discrepancy**	**268**	**−977**	**840**	**754**	**948**	**731**	**−171**	**1,118**	**−248**	**456**

1. In principle gross private saving plus government surplus on income and product transactions equals gross investment. Because of estimating errors, it differs from it by the amount of the statistical discrepancy.

Table 3.—*Personal Income and Disposition of Income, 1939–53*

[Millions of dollars]

1939	1940	1941	1942	1943	1944	1945	1946	1947	1948	1949	1950	1951	1952	1953	Line
72,884	78,680	96,275	123,497	151,392	165,696	171,222	177,990	190,522	208,743	206,818	227,050	255,340	271,242	286,066	1
45,941	49,818	62,086	82,109	105,619	117,016	117,563	111,866	122,843	135,142	134,379	146,526	170,776	185,068	198,056	2
627	687	720	860	1,082	1,526	1,799	1,891	2,334	2,713	3,021	3,823	4,786	5,510	6,336	3
14,352	15,895	20,866	28,454	33,284	34,978	36,469	41,473	40,943	45,587	42,023	44,613	49,938	49,939	49,040	4
3,788	4,043	4,458	4,289	4,484	4,673	4,691	5,784	6,521	7,248	7,458	9,207	9,090	9,128	9,365	5
5,809	5,781	5,833	5,808	5,798	6,151	6,868	7,576	8,212	8,950	9,768	10,628	11,592	12,318	13,475	6
2,963	3,114	3,113	3,143	2,964	3,588	6,165	11,411	11,787	11,281	12,403	15,147	12,575	13,090	13,801	7
596	668	801	1,166	1,839	2,236	2,333	2,011	2,118	2,178	2,234	2,894	3,417	3,811	4,007	8
2,440	2,604	3,293	5,981	17,845	18,935	20,867	18,808	21,506	21,142	18,661	20,920	29,271	34,373	35,967	9
1,235	1,364	2,016	4,668	16,517	17,536	19,379	17,162	19,650	18,997	16,194	18,179	26,278	31,143	32,484	10
1,205	1,240	1,277	1,313	1,328	1,399	1,488	1,646	1,856	2,145	2,467	2,741	2,993	3,230	3,483	11
70,444	76,076	92,982	117,516	133,547	146,761	150,355	159,182	169,016	187,601	188,157	206,130	226,069	236,869	250,099	12
67,578	71,881	81,875	89,748	100,541	109,833	121,699	146,617	164,973	177,609	180,598	194,026	208,342	218,424	230,080	13
2,866	4,195	11,107	27,768	33,006	36,928	28,656	12,565	4,043	9,992	7,559	12,104	17,727	18,445	20,019	14

Table 4.—*Relation of Gross National Product, National Income, and Personal Income, 1939–53*

[Millions of dollars]

1939	1940	1941	1942	1943	1944	1945	1946	1947	1948	1949	1950	1951	1952	1953	Line
91,095	100,618	125,822	159,133	192,513	211,393	213,558	209,246	232,228	257,325	257,301	285,067	328,232	346,095	364,857	1
7,838	8,148	9,041	10,155	10,866	12,007	12,549	11,666	14,118	16,494	18,431	20,516	23,469	25,304	27,226	2
7,121	7,316	8,078	9,162	9,854	10,793	11,246	10,013	12,150	14,290	16,380	18,042	20,344	22,456	24,170	3
222	246	273	484	399	360	381	407	567	574	518	616	909	677	808	4
495	586	690	509	613	854	922	1,246	1,401	1,630	1,533	1,858	2,216	2,171	2,248	5
83,257	92,470	116,781	148,978	181,647	199,386	201,009	197,580	218,110	240,831	238,870	264,551	304,763	320,791	337,631	6
485	420	102	150	183	652	760	835	−227	−171	−181	204	187	−229	−529	7
9,365	10,021	11,296	11,769	12,735	14,127	15,522	17,349	18,658	20,390	21,644	23,741	25,637	28,049	30,037	8
451	431	502	495	505	506	532	557	674	739	781	843	985	999	1,016	9
1,173	804	375	−830	−1,720	2,766	4,467	932	1,383	−2,110	71	215	1,287	555	1,047	10
72,753	81,634	104,710	137,694	170,310	182,639	181,248	179,577	197,168	221,641	216,193	239,956	277,041	290,959	305,002	11
1,174	2,443	4,914	5,178	5,996	5,698	3,597	7,656	11,721	13,011	8,329	12,934	9,607	8,081	8,921	12
1,441	2,834	7,610	11,415	14,074	12,949	10,689	9,111	11,283	12,510	10,411	17,829	22,476	19,965	21,144	13
−714	−200	−2,471	−1,204	−773	−287	−564	−5,263	−5,899	−2,150	1,943	−4,864	−1,260	981	−964	14
2,136	2,282	2,784	3,468	4,516	5,173	6,138	5,981	5,683	5,220	5,737	6,870	8,170	8,685	8,752	15
0	0	0	0	209	−193	14	−30	15	30	−45	0	105	−29	−76	16
1,205	1,291	1,289	1,517	2,140	2,809	3,683	4,457	4,370	4,442	4,597	4,716	4,822	4,876	5,040	17
2,512	2,683	2,611	2,648	2,459	3,082	5,633	10,854	11,113	10,542	11,622	14,304	11,590	12,091	12,785	18
451	431	502	495	505	506	532	557	674	739	781	843	985	999	1,016	19
72,884	78,680	96,275	123,497	151,392	165,696	171,222	177,990	190,522	208,743	206,818	227,050	255,340	271,242	286,066	20

Table 5.—*Sources and Uses of Gross Saving, 1939–53* [1]

[Millions of dollars]

1939	1940	1941	1942	1943	1944	1945	1946	1947	1948	1949	1950	1951	1952	1953	Line
11,164	14,586	22,591	41,897	49,304	54,153	44,252	26,594	23,998	37,377	36,217	40,690	49,648	52,782	55,126	1
2,866	4,195	11,107	27,768	33,006	36,928	28,656	12,565	4,043	9,992	7,559	12,104	17,727	18,445	20,019	2
1,174	2,443	4,914	5,178	5,996	5,698	3,597	7,656	11,721	13,011	8,329	12,934	9,607	8,081	8,921	3
−714	−200	−2,471	−1,204	−773	−287	−564	−5,263	−5,899	−2,150	1,943	−4,864	−1,260	981	−964	4
7,121	7,316	8,078	9,162	9,854	10,793	11,246	10,013	12,150	14,290	16,380	18,042	20,344	22,456	24,170	5
222	246	273	484	399	360	381	407	567	574	518	616	909	677	808	6
495	586	690	509	613	854	922	1,246	1,401	1,630	1,533	1,858	2,216	2,171	2,248	7
0	0	0	0	209	−193	14	−30	15	30	−45	0	105	−29	−76	8
−2,140	−726	−3,770	−31,399	−44,229	−51,888	−39,727	4,185	13,266	7,865	−3,205	8,113	6,156	−2,846	−6,631	9
−2,234	−1,448	−5,119	−33,198	−46,714	−54,577	−42,331	2,161	12,222	7,957	−2,398	9,229	6,517	−2,863	−6,831	10
94	722	1,349	1,799	2,485	2,689	2,604	2,024	1,044	−92	−807	−1,116	−361	17	200	11
10,197	14,664	19,196	9,668	3,355	5,031	8,992	31,711	38,647	43,132	33,063	49,018	57,091	50,491	49,542	12
9,309	13,155	18,072	9,875	5,600	7,130	10,430	27,125	29,705	41,176	32,549	51,219	56,864	50,655	51,408	13
888	1,509	1,124	−207	−2,245	−2,099	−1,438	4,586	8,942	1,956	534	−2,201	227	−164	−1,866	14
1,173	804	375	−830	−1,720	2,766	4,467	932	1,383	−2,110	71	215	1,287	555	1,047	15

Table 6.—Securities and Exchange Commission Estimates of Personal Saving and Comparison with Department of Commerce Estimates of Personal Saving, 1933–39

[Billions of dollars]

Line		1933	1934	1935	1936	1937	1938	1939
1	**Personal saving in forms other than changes in equity in real property and unincorporated enterprises** [1, 2]	**−1.11**	**2.86**	**1.33**	**3.66**	**2.63**	**2.36**	**3.45**
2	Currency and bank deposits	−1.28	1.80	2.46	3.63	.43	.40	3.00
3	Currency	.16	−.10	.23	.52	.20	.04	.45
4	Demand deposits	1.21	.24	1.03	2.04	−.48	.38	1.91
5	Time and savings deposits	−2.65	1.66	1.20	1.07	.71	−.01	.64
6	Savings and loan associations	−.58	−.29	−.20	−.06	−.11	.00	.04
7	Private insurance [3]	.57	1.33	1.55	1.67	1.76	1.54	1.72
8	Securities [4]	.07	.42	−1.67	−.32	1.10	−.22	−.53
9	United States savings bonds [5]			.13	.28	.42	.41	.66
10	Other U. S. Government [4]	.63	1.12	−.54	.61	.74	−.57	−.60
11	State and local government	−.67	−.79	−.12	−.47	−.05	−.23	−.23
12	Corporate and other	.11	.09	−1.14	−.75	−.01	.17	−.36
13	Less: Increase in debt not elsewhere classified [6]	−.10	.40	.82	1.27	.55	−.64	.78
14	**Increase in equity in nonfarm residences and in real property of nonprofit institutions** [7]	**−.85**	**−1.91**	**−.87**	**−.20**	**.10**	**.13**	**.77**
15	Nonfarm dwellings	.09	.19	.54	1.27	1.63	1.83	2.79
16	New construction by nonprofit institutions	.08	.08	.09	.14	.19	.22	.22
17	Less: Increase in mortgage debt to corporations and financial intermediaries.	−.62	.55	−.13	−.09	.01	.16	.50
18	Depreciation [8]	1.64	1.63	1.63	1.70	1.71	1.76	1.74
19	**Increase in equity in nonfarm unincorporated enterprises** [7, 9]	**−.62**	**1.64**	**1.38**	**1.92**	**1.04**	**−1.64**	**.28**
20	Increase in inventories	−.50	.01	.16	.48	.21	−.13	.07
21	New construction and producers' durable equipment	.70	.94	1.26	1.68	2.03	1.36	1.68
22	Less: Increase in bank and insurance company debt	.31	−.18	−.30	−.27	−.19	.12	.18
23	Increase in net payables to other corporations	−.32	−1.38	−.56	−.44	.42	1.79	.34
24	Depreciation [8]	.83	.87	.90	.95	.97	.96	.95
25	**Increase in equity in farm enterprises** [7]	**−.58**	**−2.18**	**−.19**	**−1.40**	**.28**	**−.44**	**−.46**
26	Increase in inventories	−.26	−1.32	.54	−1.11	.52	.10	.06
27	New construction and producers' durable equipment [10]	.18	.32	.51	.68	.84	.68	.73
28	Net purchases of farms from corporations and financial institutions	−.19	−.14	−.08	−.08	.03	.01	.00
29	Less: Increase in mortgage debt to corporations and financial intermediaries.	−.26	.47	.06	−.07	−.08	−.09	−.13
30	Increase in other debt to corporations and financial intermediaries [11]	−.26	−.30	.19	−.04	.10	.20	.26
31	Depreciation [8]	.84	.87	.91	1.00	1.09	1.12	1.12
32	**Personal saving, SEC** (lines (1)+(14)+(19)+(25))	**−3.16**	**.41**	**1.65**	**3.98**	**4.05**	**.41**	**4.04**
33	**Personal saving, Commerce** (from table 3) [12]	**−.65**	**.09**	**2.03**	**3.61**	**3.74**	**1.05**	**2.87**
34	Difference between lines (32) and (33)	−2.51	.32	−.38	.37	.31	−.64	1.17
35	Statistical discrepancy in the national income and product accounts (from table 4).	.95	.73	−.17	1.12	−.25	.46	1.17
36	**Alternative estimate of personal saving, Commerce** (lines (33)+(35)) [13]	**.30**	**.82**	**1.86**	**4.73**	**3.49**	**1.51**	**4.04**
37	Difference between lines (32) and (36)	−3.46	−.41	−.21	−.75	.56	−1.10	.00

1. SEC liquid saving less changes in government insurance and pension reserves and Armed Forces leave bonds (both of which are ascribed to the government sector), and less liquidation of mortgage debt (treated separately below).

Annual amounts, in billions of dollars, of changes in government insurance and pension reserves are as follows: 1933, $0.11; 1934, $0.16; 1935, $0.24; 1936, $0.55; 1937, $1.37; 1938, $1.09; 1939, $1.30; 1940, $1.30; 1941, $1.86; 1942, $2.55; 1943, $3.92; 1944, $4.96; 1945, $5.14; 1946, $3.55; 1947, $3.49; 1948, $3.57; 1949, $2.34; 1950, $1.09; 1951, $4.21; 1952, $4.38; 1953, $3.20. Annual amounts, in billions of dollars, of Armed Forces leave bonds are as follows: 1946, $0.60; 1947, $0.16; 1948, −$0.30; 1949, −$0.12; 1950, −$0.10; 1951, −$0.15; 1952, −$0.0[illegible]; 1953, −$0.02.

2. Includes changes in assets of unincorporated business of the types specified.

3. Excludes government pension and insurance reserves. See footnote 1.

4. Excludes Armed Forces leave bonds. See footnote 1.

Table 6.—*Securities and Exchange Commission Estimates of Personal Saving and Comparison with Department of Commerce Estimates of Personal Saving, 1940–53*

[Billions of dollars]

1940	1941	1942	1943	1944	1945	1946	1947	1948	1949	1950	1951	1952	1953	Line
3.79	**9.47**	**26.84**	**34.41**	**36.39**	**32.46**	**13.19**	**7.48**	**4.33**	**4.50**	**7.98**	**14.26**	**15.46**	**16.86**	1
2.88	4.80	10.95	16.18	17.55	19.06	10.56	2.01	−1.84	−1.46	3.62	5.95	7.10	4.72	2
.77	2.18	4.12	4.72	4.55	2.96	.10	−.43	−.46	−.79	−.05	.77	1.12	.59	3
1.46	2.58	6.07	7.12	5.89	7.27	5.16	.24	−2.20	−1.54	3.23	3.22	1.73	−.10	4
.65	.04	.76	4.34	7.11	8.82	5.31	2.19	.82	.86	.44	1.96	4.25	4.23	5
.20	.36	.26	.55	.81	1.06	1.18	1.20	1.21	1.51	1.51	2.10	3.07	3.68	6
1.85	2.14	2.49	2.85	3.21	3.46	3.42	3.64	3.75	3.71	3.92	4.05	4.91	5.08	7
−.17	2.83	10.25	13.83	14.96	9.36	.29	3.35	3.52	3.14	2.14	2.70	4.23	6.21	8
.86	2.75	7.98	11.14	11.80	6.85	.90	1.78	2.13	1.53	.55	−.41	.32	.30	9
−.35	.72	2.39	3.00	3.94	3.64	−1.04	.31	−1.22	.02	−.46	−.49	−.67	1.06	10
−.46	−.28	−.22	−.12	−.05	−.20	−.21	.42	1.09	.61	.68	.42	.86	1.82	11
−.22	−.36	.09	−.20	−.73	−.92	.65	.84	1.52	.98	1.36	3.18	3.72	3.03	12
.97	.66	−2.89	−1.01	.14	.48	2.28	2.73	2.31	2.40	3.22	.54	3.85	2.83	13
.72	**1.21**	**−.03**	**−.44**	**−.88**	**−1.00**	**−1.52**	**−.46**	**1.56**	**1.81**	**2.76**	**1.98**	**2.13**	**2.15**	14
3.15	3.67	1.90	1.13	.98	1.09	3.73	5.66	7.61	7.04	11.33	10.15	10.31	10.91	15
.21	.24	.11	.03	.07	.12	.41	.51	.85	1.09	1.29	1.38	1.27	1.38	16
.84	.82	.09	−.38	−.06	.20	3.60	4.46	4.61	3.87	7.15	6.53	6.28	6.66	17
1.80	1.87	1.95	1.98	1.99	2.01	2.06	2.16	2.30	2.46	2.72	3.02	3.20	3.48	18
.73	**.30**	**2.10**	**.17**	**.41**	**−.73**	**−.20**	**.08**	**.99**	**1.02**	**−1.90**	**2.39**	**.36**	**3.79**	19
.32	.73	.18	−.12	.50	.43	.38	.06	.97	−.23	1.50	.87	.19	.55	20
2.04	2.55	1.16	.78	.96	2.05	4.19	5.69	5.10	5.75	7.42	7.10	6.79	7.99	21
.07	.64	−.14	−.35	−.12	.78	1.91	2.06	.51	2.02	4.57	.66	.75	.80	22
.54	1.28	−2.00	−.62	−.30	.92	1.10	1.24	1.82	−.84	2.61	.81	1.34	−.76	23
1.02	1.16	1.37	1.45	1.47	1.51	1.76	2.37	2.75	3.32	3.63	4.11	4.53	4.71	24
−.11	**.25**	**1.08**	**−.43**	**−.78**	**−1.20**	**−1.24**	**−2.68**	**.94**	**−1.20**	**−.16**	**.12**	**−.37**	**−1.61**	25
.27	.45	1.16	−.18	−.45	−.46	−.25	−2.29	1.14	−.88	.92	1.40	.65	−.68	26
.83	1.14	.94	.84	1.01	1.00	1.59	3.02	3.88	4.00	4.23	4.67	4.57	4.11	27
.10	.18	.17	.18	.11	.08	.05	.02							28
−.03	−.06	−.31	−.48	−.36	−.25	−.02	.11	.08	.19	.30	.28	.33	.28	29
.21	.29	−.01	.04	−.10	.03	.45	.60	.70	.41	.81	.96	.30	−.38	30
1.13	1.29	1.51	1.71	1.91	2.04	2.20	2.71	3.30	3.72	4.20	4.71	4.96	5.15	31
5.13	**11.13**	**29.99**	**33.71**	**35.14**	**29.53**	**10.23**	**4.42**	**7.82**	**6.13**	**8.68**	**18.75**	**17.59**	**21.20**	32
4.20	**11.11**	**27.77**	**33.01**	**36.93**	**28.66**	**12.57**	**4.04**	**9.99**	**7.56**	**12.10**	**17.73**	**18.44**	**20.02**	33
.93	.02	2.22	.70	−1.79	.87	−2.34	.38	−2.17	−1.43	−3.42	1.02	−.86	1.18	34
.80	.38	−.83	−1.72	2.77	4.47	.93	1.38	−2.11	.07	.22	1.29	.56	1.08	35
5.00	**11.49**	**26.94**	**31.29**	**39.70**	**33.13**	**13.50**	**5.42**	**7.88**	**7.63**	**12.32**	**19.01**	**19.00**	**21.07**	36
.13	−.36	3.05	2.42	−4.56	−3.60	−3.27	−1.00	−.06	−1.50	−3.63	−.26	−1.41	.13	37

5. Includes increase in redemption value of outstanding bonds.
6. Consists of changes in consumer debts to corporate business.
7. Represents changes in specified assets and liabilities only.
8. Includes accidental damage to fixed property.
9. Includes increase in equity of individuals in nonfarm nonresidential real property.
10. Includes farm dwellings.
11. Excludes consumer debt, which is included in line 13.
12. Equals disposable personal income less personal consumption expenditures.
13. Equals gross investment less government surplus and less gross private saving other than personal saving as given in table 5.

Source: Securities and Exchange Commission.

Table 8.—*Government Receipts, 1929–38* [1]

[Millions of dollars]

Line		1929	1930	1931	1932	1933	1934	1935	1936	1937	1938
1	**Total receipts** [1]	11,258	10,757	9,477	8,886	9,325	10,458	11,362	12,928	15,380	15,022
2	**Federal**	3,804	3,047	2,047	1,708	2,670	3,541	3,964	5,021	7,039	6,480
3	Personal tax and nontax receipts before refunds	1,323	1,183	643	366	495	609	842	1,143	1,742	1,654
4	Income taxes [3]	1,238	1,093	567	320	375	452	580	740	1,319	1,244
5	Estate and gift taxes	61	61	56	30	69	129	248	386	402	390
6	Other taxes [4]					35	15				
7	Nontaxes [5]	24	29	20	16	16	13	14	17	21	20
8	Less: Tax refunds	60	49	36	35	21	14	15	13	19	19
9	Equals: Personal tax and nontax receipts	1,263	1,134	607	331	474	595	827	1,130	1,723	1,635
10	Corporate profits tax accruals	1,224	744	423	328	462	644	820	1,252	1,337	895
11	Indirect business tax and nontax accruals before refunds	1,219	1,067	912	937	1,658	2,270	2,235	2,273	2,425	2,238
12	Excise taxes	564	537	490	635	1,246	1,833	1,730	1,693	1,775	1,709
13	Liquor	13	11	10	7	138	375	459	569	587	565
14	Tobacco	449	446	425	387	409	452	478	536	563	567
15	Other	102	80	55	241	699	1,006	793	588	625	577
16	Customs duties	599	474	373	259	296	308	371	403	469	357
17	Capital stock tax					80	92	95	138	139	127
18	Nontaxes [6]	56	56	49	43	36	37	39	39	42	45
19	Less: Tax refunds	26	22	18	13	39	89	54	22	19	22
20	Equals: Indirect business tax and nontax accruals	1,193	1,045	894	924	1,619	2,181	2,181	2,251	2,406	2,216
21	Contributions for social insurance	124	124	123	125	115	121	136	391	1,573	1,734
22	**State and local**	7,571	7,835	7,743	7,312	7,157	8,550	9,104	8,628	9,105	9,320
23	Personal tax and nontax receipts	1,350	1,373	1,251	1,124	990	1,000	1,061	1,128	1,198	1,227
24	Income taxes	139	110	74	64	67	87	121	167	204	208
25	Death and gift taxes	165	182	168	137	110	97	109	116	129	137
26	Motor vehicle licenses [7]	187	183	171	158	152	153	163	176	183	181
27	Property taxes [8]	148	154	149	144	129	126	129	130	134	137
28	Other taxes [9]	47	49	47	48	47	52	60	64	69	75
29	Nontaxes [10]	694	695	642	573	485	485	479	475	479	469
30	Corporate profits tax accruals	145	98	75	57	59	100	131	157	165	134
31	Indirect business tax and nontax accruals	5,810	6,110	5,965	5,844	5,436	5,634	6,009	6,412	6,751	6,938
32	Sales taxes	439	525	571	578	669	934	1,156	1,396	1,518	1,583
33	State [11]	414	500	545	552	641	904	1,096	1,306	1,417	1,463
34	General	(15)	(15)	7	10	61	228	300	398	440	449
35	Gasoline	414	500	524	522	526	563	620	690	748	782
36	Liquor	(15)	(15)	1	4	34	89	141	169	174	175
37	Tobacco	(15)	(15)	13	16	20	24	35	49	55	57
38	Local	25	25	26	26	28	30	60	90	101	120
39	Motor vehicle licenses [7]	153	154	148	137	133	140	153	166	170	178
40	Property taxes [8]	4,543	4,727	4,539	4,424	3,962	3,907	4,023	4,058	4,162	4,277
41	Other taxes [12]	467	488	475	452	424	406	417	529	621	612
42	Nontaxes [13]	208	216	232	253	218	247	250	263	280	285
43	Contributions for social insurance	119	129	139	153	170	183	197	207	227	213
44	Federal grants-in-aid [14]	117	125	313	134	502	1,633	1,706	724	764	778

1. Includes transactions of social insurance funds, which can be separated by use of the data furnished in table 10. For an explanation of the treatment of government enterprises, see Part II. For a list of these enterprises, see footnotes to the table on industrial classification in the Introduction to Part III.
2. Federal grants-in-aid to State and local governments are reflected in Federal expenditures and in State and local receipts and expenditures. Total Government receipts and expenditures have been adjusted to eliminate this duplication.
3. Consists of individual income tax and victory tax.
4. Consists of dividends tax and automobile use tax.
5. Consists mainly of charges for government products and services not accounted for under government enterprises; of fines and penalties; and of donations. Includes also the excess of receipts over expenditures derived from the services of enemy prisoners of war to private contractors. Receipts from the sale of surplus property are not included.
6. Consists mainly of charges for government products and services not accounted for under government enterprises, including rents and royalties; and of fines and penalties. Receipts from the sale of surplus property are not included.
7. State only. State drivers' licenses are included in personal motor vehicle license receipts.
8. Property taxes levied on houses of owner-occupants are classified as indirect business taxes.
9. Consists of poll taxes and miscellaneous licenses and permits.

Table 8.—*Government Receipts, 1939–53* [1]

[Millions of dollars]

1939	1940	1941	1942	1943	1944	1945	1946	1947	1948	1949	1950	1951	1952	1953	Line
15,382	17,741	24,983	32,633	49,170	51,184	53,216	51,249	57,130	59,262	56,453	69,360	85,564	91,072	95,900	1
6,721	8,641	15,420	22,943	39,258	41,008	42,495	39,200	43,311	43,438	39,095	50,177	64,491	68,204	71,228	2
1,260	1,393	2,044	4,696	16,540	17,880	20,710	18,815	21,323	20,783	18,562	19,888	28,078	33,279	35,084	3
874	1,036	1,622	4,062	15,923	17,133	19,848	17,987	20,446	19,825	17,751	19,167	27,247	32,357	34,095	4
371	341	401	471	461	565	663	734	830	900	754	659	751	850	922	5
			121	77	74	81	1								6
15	16	21	42	79	108	118	93	47	58	57	62	80	72	67	7
25	29	28	28	23	344	1,331	1,653	1,673	1,786	2,368	1,709	1,800	2,136	2,600	8
1,235	1,364	2,016	4,668	16,517	17,536	19,379	17,162	19,650	18,997	16,194	18,179	26,278	31,143	32,484	9
1,285	2,635	7,333	11,065	13,616	12,484	10,234	8,649	10,679	11,840	9,806	17,059	21,598	19,144	20,281	10
2,347	2,662	3,593	4,073	4,979	6,226	7,180	7,975	7,943	8,173	8,230	9,099	9,598	10,534	11,124	11
1,826	2,122	2,817	3,364	4,076	5,257	6,214	7,267	7,297	7,501	7,561	8,252	8,677	9,580	10,100	12
602	721	928	1,215	1,454	2,083	2,370	2,691	2,330	2,177	2,204	2,419	2,459	2,726	2,820	13
593	645	748	859	990	925	1,034	1,219	1,267	1,312	1,320	1,348	1,447	1,663	1,614	14
631	756	1,141	1,290	1,632	2,249	2,810	3,357	3,700	4,012	4,037	4,485	4,771	5,191	5,666	15
344	327	439	313	410	378	397	503	436	4[illegible]0	381	549	591	582	609	16
133	167	282	329	381	372	353									17
44	46	55	67	112	219	216	205	210	262	288	298	330	372	415	18
25	35	26	24	35	55	52	79	69	83	72	67	68	68	76	19
2,322	2,627	3,567	4,049	4,944	6,171	7,128	7,896	7,874	8,090	8,158	9,032	9,530	10,466	11,048	20
1,879	2,015	2,504	3,161	4,181	4,817	5,754	5,493	5,108	4,511	4,937	5,907	7,085	7,451	7,415	21
9,649	9,957	10,370	10,578	10,854	11,123	11,591	13,157	15,557	17,810	19,586	21,522	23,541	25,503	27,489	22
1,205	1,240	1,277	1,313	1,328	1,399	1,488	1,646	1,856	2,145	2,467	2,741	2,993	3,230	3,483	23
201	232	258	291	330	366	402	409	488	570	718	776	910	1,007	1,061	24
122	115	116	111	111	125	141	153	177	183	175	182	209	219	234	25
190	210	219	198	183	178	182	199	226	253	288	326	373	400	433	26
137	140	142	142	145	147	149	155	171	189	211	227	245	266	288	27
78	65	64	67	67	71	72	86	101	115	130	141	149	168	185	28
477	478	478	504	492	512	542	644	693	835	945	1,089	1,107	1,170	1,282	29
156	199	277	350	458	465	455	462	604	670	605	770	878	821	863	30
7,043	7,394	7,729	7,720	7,791	7,956	8,394	9,453	10,784	12,300	13,486	14,709	16,107	17,583	18,989	31
1,653	1,835	2,073	2,033	1,965	2,002	2,266	2,899	3,508	4,115	4,333	4,801	5,366	5,857	6,186	32
1,542	1,705	1,942	1,900	1,831	1,866	2,110	2,716	3,202	3,715	3,882	4,317	4,815	5,230	5,472	33
465	533	621	642	700	751	806	1,051	1,330	1,584	1,609	1,828	2,118	2,353	2,463	34
815	865	958	855	704	681	777	1,020	1,176	1,318	1,451	1,625	1,791	1,973	2,060	35
184	205	241	266	276	281	359	427	407	439	418	442	462	446	493	36
78	102	122	137	151	153	168	218	289	374	404	422	444	458	456	37
111	130	131	133	134	136	156	183	306	400	451	484	551	627	714	38
182	200	213	212	212	215	231	271	324	368	412	460	517	566	615	39
4,285	4,407	4,449	4,397	4,494	4,565	4,642	4,836	5,346	5,938	6,642	7,143	7,696	8,385	9,126	40
638	656	691	760	806	847	908	1,037	1,158	1,347	1,500	1,635	1,785	1,993	2,217	41
285	296	303	318	314	327	347	410	448	532	599	670	743	782	845	42
257	267	280	307	335	356	384	488	575	709	800	963	1,085	1,234	1,337	43
988	857	807	888	942	947	870	1,108	1,738	1,986	2,228	2,339	2,478	2,635	2,817	44

10. Consists of charges for government products and services not accounted for under government enterprises (such as tuition fees and public hospital fees); fines and penalties; donations; and special assessments for outlay paid by unincorporated business, including homeowners.

11. Minor State sales taxes not specified below are included in "Other taxes."

12. Consists of gross receipts taxes, franchise taxes, licenses, permits, severance taxes, documentary and stock transfer taxes, and minor State sales taxes.

13. Consists mainly of charges for government products and services not accounted for under government enterprises, including rents and royalties; of fines and penalties; special assessments for operation; and donations.

14. Includes shared receipts as well as grants-in-aid. The latter consist of highway grants, education grants (agricultural research and education, vocational education, and rehabilitation, war training and research programs, and veterans' postwar training programs), public assistance grants (mainly categorical assistance under the Social Security program), grants for the administration of the Unemployment Compensation program and of the U. S. Employment Service, Public Health grants, grants made by the Bureau of Community Facilities of the Federal Works Agency to war-congested communities, the Federal contribution to the District of Columbia, grants made by the Federal Emergency Relief Administration and the Public Works Administration, and miscellaneous other grants.

15. Small amounts included in "Other taxes."

Table 9.—*Government Expenditures, 1929–38* [1]

[Millions of dollars]

Line		1929	1930	1931	1932	1933	1934	1935	1936	1937	1938
1	**Total expenditures** [2]	**10,227**	**11,022**	**12,318**	**10,607**	**10,676**	**12,830**	**13,340**	**15,882**	**14,827**	**16,589**
2	**Federal**	**2,645**	**2,766**	**4,183**	**3,188**	**3,986**	**6,394**	**6,527**	**8,501**	**7,225**	**8,451**
3	Purchases of goods and services	1,311	1,410	1,537	1,480	2,018	2,991	2,931	4,815	4,552	5,280
4	Compensation of employees	879	915	921	880	1,164	1,694	1,768	3,570	3,013	3,505
5	Net purchases from business	362	424	536	540	805	1,258	1,108	1,180	1,445	1,711
6	New construction [3]	155	209	271	333	346	426	473	509	540	489
7	Other	207	215	265	207	459	832	635	671	905	1,222
8	*Less*: Domestic sales of surplus consumption goods										
9	Net purchases from abroad	70	71	80	60	49	39	55	65	94	64
10	Purchases from abroad	103	93	92	64	53	45	59	68	99	70
11	*Less*: Sales to abroad	33	22	12	4	4	6	4	3	5	6
12	Transfer payments	691	735	1,716	931	698	600	634	2,064	828	1,196
13	Grants-in-aid to State and local governments [4]	117	125	313	134	502	1,633	1,706	724	764	778
14	Net interest paid	441	380	444	479	517	590	526	485	616	619
15	Interest paid	733	684	679	718	845	1,016	1,025	1,062	1,240	1,158
16	*Less*: Interest received	292	304	235	239	328	426	499	577	624	539
17	Subsidies less current surplus of government enterprises [2]	85	116	173	164	251	580	730	413	465	578
18	**State and local**	**7,699**	**8,381**	**8,448**	**7,553**	**7,192**	**8,069**	**8,519**	**8,105**	**8,366**	**8,916**
19	Purchases of goods and services	7,171	7,772	7,681	6,598	6,013	6,773	7,059	7,001	7,160	7,536
20	Compensation of employees	3,456	3,630	3,737	3,565	3,531	3,884	4,178	3,696	3,889	4,121
21	Purchases from business	3,715	4,142	3,944	3,033	2,482	2,889	2,881	3,305	3,271	3,415
22	New construction [3]	2,331	2,649	2,388	1,529	1,032	1,186	1,122	1,744	1,607	1,622
23	Other	1,384	1,493	1,556	1,504	1,450	1,703	1,759	1,561	1,664	1,793
24	Transfer payments	218	264	349	502	759	953	1,172	862	1,023	1,209
25	Net interest paid	542	584	640	662	653	640	615	616	588	573
26	Interest paid	773	829	842	856	844	833	806	806	779	762
27	*Less*: Interest received	231	245	202	194	191	193	191	190	191	189
28	*Less*: Current surplus of government enterprises	232	239	222	209	233	297	327	374	405	402

1. See footnote 1 to table 8. 2. See footnote 2 to table 8.
3. For 1933–43, the sum of Federal and State and local new construction is smaller than New public construction shown in table 31, because work relief construction, as estimated by the National Income Division, has been excluded. The value of work relief construction is reflected in compensation of employees and "Other purchases from business."
4. See footnote 14 to table 8.

Table 10.—*Social Insurance Funds, 1929–38* [1]

[Millions of dollars]

Line		1929	1930	1931	1932	1933	1934	1935	1936	1937	1938
	Federal										
1	Contributions for social insurance	124	124	123	125	115	121	136	391	1,573	1,734
2	Employee contributions	95	96	96	95	89	92	92	104	480	458
3	Employer contributions	29	28	27	30	26	29	44	287	1,093	1,276
4	Government and government enterprises	29	28	27	30	26	26	37	47	66	79
5	Private						3	7	240	1,027	1,197
6	Self-employed persons' contributions										
7	*Less*: Transferred to general government						3	7	52	133	138
8	*Equals*: Retained by social insurance funds	124	124	123	125	115	118	129	339	1,440	1,596
9	*Plus*: Investment income	21	26	26	19	25	25	26	37	154	94
10	*Equals*: Net receipts	145	150	149	144	140	143	155	376	1,594	1,690
11	*Less*: Benefit payments	44	51	60	72	82	94	93	95	142	606
12	*Equals*: Surplus (+) or deficit (−)	101	99	89	72	58	49	62	281	1,452	1,084
	State and Local										
13	Contributions for social insurance	119	129	139	153	170	183	197	207	227	243
14	Employees	47	51	55	57	63	65	70	76	86	96
15	Employer (government and government enterprises) [2]	72	78	84	96	107	118	127	131	141	147
16	*Less*: Transferred to general government	1	1	1	1	2	2	2	2	2	3
17	*Equals*: Retained by social insurance funds	118	128	138	152	168	181	195	205	225	240
18	*Plus*: Investment income	16	19	21	24	28	31	35	39	43	48
19	*Equals*: Net receipts	134	147	159	176	196	212	230	244	268	288
20	*Less*: Benefit payments	72	78	86	95	110	119	127	137	144	151
21	*Equals*: Surplus (+) or deficit (−)	62	69	73	81	86	93	103	107	124	137

1. For a listing of social insurance funds and for detail on employer and employee contributions, and benefit payments, see tables 34, 35, and 36.
2. Includes contributions by private employers to State cash sickness compensation funds as follows, in millions of dollars: 1949, $2; 1950, $7; 1951, $2; 1952, $2; 1953, $3.

Table 9.—*Government Expenditures, 1939–53* [1]

[Millions of dollars]

1939	1940	1941	1942	1943	1944	1945	1946	1947	1948	1949	1950	1951	1952	1953	Line
17,522	**18,467**	**28,753**	**64,032**	**93,399**	**103,072**	**92,943**	**47,064**	**43,864**	**51,397**	**59,658**	**61,247**	**79,398**	**93,918**	**102,531**	1
8,955	**10,089**	**20,539**	**56,141**	**85,972**	**95,585**	**84,826**	**37,039**	**31,089**	**35,481**	**41,493**	**40,948**	**57,974**	**71,067**	**78,059**	2
5,157	6,170	16,923	52,027	81,223	89,006	74,796	20,934	15,776	21,019	25,445	22,138	40,995	53,951	60,105	3
3,414	3,489	5,027	10,645	20,899	27,250	29,786	14,545	9,343	8,872	9,926	10,649	16,164	18,708	18,132	4
1,679	2,597	11,566	40,189	58,913	60,831	44,067	7,193	6,486	9,955	11,676	8,067	21,642	32.208	38,486	5
543	965	3,596	9,309	5,608	2,505	1,737	931	951	1,187	1,488	1,625	2,982	4,186	4,153	6
1,140	1,638	7,977	30,896	53,372	58,535	42,752	6,978	5,828	8,911	10,271	6,488	18,721	28,086	34,403	7
4	6	7	16	67	209	422	716	293	143	83	46	61	64	70	8
64	84	330	1,193	1,411	925	943	−804	−53	2,192	3,843	3,422	3,189	3,035	3,487	9
69	87	367	1,381	1,985	1,877	2,679	1,203	978	2,584	4,173	3,631	3,547	3,326	3,819	10
5	3	37	188	574	952	1,736	2,007	1,031	392	330	209	358	291	332	11
1,240	1,421	1,369	1,419	1,239	1,841	4,310	9,214	8,887	7,652	8,754	10,884	8,663	8,940	9,660	12
988	857	807	888	942	947	870	1,108	1,738	1,986	2,228	2,339	2,478	2,635	2,817	13
643	726	774	1,038	1,707	2,420	3,334	4,164	4,117	4,179	4,327	4,431	4,558	4,589	4,732	14
1,189	1,298	1,379	1,726	2,481	3,282	4,335	5,217	5,230	5,354	5,611	5,804	5,996	6,290	6,633	15
546	572	605	688	774	842	1,001	1,053	1,113	1,175	1,284	1,373	1,438	1,701	1,901	16
927	915	666	769	861	1,371	1,516	1,619	571	645	739	1,156	1,280	952	745	17
9,555	**9,235**	**9,021**	**8,779**	**8,369**	**8,434**	**8,987**	**11,133**	**14,513**	**17,902**	**20,393**	**22,638**	**23,902**	**25,486**	**27,289**	18
8,163	7,903	7,828	7,690	7,394	7,523	8,071	9,984	12,832	15,565	18,175	19,885	21,804	23,229	25,130	19
4,185	4,289	4,388	4,473	4,663	4,938	5,370	6,177	7,320	8,502	9,422	10,124	11,069	12,265	13,305	20
3,978	3,614	3,440	3,217	2,731	2,585	2,701	3,807	5,512	7,063	8,753	9,761	10,735	10,964	11,825	21
2,129	1,733	1,424	1,066	681	568	661	1,431	2,482	3,638	4,917	5,375	6,436	6,715	7,226	22
1,849	1,881	2,016	2,151	2,050	2,017	2,040	2,376	3,030	3,425	3,836	4,386	4,299	4,249	4,599	23
1,272	1,282	1,242	1,229	1,220	1,241	1,323	1,640	2,226	2,890	2,868	3,420	2,927	3,151	3,125	24
562	565	515	479	433	389	349	293	253	263	270	285	264	287	308	25
752	761	709	681	660	633	599	555	521	550	585	624	656	733	808	26
190	196	194	202	227	244	250	262	268	287	315	339	392	446	500	27
442	495	564	619	678	719	756	784	798	816	920	952	1,093	1,181	1,274	28

5. Subsidies reflected consist of government payments to farmers, payments for the exportation and diversion of surplus agricultural commodities, shipping and housing subsidies, the wartime subsidy programs administered mainly by the Commodity Credit Corporation and the Reconstruction Finance Corporation, and subsidy payments to air carriers.

Table 10.—*Social Insurance Funds, 1939–53* [1]

[Millions of dollars]

1939	1940	1941	1942	1943	1944	1945	1946	1947	1948	1949	1950	1951	1952	1953	Line
1,879	2,015	2,504	3,161	4,181	4,817	5,754	5,493	5,108	4,511	4,937	5,907	7,085	7,451	7,415	1
491	546	686	1,044	1,706	2,092	2,174	1,773	1,833	1,829	1,856	2,448	2,904	3,032	3,153	2
1,388	1,469	1,818	2,117	2,475	2,725	3,580	3,720	3,275	2,682	3,081	3,459	4,181	4,212	4,042	3
86	95	104	138	174	447	1,495	1,654	840	342	732	396	486	547	334	4
1,302	1,374	1,714	1,979	2,301	2,278	2,085	2,066	2,435	2,340	2,349	3,063	3,695	3,665	3,708	5
													207	220	6
160	147	186	172	212	182	196	244	114	175	226	338	388	305	317	7
1,719	1,868	2,318	2,989	3,969	4,635	5,558	5,249	4,994	4,336	4,711	5,569	6,697	7,146	7,098	8
122	152	183	224	279	365	492	608	667	756	853	884	887	1,008	1,118	9
1,841	2,020	2,501	3,213	4,248	5,000	6,050	5,857	5,661	5,092	5,564	6,453	7,584	8,154	8,216	10
696	835	707	747	538	655	1,322	2,348	2,123	2,226	3,492	6,100	4,352	4,791	5,607	11
1,145	1,185	1,794	2,466	3,710	4,345	4,728	3,509	3,538	2,866	2,072	353	3,232	3,363	2,609	12
257	267	280	307	335	356	384	488	575	709	800	963	1,085	1,234	1,337	13
105	112	115	122	133	144	159	238	285	349	378	446	513	572	634	14
152	155	165	185	202	212	225	250	290	360	422	517	572	662	708	15
3	3	3	4	4	4	5	6	7	11	16	17	17	18	19	16
254	264	277	303	331	352	379	482	568	698	784	946	1,068	1,216	1,318	17
53	59	66	69	74	78	82	86	91	101	122	142	168	199	220	18
307	323	343	372	405	430	461	568	659	799	906	1,088	1,236	1,415	1,538	19
157	163	175	194	213	223	240	260	297	326	356	398	466	542	610	20
150	160	168	178	192	207	221	308	362	473	550	690	770	873	928	21

Table 13.—*National Income by Industrial Origin, 1929–38* [1]

[Millions of dollars]

Line		1929	1930	1931	1932	1933	1934	1935	1936	1937	1938
1	**All industries, total**	87,814	75,729	59,708	42,547	40,159	48,959	57,057	64,911	73,618	67,581
2	**Agriculture, forestry, and fisheries**	8,278	6,236	4,895	3,332	3,713	3,728	6,411	5,405	7,214	5,907
3	Farms	8,083	6,044	4,727	3,199	3,590	3,603	6,268	5,266	7,029	5,741
4	Agricultural services, forestry, and fisheries	195	182	168	133	123	120	143	139	185	166
5	**Mining**	2,048	1,638	969	673	647	1,158	1,211	1,520	1,912	1,470
6	Metal mining	466	275	106	20	38	123	166	263	452	271
7	Anthracite mining	284	282	229	151	130	172	139	146	137	114
8	Bituminous and other soft-coal mining	649	531	374	241	257	417	446	535	600	458
9	Crude petroleum and natural gas	447	348	150	211	181	376	378	461	581	523
10	Nonmetallic mining and quarrying	202	192	110	50	41	70	82	115	142	104
11	**Contract construction**	3,808	3,179	2,203	1,056	755	1,066	1,297	1,983	2,078	1,993
12	**Manufacturing**	21,888	18,232	12,419	7,207	7,562	10,905	13,265	16,182	19,305	15,006
13	Food and kindred products	2,135	2,394	1,860	1,409	1,331	1,599	1,873	2,076	2,401	2,252
14	Tobacco manufactures	256	299	322	312	142	146	203	134	196	223
15	Textile-mill products	1,796	1,405	1,148	714	699	1,102	1,201	1,361	1,601	1,094
16	Apparel and other finished fabric products	1,262	1,003	808	498	542	784	850	973	992	917
17	Lumber and furniture products [2]	1,528	1,122	653	329	305	547	669	891	1,072	852
18	Lumber and wood products, except furniture	-----	-----	-----	-----	-----	-----	-----	-----	-----	-----
19	Furniture and fixtures	-----	-----	-----	-----	-----	-----	-----	-----	-----	-----
20	Lumber and timber basic products	852	615	281	118	123	264	328	449	564	430
21	Furniture and finished lumber products	676	507	372	211	182	283	341	442	508	422
22	Paper and allied products	562	504	388	270	290	418	461	505	565	573
23	Printing, publishing, and allied industries	1,589	1,501	1,220	883	793	928	1,042	1,171	1,253	1,137
24	Chemicals and allied products [2]	1,129	1,036	830	561	621	726	806	961	1,167	1,007
25	Products of petroleum and coal [2]	917	809	309	121	76	120	208	317	542	491
26	Rubber products	355	274	232	113	102	134	213	214	292	204
27	Leather and leather products	602	491	390	305	271	413	376	424	461	403
28	Stone, clay, and glass products	799	613	439	123	208	330	409	576	653	503
29	Metals, metal products, and miscellaneous [2]	4,323	3,347	1,861	768	1,031	1,781	2,345	3,084	3,806	2,479
30	Primary metal industries	-----	-----	-----	-----	-----	-----	-----	-----	-----	-----
31	Fabricated metal products, including ordnance	-----	-----	-----	-----	-----	-----	-----	-----	-----	-----
32	Instruments	-----	-----	-----	-----	-----	-----	-----	-----	-----	-----
33	Miscellaneous manufacturing	-----	-----	-----	-----	-----	-----	-----	-----	-----	-----
34	Iron and steel and their products, including ordnance	2,970	2,217	1,110	410	684	1,086	1,478	2,069	2,597	1,600
35	Nonferrous metals and their products	757	634	412	196	153	381	461	557	699	438
36	Miscellaneous manufacturing	596	496	339	162	194	314	406	458	510	441
37	Machinery, except electrical [2]	1,890	1,481	753	299	424	733	1,014	1,398	1,760	1,247
38	Electrical machinery [2]	1,045	824	503	245	276	376	526	710	912	661
39	Transportation equipment, except automobiles	315	288	142	89	69	119	139	232	332	263
40	Automobiles and automobile equipment	1,385	841	561	168	382	649	930	1,155	1,300	700
41	**Wholesale and retail trade**	13,358	12,229	9,743	6,354	5,485	8,056	9,200	10,590	12,212	11,943
42	Wholesale trade	4,222	4,053	3,181	2,158	1,781	2,476	2,919	3,234	3,926	3,779
43	Retail trade and automobile services	9,136	8,176	6,562	4,196	3,704	5,580	6,281	7,356	8,286	8,164
44	**Finance, insurance, and real estate**	12,693	10,592	8,646	6,753	5,745	5,633	5,933	6,580	7,237	7,676
45	Banking	1,957	1,480	985	733	495	541	665	778	895	846
46	Security and commodity brokers, dealers and exchanges	655	144	70	98	260	215	183	279	243	159
47	Finance, n. e. c.	200	6	−28	−63	0	19	77	140	151	220
48	Insurance carriers	888	808	718	576	571	650	720	801	906	922
49	Insurance agents and combination offices	421	402	366	328	289	315	330	347	386	383
50	Real estate	8,572	7,752	6,535	5,081	4,130	3,893	3,958	4,235	4,656	5,146
51	**Transportation**	6,636	5,604	4,369	3,210	3,036	3,415	3,700	4,277	4,634	4,052
52	Railroads	4,597	3,766	2,828	1,979	1,866	2,062	2,250	2,635	2,808	2,370
53	Local and highway passenger transportation	825	766	633	512	450	485	478	535	546	499
54	Local railways and buslines	-----	-----	-----	-----	-----	-----	-----	-----	-----	-----
55	Highway passenger transportation, n. e. c.	-----	-----	-----	-----	-----	-----	-----	-----	-----	-----
56	Highway freight transportation and warehousing	560	533	481	418	416	466	526	587	654	658
57	Water transportation	266	216	173	127	153	178	200	243	293	206
58	Air transportation (common carriers)	−3	−10	4	10	10	8	14	22	26	30
59	Pipeline transportation	129	105	81	56	47	103	106	107	130	120
60	Services allied to transportation	262	228	169	108	94	113	126	148	177	169
61	**Communications and public utilities**	2,864	2,790	2,628	2,286	2,000	2,198	2,280	2,487	2,725	2,717
62	Telephone, telegraph, and related services	1,125	1,097	991	794	691	741	777	842	925	947
63	Radio broadcasting and television	28	9	16	21	14	32	38	53	66	65
64	Utilities: electric and gas	1,631	1,608	1,563	1,410	1,237	1,359	1,401	1,528	1,668	1,642
65	Local utilities and public services, n. e. c.	80	76	58	61	58	66	64	64	66	63
66	**Services**	10,338	9,187	7,863	6,133	5,567	6,231	6,669	7,479	8,246	7,907
67	Hotels and other lodging places	599	543	442	305	271	341	371	413	471	456
68	Personal services	1,279	1,203	1,030	800	695	782	857	958	1,110	1,024
69	Private households	3,253	2,363	1,815	1,362	1,199	1,336	1,428	1,662	1,930	1,718
70	Commercial and trade schools and employment agencies	40	38	31	22	20	23	29	32	39	34
71	Business services, n. e. c.	561	559	445	356	330	424	473	574	607	599
72	Miscellaneous repair services and hand trades	312	301	273	224	191	203	218	230	247	259
73	Motion pictures	440	438	361	194	210	283	329	391	437	426
74	Amusement and recreation, except motion pictures	381	337	269	178	154	197	211	263	305	266
75	Medical and other health services	1,536	1,476	1,306	1,037	948	1,036	1,115	1,253	1,323	1,330
76	Legal services	689	683	701	591	561	600	624	647	680	666
77	Engineering and other professional services, n. e. c.	206	184	152	102	98	113	121	144	156	164
78	Educational services, n. e. c.	402	413	412	393	363	361	365	376	394	409
79	Nonprofit membership organizations, n. e. c.	640	649	626	569	527	532	528	546	547	556
80	**Government and government enterprises**	5,093	5,316	5,426	5,150	5,326	6,271	6,724	8,108	7,772	8,524
81	Federal—general government	879	915	921	880	1,164	1,694	1,768	3,570	3,013	3,505
82	Civilian, except work relief	-----	-----	-----	-----	-----	-----	-----	-----	-----	-----
83	Military	-----	-----	-----	-----	-----	-----	-----	-----	-----	-----
84	Work relief	-----	-----	-----	-----	-----	-----	-----	-----	-----	-----
85	Federal—government enterprises	581	584	582	544	485	540	614	662	675	698
86	State and local—general government	3,456	3,630	3,737	3,565	3,531	3,884	4,178	3,696	3,889	4,121
87	Public education	-----	-----	-----	-----	-----	-----	-----	-----	-----	-----
88	Nonschool, except work relief	-----	-----	-----	-----	-----	-----	-----	-----	-----	-----
89	Work relief	-----	-----	-----	-----	-----	-----	-----	-----	-----	-----
90	State and local—government enterprises	177	187	186	161	146	153	164	180	195	200
91	**Rest of the world**	810	746	547	393	323	303	367	380	283	386

1. National income originating in each industry is the sum of factor costs incurred by the industry in production. Hence, it is the net value added to production by the industry, measured at factor costs. In the business sector of the economy, except government enterprises, it is equal to the excess of the market value of the industry's product and the subsidies it receives over the sum of the following costs: purchases of goods and services from other enterprises, indirect business tax and nontax liability, business transfer payments, and capital consumption charges. In the other sectors of the economy (government, personal, and rest-of-the-world) and also in government enterprises, this value added in production (as measured in the present series) can be described only as factor costs incurred. "National income originating" is a more net concept of value-added than that used by the Bureau of the Census in compiling the Census of Manufactures. "Value added by manufacture" was obtained in the 1947 Census of Manufactures by deducting from the value of products only "the cost of materials, supplies, containers, fuel, purchased electric energy, and contract work." National income by industrial origin is obtained statistically by aggregating the data

Table 13.—*National Income by Industrial Origin, 1939–53* [1]

[Millions of dollars

1939	1940	1941	1942	1943	1944	1945	1946	1947	1948	1949	1950	1951	1952	1953	Line
72,753	81,634	104,710	137,694	170,310	182,639	181,248	179,577	197,168	221,641	216,193	239,956	277,041	290,959	305,002	1
5,933	6,247	8,470	12,403	14,143	14,483	14,889	17,344	18,244	20,815	16,646	17,232	20,285	18,653	16,821	2
5,761	6,073	8,269	12,148	13,864	14,152	14,526	16,927	17,777	20,290	16,117	16,673	19,648	17,955	16,102	3
172	174	201	255	279	331	363	417	467	525	529	559	637	698	719	4
1,582	1,868	2,299	2,571	2,741	2,891	2,717	2,970	4,191	5,246	4,355	4,998	5,551	5,320	5,507	5
343	440	504	581	498	403	334	302	515	640	513	693	815	836	932	6
126	138	165	192	213	239	219	283	300	342	259	277	276	249	183	7
501	621	805	989	1,133	1,263	1,195	1,242	1,815	2,087	1,460	1,701	1,809	1,544	1,493	8
482	518	620	556	646	757	741	839	1,178	1,729	1,670	1,816	2,062	2,081	2,250	9
130	151	205	253	251	229	228	304	383	448	453	511	589	610	649	10
2,323	2,569	4,195	6,471	5,460	4,135	4,280	6,477	8,401	10,305	10,369	11,461	13,551	14,518	15,199	11
17,925	22,336	33,027	45,343	58,149	60,124	52,008	48,479	58,717	66,630	62,757	74,235	87,734	89,831	97,323	12
2,269	2,462	2,737	3,693	4,396	4,951	5,010	5,539	5,803	6,646	6,508	6,753	6,999	7,629	8,057	13
297	260	220	185	189	283	236	326	364	399	512	512	525	572	615	14
1,261	1,509	2,067	2,852	3,014	2,965	3,015	4,005	4,657	5,163	4,139	4,551	5,176	4,541	4,366	15
1,028	1,138	1,463	1,928	2,418	2,705	2,914	3,355	3,383	3,500	3,331	3,424	3,702	3,849	3,998	16
1,001	1,154	1,691	1,973	2,089	2,170	2,133	2,811	3,455	[3] 3,831	3,349	4,187	4,631	4,368	4,353	17
----	----	----	----	----	----	----	----	----	2,639	2,189	2,795	3,118	2,839	2,765	18
----	----	----	----	----	----	----	----	----	1,192	1,160	1,392	1,513	1,529	1,588	19
494	591	907	1,090	1,138	1,142	1,080	1,448	1,938	----	----	----	----	----	----	20
507	563	784	883	951	1,028	1,053	1,363	1,517	----	----	----	----	----	----	21
556	665	1,030	1,124	1,257	1,348	1,341	1,696	2,208	2,340	2,162	2,685	3,355	3,144	3,338	22
1,213	1,254	1,363	1,434	1,739	2,029	2,234	2,697	3,055	3,286	3,426	3,620	3,870	4,070	4,389	23
1,202	1,488	1,940	2,774	3,349	3,350	3,221	3,271	3,763	[3] 4,278	4,308	5,103	6,146	6,109	6,481	24
434	639	826	1,152	1,459	1,326	1,244	1,510	2,209	[3] 3,306	2,527	2,889	3,620	3,217	3,426	25
278	321	489	594	898	1,019	928	1,082	1,124	1,066	954	1,045	1,626	1,738	1,730	26
424	461	617	778	859	884	925	1,082	1,114	1,249	1,111	1,132	1,346	1,363	1,385	27
663	760	1,070	1,171	1,192	1,134	1,146	1,561	1,852	2,133	2,076	2,631	3,004	2,827	3,037	28
3,377	4,502	7,165	9,593	12,589	12,598	10,679	8,851	11,094	[3] 13,009	11,965	15,370	18,809	18,207	21,082	29
----	----	----	----	----	----	----	----	----	5,896	5,387	7,112	8,995	7,900	9,404	30
----	----	----	----	----	----	----	----	----	4,387	3,986	5,085	6,178	6,504	7,451	31
----	----	----	----	----	----	----	----	----	1,016	996	1,242	1,585	1,767	1,960	32
----	----	----	----	----	----	----	----	----	1,710	1,597	1,931	2,051	2,036	2,267	33
2,267	3,078	5,076	6,895	9,068	9,045	7,389	5,531	7,566	----	----	----	----	----	----	34
591	790	1,200	1,491	1,945	1,934	1,686	1,753	1,912	----	----	----	----	----	----	35
519	634	889	1,207	1,576	1,619	1,604	1,567	1,616	----	----	----	----	----	----	36
1,490	2,179	3,844	5,395	5,917	5,807	5,084	4,717	6,192	[3] 6,889	6,198	7,247	9,796	10,585	10,598	37
852	1,134	1,893	2,474	3,347	3,708	3,051	2,376	3,398	[3] 3,628	3,456	4,404	5,450	6,184	6,985	38
398	810	2,262	6,214	12,105	12,446	7,730	1,691	1,524	1,867	1,918	2,051	3,349	4,945	5,785	39
1,184	1,600	2,350	2,009	1,333	1,401	1,117	1,909	3,522	4,040	4,817	6,631	6,330	6,483	7,698	40
12,483	14,337	17,254	20,312	23,831	25,745	27,997	34,417	37,341	41,522	40,504	43,449	47,880	50,938	52,350	41
3,830	4,463	5,228	6,195	6,911	7,640	8,242	10,393	11,651	13,049	12,299	13,694	15,922	16,781	17,138	42
8,623	9,874	12,026	14,117	16,920	18,105	19,755	24,024	25,690	28,473	28,205	29,755	31,958	34,157	35,212	43
7,920	8,208	9,172	10,649	11,569	12,197	12,830	14,479	15,250	17,355	18,890	20,671	22,407	24,434	26,384	44
882	981	1,097	1,188	1,410	1,661	1,829	2,167	2,159	2,406	2,568	2,893	3,310	3,711	4,123	45
165	139	109	78	173	178	315	283	132	184	180	355	350	259	235	46
168	192	225	364	283	273	272	333	403	540	697	801	985	1,114	1,222	47
926	893	918	1,021	1,101	1,087	1,077	1,183	1,403	1,869	2,260	2,250	2,199	2,370	2,639	48
390	405	444	468	488	529	568	750	852	933	949	1,057	1,147	1,226	1,329	49
5,389	5,598	6,379	7,530	8,114	8,469	8,769	9,763	10,301	11,423	12,236	13,315	14,416	15,754	16,836	50
4,642	5,040	6,300	8,598	10,784	11,245	10,536	10,245	11,498	12,644	11,969	13,266	14,884	15,618	16,008	51
2,737	2,944	3,778	5,568	6,971	6,899	6,009	5,466	6,294	7,104	6,369	7,109	7,792	7,980	7,789	52
515	526	582	904	1,218	1,293	1,306	1,412	1,393	1,378	1,351	1,336	1,432	1,460	1,510	53
----	----	----	----	----	----	----	----	----	----	----	----	----	----	----	54
----	----	----	----	----	----	----	----	----	----	----	----	----	----	----	55
739	815	1,021	1,183	1,308	1,354	1,390	1,699	1,993	2,272	2,377	2,780	3,128	3,456	3,851	56
280	336	432	425	595	857	989	823	814	810	750	746	966	998	1,052	57
44	57	77	113	151	175	192	217	243	306	349	432	540	638	690	58
131	131	145	117	129	145	131	126	151	192	202	255	281	308	319	59
196	231	265	288	412	522	519	502	610	582	571	608	745	778	797	60
2,863	3,056	3 324	3,669	3,934	4,062	4,244	4,792	5,114	5,894	6,566	7,172	8,256	9,206	10,195	61
1,005	1,025	1,135	1,367	1,547	1,652	1,751	1,973	2,077	2,462	2,672	2,958	3,333	3,696	4,118	62
76	91	106	109	139	175	186	203	226	253	283	314	388	433	481	63
1,717	1,872	2,011	2,121	2,169	2,152	2,218	2,523	2,709	3,065	3,512	3,779	4,399	4,923	5,430	64
65	68	72	72	79	83	89	93	102	114	119	121	136	154	166	65
8,276	8,854	9,806	10,981	12,295	13,618	14,614	17,205	18,919	20,496	21,180	22,757	24,754	26,638	28,847	66
481	530	584	674	877	983	1,085	1,322	1,287	1,328	1,287	1,309	1,380	1,491	1,561	67
1,049	1,150	1,286	1,548	1,893	2,012	2,121	2,552	2,634	2,765	2,807	2,861	3,012	3,138	3,291	68
1,866	2,056	2,188	2,201	2,107	2,360	2,635	2,766	3,272	3,617	3,885	4,539	4,941	5,217	5,981	69
34	34	57	112	159	134	72	89	114	135	151	169	166	160	153	70
638	666	779	826	915	1,055	1,179	1,471	1,634	1,847	1,864	2,034	2,324	2,619	2,923	71
261	261	350	419	610	701	703	843	938	965	933	971	1,110	1,261	1,350	72
434	449	513	652	830	883	930	1,133	1,054	921	898	844	857	837	835	73
288	310	368	388	436	507	613	810	794	824	787	792	848	889	958	74
1,381	1,463	1,575	1,806	1,988	2,341	2,459	3,024	3,544	3,910	4,147	4,496	4,935	5,387	5,802	75
692	719	763	793	814	874	930	954	1,033	1,180	1,231	1,317	1,373	1,417	1,499	76
181	193	264	385	344	320	335	454	560	665	662	727	930	1,135	1,240	77
415	424	439	461	503	532	569	660	813	981	1,075	1,135	1,174	1,245	1,299	78
556	599	640	716	819	916	983	1,127	1,242	1,358	1,453	1,563	1,704	1,842	1,955	79
8,523	8,762	10,500	16,332	27,037	33,716	36,764	22,592	18,619	19,658	21,879	23,449	30,192	34,340	34,868	80
3,414	3,489	5,027	10,645	20,899	27,250	29,786	14,545	9,343	8,872	9,926	10,649	16,164	18,708	18,132	81
----	----	----	----	----	----	----	----	----	----	----	----	----	----	----	82
----	----	----	----	----	----	----	----	----	----	----	----	----	----	----	83
----	----	----	----	----	----	----	----	----	----	----	----	----	----	----	84
719	746	808	918	1,139	1,188	1,248	1,448	1,440	1,627	1,806	1,897	2,081	2,357	2,331	85
4,185	4,269	4,388	4,473	4,663	4,938	5,370	6,177	7,320	8,502	9,422	10,124	11,069	12,265	13,305	86
----	----	----	----	----	----	----	----	----	----	----	----	----	----	----	87
----	----	----	----	----	----	----	----	----	----	----	----	----	----	----	88
----	----	----	----	----	----	----	----	----	----	----	----	----	----	----	89
205	238	277	296	336	340	360	422	516	657	725	779	878	1,010	1,100	90
313	357	363	365	367	423	369	577	874	1,076	1,078	1,266	1,547	1,463	1,500	91

presented in tables 14 and 18 and the industry detail underlying tables 17, 23, and 24 together with the rental income of persons (shown in table 12 and classified in the real estate industry.) Footnotes to these tables are, therefore, relevant also to table 13.

2. For certain manufacturing industries, the 1929–47 values shown are not comparable with those given for 1948 and subsequent years. The discontinuities stem from changes in the industrial classification system on which the tabulations of basic data are prepared. See Introduction to Part III and notes to tables 15 and 18. Of the industry series principally involved here, five have been terminated in 1947, the others are indicated by footnotes.

3. See note 2. Estimates of 1948 national income comparable to those shown for 1947 in the specified industries are as follows: Lumber and furniture products, $3,954 million; Chemicals and allied products, $4,427 million; Products of petroleum and coal, $3,290 million; Metals, metal products and miscellaneous, $12,546 million; Machinery, except electrical, $7,011: and Electrical machinery, $3,693 million.

Table 14.—Compensation of Employees, by Industry, 1929–38 [1]

[Millions of dollars]

Line		1929	1930	1931	1932	1933	1934	1935	1936	1937	1938
1	**All industries, total**	51,085	46,844	39,740	31,054	29,539	34,295	37,340	42 910	47,934	44,994
2	**Agriculture, forestry, and fisheries**	1,406	1,290	1,011	747	687	748	859	950	1,105	1,083
3	Farms	1,291	1,180	907	663	612	675	773	867	992	981
4	Agricultural services, forestry, and fisheries	115	110	104	84	75	73	86	83	113	102
5	**Mining**	1,539	1,349	1,011	698	700	927	985	1,162	1,368	1,170
6	Metal mining	204	169	104	54	53	69	89	130	206	148
7	Anthracite mining	265	256	208	153	134	162	143	142	141	123
8	Bituminous and other soft-coal mining	618	515	387	266	284	394	430	515	573	462
9	Crude petroleum and natural gas	326	298	228	172	182	245	262	296	351	356
10	Nonmetallic mining and quarrying	126	111	84	53	47	57	61	79	97	81
11	**Contract construction**	2,540	2,142	1,529	863	639	788	920	1,350	1,463	1,348
12	**Manufacturing**	16,243	13,991	10,933	7,783	7,921	9,746	10,961	12,672	15,186	12,493
13	Food and kindred products	1,586	1,540	1,346	1,115	1,149	1,344	1,411	1,532	1,731	1,644
14	Tobacco manufactures	143	131	109	85	74	84	84	90	101	98
15	Textile-mill products	1,465	1,207	1,072	774	903	1,012	1,117	1,178	1,303	1,061
16	Apparel and other finished fabric products	1,055	916	784	561	572	693	783	850	895	843
17	Lumber and furniture products [2]	1,330	1,038	698	434	456	533	632	783	923	788
18	Lumber and wood products, except furniture										
19	Furniture and fixtures										
20	Lumber and timber basic products	713	547	309	179	201	255	303	384	459	393
21	Furniture and finished lumber products	617	491	389	255	255	278	329	399	464	395
22	Paper and allied products	435	417	355	277	283	337	362	403	476	432
23	Printing, publishing, and allied industries	1,243	1,248	1,071	843	722	813	872	958	1,076	1,026
24	Chemicals and allied products [2]	671	629	536	420	428	502	532	584	701	653
25	Products of petroleum and coal [2]	248	248	200	166	156	181	204	219	265	272
26	Rubber products	283	224	169	133	142	178	184	213	243	194
27	Leather and leather products	494	420	366	293	305	354	369	381	423	377
28	Stone, clay, and glass products	627	533	390	243	231	290	334	410	506	428
29	Metals, metal products, and miscellaneous [2]	3,141	2,643	1,880	1,164	1,248	1,622	1,939	2,432	3,081	2,233
30	Primary metal industries										
31	Fabricated metal products, including ordnance										
32	Instruments										
33	Miscellaneous manufacturing										
34	Iron and steel and their products, including ordnance	2,147	1,820	1,230	736	821	1,089	1,314	1,703	2,196	1,494
35	Nonferrous metals and their products	544	421	326	207	207	267	321	383	484	377
36	Miscellaneous manufacturing	450	402	324	221	220	266	304	346	401	362
37	Machinery, except electrical [2]	1,408	1,185	783	497	500	685	832	1,050	1,391	1,009
38	Electrical machinery [2]	868	720	491	290	306	413	466	582	778	569
39	Transportation equipment, except automobiles	264	256	168	118	94	134	146	209	286	235
40	Automobiles and automobile equipment	982	636	515	370	352	571	694	798	1,007	631
41	**Wholesale and retail trade**	9,374	8,766	7,634	5,956	5,331	6,159	6,683	7,341	8,442	8,340
42	Wholesale trade	3,397	3,220	2,757	2,152	1,895	2,192	2,382	2,597	2,984	3,000
43	Retail trade and automobile services	5,977	5,546	4,877	3,804	3,436	3,967	4,301	4,744	5,458	5,340
44	**Finance, insurance, and real estate**	2,989	2,808	2,527	2,145	1,939	2,031	2,111	2,313	2,524	2,460
45	Banking	784	739	670	582	499	516	524	542	574	586
46	Security and commodity brokers, dealers and exchanges	409	321	267	235	245	234	206	252	260	197
47	Finance, n. e. c.	257	247	223	198	178	184	201	233	256	234
48	Insurance carriers	821	828	777	648	579	604	645	659	718	769
49	Insurance agents and combination offices	240	232	210	187	166	180	190	206	224	228
50	Real estate	479	441	380	295	272	313	345	391	452	446
51	**Transportation**	4,813	4,332	3,622	2,736	2,537	2,766	2,961	3,357	3,762	3,380
52	Railroads	3,303	2,926	2,407	1,752	1,628	1,782	1,894	2,154	2,377	2,100
53	Local and highway passenger transportation	661	621	541	435	373	389	405	435	471	450
54	Local railways and buslines	482	453	402	329	283	296	307	326	349	327
55	Highway passenger transportation, n. e. c.	179	168	139	106	90	93	98	109	122	123
56	Highway freight transportation and warehousing	333	322	295	263	258	286	327	366	426	416
57	Water transportation	215	195	168	137	144	154	162	198	238	180
58	Air transportation (common carriers)	5	9	13	14	14	14	17	22	28	31
59	Pipeline transportation	48	42	38	29	29	34	36	40	49	46
60	Services allied to transportation	248	217	160	106	91	107	120	142	173	157
61	**Communications and public utilities**	1,549	1,572	1,437	1,217	1,090	1,170	1,231	1,346	1,525	1,549
62	Telephone, telegraph, and related services	756	754	674	565	499	529	542	587	668	684
63	Radio broadcasting and television	10	15	21	24	21	25	27	34	45	49
64	Utilities: electric and gas	751	771	712	602	547	591	636	697	785	790
65	Local utilities and public services, n. e. c.	32	32	30	26	23	25	26	28	27	26
66	**Services**	5,538	5,277	4,609	3,758	3,368	3,688	3,904	4,310	4,786	4,646
67	Hotels and other lodging places	427	409	343	258	219	272	289	318	363	368
68	Personal services	755	730	646	526	459	500	529	584	652	634
69	Private households	1,718	1,485	1,148	836	733	851	912	1,017	1,190	1,026
70	Commercial and trade schools and employment agencies	34	33	27	19	16	18	22	26	31	29
71	Business services, n. e. c.	359	371	311	262	243	294	326	392	414	412
72	Miscellaneous repair services and hand trades	108	106	98	83	73	76	81	84	91	95
73	Motion pictures	310	313	307	241	227	253	282	317	360	346
74	Amusement and recreation, except motion pictures	323	299	256	191	161	176	180	205	239	216
75	Medical and other health services	398	406	386	346	317	324	349	388	433	468
76	Legal services	124	131	132	126	118	116	121	126	135	138
77	Engineering and other professional services, n. e. c.	81	75	55	36	34	37	40	51	57	65
78	Educational services, n. e. c.	296	307	311	303	281	279	284	295	312	330
79	Nonprofit membership organizations, n. e. c.	605	612	589	531	487	492	489	507	509	519
80	**Government and government enterprises**	5,093	5,316	5,426	5,150	5,326	6,271	6,724	8,108	7,772	8,524
81	Federal—general government	879	915	921	880	1,164	1,694	1,768	3,570	3,013	3,505
82	Civilian, except work relief										
83	Military										
84	Work relief										
85	Federal—government enterprises	581	584	582	544	485	540	614	662	675	698
86	State and local—general government	3,456	3,630	3,737	3,565	3,531	3,884	4,178	3,696	3,889	4,121
87	Public education										
88	Nonschool, except work relief										
89	Work relief										
90	State and local—government enterprises	177	187	186	161	146	153	164	180	195	200
91	**Rest of the world**	1	1	1	1	1	1	1	1	1	1
92	**Addendum: All private industries**	45,991	41,527	34,313	25,903	24,212	28,023	30,615	34,801	40,161	36,469

1. Compensation of employees is the sum of wages and salaries (table 15) and supplements to wages and salaries (table 16). Footnotes to tables 15 and 16 are, therefore, relevant also to table 14.

2. See note 1, table 15. Estimates of 1948 employee compensation approximately comparable to those shown for 1947 in the specified industries are as follows: Lumber and furniture products, $3,043 million; Chemicals and allied products, $2,602 million; Products of petroleum and coal, $1,125 million; Metals, metal products, and miscellaneous, $9,733 million; Machinery, except electrical, $5,600 million; and Electrical machinery $2,996 million.

Table 14.—Compensation of Employees, by Industry, 1939–53 [1]

[Millions of dollars]

1939	1940	1941	1942	1943	1944	1945	1946	1947	1948	1949	1950	1951	1952	1953	Line
48,108	52,129	64,789	85,271	109,587	121,286	123,181	117,697	128,757	140,927	140,858	154 325	180,420	195,423	209,061	1
1,097	1,141	1,375	1,797	2,206	2,412	2,523	2,801	3,097	3,333	3,157	3,043	3,288	3,393	3,457	2
992	1,035	1,257	1,645	2,042	2,218	2,315	2,563	2,829	3,040	2,867	2,735	2,943	3,019	3,074	3
105	106	118	152	164	194	208	238	268	293	290	308	345	374	383	4
1,204	1,360	1,621	1,855	2,072	2,285	2,261	2,470	3,070	3,543	3,127	3,440	3,910	3,966	4,074	5
168	203	246	287	324	277	240	242	309	353	339	368	448	502	560	6
130	124	143	165	187	209	203	248	262	293	238	254	260	246	198	7
480	570	712	858	957	1,091	1,056	1,111	1,463	1,652	1,277	1,465	1,619	1,432	1,403	8
335	357	383	374	425	538	595	651	775	953	975	1,023	1,195	1,368	1,461	9
91	106	137	171	179	170	167	218	261	292	298	330	388	418	452	10
1,650	1,821	3,074	4,925	4,120	3,037	3,107	4,621	6,108	7,409	7,257	8,311	10,287	11,173	11,637	11
14,321	16,397	22,775	32,248	42,658	44,960	40,182	38,178	44,537	48,604	46,124	52,535	62,373	67,528	75,052	12
1,707	1,790	2,018	2,392	2,764	3,106	3,269	3,750	4,282	4,560	4,629	4,908	5,423	5,699	6,048	13
102	108	119	125	152	165	179	197	207	215	226	236	272	289	304	14
1,224	1,261	1,673	2,001	2,137	2,127	2,199	2,803	3,219	3,663	3,278	3,744	3,881	3,756	3,788	15
967	980	1,261	1,497	1,786	1,965	2,078	2,555	2,744	2,993	2,891	3,118	3,263	3,400	3,619	16
890	981	1,284	1,496	1,648	1,710	1,715	2,192	2,767	[2] 2,950	2,680	3,229	3,597	3,670	3,740	17
-----	-----	-----	-----	-----	-----	-----	-----	-----	1,948	1,724	2,060	2,364	2,362	2,352	18
-----	-----	-----	-----	-----	-----	-----	-----	-----	1,002	956	1,169	1,233	1,308	1,388	19
432	489	654	795	882	910	884	1,090	1,395	-----	-----	-----	-----	-----	-----	20
458	492	630	701	766	800	831	1,102	1,372	-----	-----	-----	-----	-----	-----	21
468	515	652	731	849	920	976	1,187	1,408	1,572	1,541	1,780	2,045	2,134	2,368	22
1,037	1,044	1,119	1,134	1,225	1,353	1,526	1,981	2,344	2,607	2,752	2,928	3,143	3,371	3,644	23
702	849	1,150	1,731	2,118	2,172	2,210	2,[illegible]72	2,394	[2] 2,5[illegible]3	2,505	2,752	3,321	3,613	4,041	24
2[illegible]0	326	388	477	576	705	773	822	991	[2] 1,154	1,186	1,214	1,453	1,585	1,702	25
236	258	351	414	575	670	662	778	866	844	778	918	1,089	1,189	1,292	26
405	401	530	607	648	674	727	905	978	1,010	971	1,047	1,062	1,147	1,190	27
494	542	710	808	875	880	899	1,180	1,402	1,593	1,530	1,765	2,108	2,097	2,293	28
2,781	3,376	4,805	6,706	9,360	9,682	8,614	7,477	8,923	[2] 10,034	9,187	11,055	13,459	14,469	16,734	29
-----	-----	-----	-----	-----	-----	-----	-----	-----	4,393	3,931	4,864	6,0[illegible]0	6,057	6,937	30
-----	-----	-----	-----	-----	-----	-----	-----	-----	3,473	3,210	3,827	4,699	5,421	6,393	31
-----	-----	-----	-----	-----	-----	-----	-----	-----	828	794	931	1,193	1,366	1,546	32
-----	-----	-----	-----	-----	-----	-----	-----	-----	1,340	1,252	1,433	1,567	1,625	1,858	33
1,907	2,334	3,347	4,724	6,817	7,089	6,090	4,704	5,942	-----	-----	-----	-----	-----	-----	34
453	547	780	1,066	1,360	1,393	1,304	1,412	1,491	-----	-----	-----	-----	-----	-----	35
421	495	678	916	1,183	1,200	1,220	1,361	1,490	-----	-----	-----	-----	-----	-----	36
1,167	1,505	2,435	3,712	4,319	4,356	4,069	4,142	5,641	[2] 5,499	4,781	5,379	7,262	8,045	8,605	37
673	808	1,224	1,805	2,479	2,834	2,544	2,352	2,859	[2] 2,949	2,678	3,177	4,048	4,698	5,519	38
324	555	1,518	4,899	10,146	10,545	6,797	1,846	1,674	1,771	1,726	1,753	2,982	4,283	5,072	39
864	1,098	1,538	1,713	1,001	1,096	945	1,939	2,438	2,687	2,785	3,532	3,965	4,083	5,093	40
8,729	9,374	10,773	11,349	12,289	13,426	15,166	20,195	23,622	26,053	26,434	28,330	31,123	32,947	35,055	41
3,141	3,358	3,935	4,182	4,366	4,755	5,307	6,901	8,248	9,159	9,131	9,869	11,077	11,753	12,603	42
5,588	6,016	6,838	7,167	7,923	8,671	9,859	13,294	15,374	16,894	17,303	18,461	20,046	21,194	22,452	43
2,522	2,599	2,752	2,864	3,013	3,166	3,436	4,307	4,722	5,295	5,554	6,159	6,762	7,314	7,955	44
600	622	654	710	765	829	903	1,086	1,227	1,350	1,432	1,545	1,739	1,914	2,102	45
180	170	158	131	154	167	228	286	237	246	240	312	338	336	346	46
232	245	271	270	251	243	247	314	361	413	457	498	576	656	725	47
797	820	870	910	942	968	1,033	1,296	1,481	1,676	1,823	2,003	2,191	2,416	2,676	48
232	231	245	266	284	298	324	430	467	535	566	643	700	747	809	49
481	511	554	577	617	661	701	895	949	1,075	1,036	1,158	1,218	1,245	1,297	50
3,644	3,866	4,520	5,596	6,956	7,989	8,388	9,016	9,664	10,248	9,875	10,430	11,978	12,521	13,042	51
2,240	2,373	2,803	3,532	4,264	4,713	4,758	5,144	5,446	5,777	5,387	5,596	6,425	6,465	6,442	52
455	441	472	609	785	880	958	1,125	1,195	1,174	1,166	1,148	1,211	1,249	1,276	53
327	301	300	353	433	477	511	571	605	553	561	548	568	575	585	54
128	140	172	256	352	403	447	554	590	621	605	600	643	674	691	55
465	524	643	771	883	965	1,053	1,255	1,459	1,670	1,758	2,083	2,399	2,659	3,006	56
224	240	274	314	487	760	902	701	636	665	599	589	712	774	855	57
36	45	57	80	118	135	160	246	286	309	325	349	423	520	583	58
44	46	51	58	69	82	87	93	111	132	130	124	143	160	164	59
180	197	220	232	350	454	470	452	531	521	510	541	665	694	716	60
1,576	1,657	1,806	1,903	2,024	2,166	2,410	3,067	3,563	4,119	4,376	4,619	5,111	5,636	6,154	61
695	720	807	890	1,006	1,083	1,227	1,615	1,816	2,096	2,188	2,239	2,465	2,730	2,985	62
55	62	71	76	87	105	122	147	173	206	227	258	302	335	371	63
798	845	897	904	898	942	1,021	1,259	1,522	1,760	1,902	2,060	2,277	2,496	2,716	64
28	30	31	33	33	36	40	46	52	57	59	62	67	75	82	65
4,840	5,149	5,587	6,392	7,198	8,117	8,933	10,433	11,738	12,649	13,059	13,991	15,376	16,580	17,747	66
376	402	430	459	541	631	695	849	912	955	960	980	1,044	1,109	1,160	67
638	712	799	925	1,078	1,182	1,311	1,632	1,750	1,819	1,822	1,880	1,997	2,093	2,184	68
1,132	1,221	1,240	1,480	1,600	1,890	2,145	2,123	2,350	2,384	2,415	2,671	2,846	2,871	3,065	69
28	28	46	91	133	102	59	69	92	110	125	139	133	126	118	70
433	443	491	507	554	652	753	961	1,104	1,258	1,284	1,403	1,599	1,806	2,011	71
97	94	125	148	214	243	245	308	358	369	357	367	466	531	553	72
353	353	386	425	477	531	573	702	718	681	684	681	705	721	711	73
230	246	270	281	291	337	384	523	565	610	609	622	648	683	731	74
478	513	558	641	744	845	932	1,134	1,410	1,610	1,753	1,990	2,303	2,600	2,903	75
142	144	151	150	149	159	169	184	209	230	248	266	297	328	362	76
75	80	123	214	199	197	221	275	334	408	410	437	610	790	869	77
337	348	362	389	433	465	494	578	727	890	977	1,034	1,068	1,127	1,174	78
521	565	606	682	785	883	952	1,095	1,209	1,325	1,415	1,521	1,660	1,795	1,906	79
8,523	8,762	10,500	16,332	27,037	33,716	36,764	22,592	18,619	19,658	21,879	23,449	30,192	34,340	34,868	80
3,414	3,489	5,027	10,645	20,899	27,250	29,786	14,545	9,343	8,872	9,926	10,649	16,164	18,708	18,132	81
-----	-----	-----	-----	-----	-----	-----	-----	-----	-----	-----	-----	-----	-----	-----	82
-----	-----	-----	-----	-----	-----	-----	-----	-----	-----	-----	-----	-----	-----	-----	83
-----	-----	-----	-----	-----	-----	-----	-----	-----	-----	-----	-----	-----	-----	-----	84
719	746	808	918	1,139	1,188	1,248	1,448	1,440	1,627	1,806	1,897	2,081	2,357	2,331	85
4,185	4,289	4,388	4,473	4,663	4,938	5,370	6,177	7,320	8,502	9,422	10,124	11,069	12,265	13,305	86
-----	-----	-----	-----	-----	-----	-----	-----	-----	-----	-----	-----	-----	-----	-----	87
-----	-----	-----	-----	-----	-----	-----	-----	-----	-----	-----	-----	-----	-----	-----	88
-----	-----	-----	-----	-----	-----	-----	-----	-----	-----	-----	-----	-----	-----	-----	89
205	238	277	296	336	340	300	422	516	657	725	779	878	1,010	1,100	90
2	3	6	10	14	12	11	17	17	16	16	18	20	25	20	91
39,583	43,364	54,283	68,929	82,536	87,558	86,406	95,088	110,121	121,253	118,963	130,858	150,208	161,058	174,173	92

Table 17.—*Income of Unincorporated Enterprises, by Industry Division, 1929–38* [1]

[Millions of dollars]

Line		1929	1930	1931	1932	1933	1934	1935	1936	1937	1938
1	**All industries, total** [2]	14,617	10,785	8,123	5,021	6,124	7,064	10,437	10,602	12,729	10,907
2	Agriculture, forestry, and fisheries	6,033	4,194	3,212	1,979	2,476	2,489	5,087	4,002	5,684	4,394
3	Mining	54	28	−15	8	6	33	37	56	74	48
4	Contract construction	1,127	865	608	237	191	304	376	607	581	611
5	Manufacturing	565	292	120	18	201	240	299	404	367	268
6	Wholesale and retail trade	2,867	1,947	1,257	527	1,103	1,658	2,051	2,627	2,904	2,652
7	Finance, insurance, and real estate	762	450	294	223	313	250	305	356	357	316
8	Transportation	220	209	184	159	154	172	195	216	231	229
9	Communications and public utilities	9	9	7	3	1	3	3	4	7	7
10	Services	2,980	2,791	2,456	1,867	1,679	1,915	2,084	2,330	2,515	2,382

1. "Income of unincorporated enterprises" measures the net income of sole proprietorships and partnerships except that the series for trade includes estimated patronage refunds and stock dividends paid by farmers' cooperatives (shown separately in table 12). "Income of unincorporated enterprises" excludes the inventory valuation adjustment which is shown by industry division in table 23.

2. Exhibit 2, section 3, of Part III, provides a breakdown of the industry division totals for the years 1929, 1939, 1945, and 1949.

Table 21.—*Net Corporate Dividend Payments, by Industry, 1929–38*

[Millions of dollars]

Line		1929	1930	1931	1932	1933	1934	1935	1936	1937	1938
1	**All industries, total** [1]	5,813	5,490	4,088	2,565	2,056	2,587	2,863	4,548	4,685	3,187
2	**Agriculture, forestry, and fisheries**	14	8	15	7	0	17	19	36	29	11
3	Farms	9	4	13	6	−1	16	17	34	27	10
4	Agricultural services, forestry, and fisheries	5	4	2	1	1	1	2	2	2	1
5	**Mining**	338	230	120	72	65	174	148	192	257	167
6	Metal mining	194	92	38	11	13	31	41	79	128	65
7	Anthracite mining	16	13	9	6	1	3	3	3	1	1
8	Bituminous and other soft-coal mining	27	24	16	7	4	28	11	16	12	7
9	Crude petroleum and natural gas	69	79	37	36	38	98	73	70	91	79
10	Nonmetallic mining and quarrying	32	22	20	12	9	14	20	24	25	15
11	**Contract construction**	60	67	40	19	19	15	21	36	42	21
12	**Manufacturing**	2,647	2,539	1,862	1,102	991	1,186	1,516	2,332	2,358	1,211
13	Food and kindred products	305	328	263	198	190	242	247	337	296	254
14	Tobacco manufactures	83	95	99	92	86	90	80	99	99	91
15	Textile-mill products	142	103	79	46	50	81	77	121	120	44
16	Apparel and other finished fabric products	36	26	18	9	8	11	15	27	22	14
17	Lumber and furniture products [2]	101	68	33	16	14	32	34	57	63	34
18	Lumber and wood products, except furniture	-----	-----	-----	-----	-----	-----	-----	-----	-----	-----
19	Furniture and fixtures	-----	-----	-----	-----	-----	-----	-----	-----	-----	-----
20	Lumber and timber basic products	69	46	20	8	9	24	23	35	40	15
21	Furniture and finished lumber products	32	22	13	8	5	8	11	22	23	19
22	Paper and allied products	56	51	36	20	27	39	46	61	75	39
23	Printing, publishing, and allied industries	132	127	95	59	35	66	72	104	93	63
24	Chemicals and allied products [2]	217	269	196	169	174	156	264	249	257	172
25	Products of petroleum and coal [2]	254	320	258	109	119	7	38	192	147	67
26	Rubber products	29	26	20	13	6	−1	7	31	27	12
27	Leather and leather products	37	38	28	20	19	21	22	28	28	19
28	Stone, clay, and glass products	83	73	53	27	22	39	50	95	101	45
29	Metals, metal products, and miscellaneous [2]	541	476	289	152	103	200	345	389	448	144
30	Primary metal industries	-----	-----	-----	-----	-----	-----	-----	-----	-----	-----
31	Fabricated metal products, including ordnance	-----	-----	-----	-----	-----	-----	-----	-----	-----	-----
32	Instruments	-----	-----	-----	-----	-----	-----	-----	-----	-----	-----
33	Miscellaneous manufacturing	-----	-----	-----	-----	-----	-----	-----	-----	-----	-----
34	Iron and steel and their products, including ordnance	360	331	181	82	37	101	225	201	260	84
35	Nonferrous metals and their products	106	79	58	42	40	67	60	124	122	29
36	Miscellaneous manufacturing	75	66	50	28	26	32	60	64	66	31
37	Machinery, except electrical [2]	256	214	137	70	47	81	105	182	220	140
38	Electrical machinery [2]	90	81	65	22	24	22	12	82	111	59
39	Transportation equipment, except automobiles	40	39	25	10	3	26	25	23	38	12
40	Automobiles and automobile equipment	245	205	168	70	64	74	77	255	213	2
41	**Wholesale and retail trade**	537	474	376	210	173	328	419	616	607	347
42	Wholesale trade	193	177	134	71	61	160	194	270	270	111
43	Retail trade and automobile services	344	297	242	139	112	168	225	376	347	236
44	**Finance, insurance, and real estate**	835	625	510	310	145	−26	−318	307	323	307
45	Banking	410	389	334	246	134	166	170	168	173	181
46	Security and commodity brokers, dealers and exchanges	5	6	5	5	4	5	6	21	1	7
47	Finance, n. e. c.	0	−81	−91	−90	−94	−351	−689	−81	−74	−59
48	Insurance carriers	64	56	56	24	18	18	31	17	16	37
49	Insurance agents and combination offices	16	15	16	8	7	8	10	9	10	11
50	Real estate	340	240	190	117	76	128	154	173	197	130
51	**Transportation**	571	581	378	177	124	233	320	287	287	174
52	Railroads	303	353	219	26	20	78	73	119	125	45
53	Local and highway passenger transportation	115	79	66	64	55	50	56	35	31	16
54	Highway freight transportation and warehousing	12	11	8	8	7	7	8	9	9	11
55	Water transportation	29	30	20	12	8	24	56	40	41	20
56	Air transportation (common carriers)	0	0	0	0	0	3	3	3	2	1
57	Pipeline transportation	92	90	49	53	23	59	112	66	64	64
58	Services allied to transportation	20	18	16	14	11	12	12	15	15	17
59	**Communications and public utilities**	634	861	772	677	510	618	644	649	692	671
60	Telephone, telegraph, and related services	167	201	217	192	190	187	191	174	179	187
61	Radio broadcasting and television	4	6	5	1	1	3	8	11	12	9
62	Utilities: electric and gas	449	601	526	471	333	411	428	446	485	459
63	Local utilities and public services, n. e. c.	14	53	24	13	16	17	17	18	16	16
64	**Services**	88	79	52	35	21	34	34	71	79	61
65	Hotels and other lodging places	6	4	2	1	0	1	1	2	2	3
66	Personal services	11	7	5	3	2	2	3	5	5	6
67	Business services, n. e. c.	37	24	13	16	11	17	16	25	29	21
68	Miscellaneous repair services and hand trades	3	2	1	1	0	1	1	1	1	1
69	Motion pictures	17	33	26	10	5	7	6	26	28	21
70	Amusement and recreation, except motion pictures	11	8	4	2	1	3	4	8	9	6
71	Engineering and other professional services, n. e. c.	3	1	1	2	2	3	3	4	5	3
72	**Rest of the world**	89	26	−37	−44	−22	8	60	−8	11	217

1. See table 18, footnote 2.

2. Estimates for 1948–53 not strictly comparable with earlier years. See table 18, footnote 3.

Table 17.—*Income of Unincorporated Enterprises, by Industry Division, 1939–53*

[Millions of dollars]

1939	1940	1941	1942	1943	1944	1945	1946	1947	1948	1949	1950	1951	1952	1953	Line
11,776	13,065	18,016	24,274	28,343	29,634	30,941	36,970	35,904	38,801	33,681	37,274	41,153	38,710	38,639	1
4,378	4,633	6,578	10,105	11,473	11,656	11,972	14,115	14,678	16,965	12,963	13,532	16,305	14,509	12,560	2
61	59	88	122	160	145	108	143	244	335	243	213	219	197	207	3
646	689	958	1,241	1,112	986	1,068	1,720	2,119	2,397	2,541	2,739	2,714	2,824	2,984	4
400	515	985	1,434	1,878	2,195	2,361	2,279	1,626	1,394	1,238	1,728	1,578	1,306	1,172	5
3,193	3,863	5,675	7,098	8,749	9,201	9,676	12,070	10,437	10,379	9,281	11,156	12,005	12,091	12,391	6
346	365	401	431	534	598	757	818	720	798	775	996	1,021	1,007	1,079	7
249	285	358	415	476	463	426	486	553	576	602	607	688	741	798	8
7	7	10	12	15	19	23	24	26	28	29	29	29	30	30	9
2,496	2,639	2,963	3,416	3,946	4,371	4,530	5,315	5,501	5,929	6,019	6,274	6,594	7,006	7,418	10

Table 21.—*Net Corporate Dividend Payments, by Industry, 1939–53*

[Millions of dollars]

1939	1940	1941	1942	1943	1944	1945	1946	1947	1948	1949	1950	1951	1952	1953	Line
3,788	4,043	4,458	4,289	4,484	4,673	4,691	5,784	6,521	7,248	7,458	9,207	9,090	9,128	9,365	1
15	19	22	22	27	24	14	28	52	54	53	60	70	51	30	2
13	17	19	20	23	22	13	23	50	52	51	57	67	-----	-----	3
2	2	3	2	4	2	1	5	2	2	2	3	3	-----	-----	4
175	238	265	237	175	157	138	177	260	361	338	455	583	544	531	5
94	109	107	145	70	61	44	53	84	117	92	131	142	-----	-----	6
0	3	4	7	6	7	6	13	10	9	8	5	1	-----	-----	7
9	15	16	21	23	23	26	28	37	60	51	53	46	-----	-----	8
54	92	116	44	57	48	45	60	98	141	154	224	272	-----	-----	9
18	19	22	20	19	18	17	23	31	34	33	42	42	-----	-----	10
22	22	27	25	23	21	18	30	36	56	62	68	61	64	72	11
1,741	1,930	2,271	2,129	2,271	2,397	2,421	2,856	3,414	3,736	3,939	4,836	4,581	4,568	4,620	12
272	268	296	282	304	301	313	405	439	419	402	430	445	-----	-----	13
89	85	90	67	63	68	62	69	75	86	90	92	91	-----	-----	14
67	73	104	100	106	111	110	200	237	267	201	232	224	-----	-----	15
18	19	23	21	27	37	25	52	49	55	43	46	35	-----	-----	16
49	61	79	67	62	60	60	80	109	[3] 121	104	141	129	-----	-----	17
-----	-----	-----	-----	-----	-----	-----	-----	-----	89	74	100	97	-----	-----	18
-----	-----	-----	-----	-----	-----	-----	-----	-----	32	30	41	32	-----	-----	19
24	35	51	43	38	35	38	44	62	-----	-----	-----	-----	-----	-----	20
25	26	28	24	24	25	22	36	47	-----	-----	-----	-----	-----	-----	21
48	58	83	65	71	67	70	96	136	154	130	170	200	-----	-----	22
74	73	70	63	78	93	88	123	123	132	123	123	112	-----	-----	23
251	254	260	237	262	271	298	380	401	[3] 398	450	576	539	-----	-----	24
79	82	104	245	236	274	255	291	375	[3] 416	521	478	552	-----	-----	25
22	16	25	19	29	33	35	44	35	29	37	40	35	-----	-----	26
22	21	27	26	27	27	26	34	43	40	37	37	34	-----	-----	27
80	84	95	62	62	52	58	85	97	111	124	156	149	-----	-----	28
243	261	359	372	392	426	425	432	552	[3] 628	616	810	781	-----	-----	29
-----	-----	-----	-----	-----	-----	-----	-----	-----	314	311	455	428	-----	-----	30
-----	-----	-----	-----	-----	-----	-----	-----	-----	194	186	218	220	-----	-----	31
-----	-----	-----	-----	-----	-----	-----	-----	-----	52	57	69	66	-----	-----	32
-----	-----	-----	-----	-----	-----	-----	-----	-----	68	62	68	67	-----	-----	33
145	171	246	275	273	295	287	278	370	-----	-----	-----	-----	-----	-----	34
56	52	62	60	81	92	90	97	129	-----	-----	-----	-----	-----	-----	35
42	38	51	37	38	39	48	57	53	-----	-----	-----	-----	-----	-----	36
154	200	238	211	188	189	182	230	299	[3] 348	332	400	400	-----	-----	37
96	132	131	88	120	109	122	125	162	[3] 177	186	253	255	-----	-----	38
82	64	84	172	213	259	260	83	72	85	85	94	94	-----	-----	39
145	179	204	43	31	30	23	147	210	270	458	758	506	-----	-----	40
425	432	501	447	485	490	499	816	867	949	853	1,062	946	907	830	41
155	149	200	169	174	179	176	300	332	374	324	401	382	-----	-----	42
270	283	301	278	311	311	323	516	535	575	529	601	564	-----	-----	43
301	243	245	426	436	483	522	631	570	643	656	826	815		886	44
191	209	216	203	218	243	263	290	310	327	348	401	412	-----	-----	45
4	13	7	0	−4	−1	−2	6	−1	0	−1	−2	−3	-----	-----	46
−86	−173	−174	69	33	58	84	103	45	74	40	135	187	-----	-----	47
43	35	23	25	49	30	30	27	11	23	47	57	4	-----	-----	48
11	13	14	9	10	9	8	10	14	20	17	23	21	-----	-----	49
138	146	159	120	130	144	139	195	191	199	205	211	194	-----	-----	50
228	259	271	283	267	292	292	285	246	312	271	366	383	413	429	51
77	114	83	131	150	189	203	167	127	197	154	199	250	-----	-----	52
15	19	23	22	29	29	29	49	35	33	30	29	33	-----	-----	53
14	12	13	16	12	12	11	15	16	19	21	27	23	-----	-----	54
32	43	51	28	23	24	21	24	37	34	32	37	40	-----	-----	55
0	1	3	4	8	6	5	3	4	4	4	10	15	-----	-----	56
69	50	78	17	19	17	10	15	15	13	18	51	21	-----	-----	57
21	20	20	15	16	15	13	12	12	12	12	13	11	-----	-----	58
683	685	675	591	592	624	623	687	714	741	831	1,032	1,151	1,282	1,427	59
174	175	174	185	171	181	189	192	180	181	201	253	294	-----	-----	60
11	12	14	9	12	12	10	14	14	12	8	18	10	-----	-----	61
483	483	472	386	400	421	414	470	510	539	611	748	835	-----	-----	62
15	15	15	11	9	10	10	11	10	9	11	13	12	-----	-----	63
61	66	72	62	81	82	89	145	141	142	150	137	152	128	134	64
5	5	6	6	9	9	10	18	16	20	17	20	18	-----	-----	65
7	7	7	7	8	10	10	13	12	13	14	14	11	-----	-----	66
22	25	23	15	18	19	20	26	29	31	37	37	37	-----	-----	67
1	1	1	0	1	1	1	1	1	1	1	2	3	-----	-----	68
15	18	24	26	35	33	35	64	61	55	59	40	57	-----	-----	69
6	6	8	4	5	6	10	18	16	15	15	16	17	-----	-----	70
5	4	3	4	5	4	3	5	6	7	7	8	9	-----	-----	71
137	149	169	167	137	163	75	129	221	254	305	436	418	382	406	72

Table 25.—Number of Full-Time Equivalent Employees, by Industry 1929–38 [1]

[Data in thousands]

Line		1929	1930	1931	1932	1933	1934	1935	1936	1937	1938
1	**All industries, total**	**35,896**	**33,769**	**30,690**	**27,215**	**27,681**	**30,905**	**32,263**	**35,413**	**36,662**	**34,945**
2	**Agriculture, forestry, and fisheries**	**3,530**	**3,312**	**3,225**	**3,004**	**2,973**	**2,968**	**2,990**	**3,085**	**3,054**	**2,922**
3	Farms	3,403	3,190	3,103	2,894	2,865	2,862	2,878	2,981	2,924	2,807
4	Agricultural services, forestry, and fisheries	127	122	122	110	108	106	112	104	130	115
5	**Mining**	**993**	**932**	**813**	**672**	**693**	**822**	**840**	**897**	**955**	**859**
6	Metal mining	124	107	79	50	50	60	71	92	119	95
7	Anthracite mining	151	144	128	104	92	106	99	98	98	89
8	Bituminous and other soft coal mining	471	452	418	358	373	431	443	457	470	416
9	Crude petroleum and natural gas	159	148	118	105	124	163	165	180	192	192
10	Nonmetallic mining and quarrying	88	81	70	55	54	62	62	70	76	67
11	**Contract construction**	**1,484**	**1,366**	**1,198**	**907**	**703**	**806**	**866**	**1,104**	**1,082**	**1,055**
12	**Manufacturing**	**10,428**	**9,309**	**7,895**	**6,678**	**7,204**	**8,364**	**8,904**	**9,615**	**10,531**	**9,131**
13	Food and kindred products	1,041	1,020	914	841	939	1,085	1,105	1,157	1,223	1,166
14	Tobacco manufactures	145	133	120	108	102	112	108	109	111	108
15	Textile-mill products	1,262	1,095	1,025	907	1,081	1,139	1,196	1,218	1,203	1,092
16	Apparel and other finished fabric products	772	722	672	593	632	699	768	829	843	807
17	Lumber and furniture products [2]	1,041	840	624	486	549	609	689	779	857	740
18	Lumber and wood products, except furniture	-----	-----	-----	-----	-----	-----	-----	-----	-----	-----
19	Furniture and fixtures	-----	-----	-----	-----	-----	-----	-----	-----	-----	-----
20	Lumber and timber basic products	604	469	303	225	270	320	360	415	459	398
21	Furniture and finished lumber products	437	371	321	261	279	289	329	364	398	342
22	Paper and allied products	284	277	250	226	244	280	289	300	325	301
23	Printing, publishing, and allied industries	615	617	548	481	449	492	510	554	604	578
24	Chemicals and allied products [3]	397	377	329	291	321	369	379	393	431	383
25	Products of petroleum and coal [3]	128	125	105	97	99	115	121	124	132	131
26	Rubber products	176	142	120	110	124	141	134	142	154	127
27	Leather and leather products	370	344	315	300	320	345	352	359	375	353
28	Stone, clay, and glass products	397	345	277	204	212	262	281	317	356	310
29	Metals, metal products, and miscellaneous [3]	1,827	1,621	1,298	1,040	1,118	1,358	1,487	1,686	1,914	1,552
30	Primary metal industries	-----	-----	-----	-----	-----	-----	-----	-----	-----	-----
31	Fabricated metal products, including ordnance	-----	-----	-----	-----	-----	-----	-----	-----	-----	-----
32	Instruments	-----	-----	-----	-----	-----	-----	-----	-----	-----	-----
33	Miscellaneous manufacturing	-----	-----	-----	-----	-----	-----	-----	-----	-----	-----
34	Iron and steel and their products, including ordnance	1,217	1,092	857	687	749	917	996	1,147	1,317	1,026
35	Nonferrous metals and their products	325	269	222	175	182	220	249	277	313	256
36	Miscellaneous manufacturing	285	260	219	178	187	221	242	262	284	270
37	Machinery, except electrical [3]	764	671	509	373	392	505	577	664	791	626
38	Electrical machinery [3]	519	430	332	242	251	319	338	385	461	353
39	Transportation equipment, except automobiles	150	147	105	80	71	101	105	137	171	141
40	Automobiles and automobile equipment	540	403	352	299	300	433	464	492	580	363
41	**Wholesale and retail trade**	**5,846**	**5,551**	**5,074**	**4,496**	**4,472**	**4,982**	**5,186**	**5,584**	**6,046**	**5,923**
42	Wholesale trade	1,631	1,571	1,418	1,279	1,275	1,406	1,443	1,550	1,706	1,707
43	Retail trade and automobile services	4,215	3,980	3,656	3,217	3,197	3,576	3,743	4,034	4,340	4,216
44	**Finance, insurance, and real estate**	**1,415**	**1,390**	**1,328**	**1,266**	**1,219**	**1,242**	**1,261**	**1,305**	**1,346**	**1,342**
45	Banking	385	375	345	311	281	284	277	276	285	286
46	Security and commodity brokers, dealers and exchanges	128	103	88	80	89	83	74	85	83	68
47	Finance, n. e. c.	130	128	120	114	108	106	108	114	116	102
48	Insurance carriers	358	368	361	355	341	348	364	368	383	396
49	Insurance agents and combination offices	120	122	119	117	112	113	112	114	115	117
50	Real estate	294	294	295	289	288	308	326	348	364	373
51	**Transportation**	**2,873**	**2,632**	**2,280**	**1,934**	**1,841**	**1,910**	**1,933**	**2,046**	**2,159**	**1,897**
52	Railroads	1,845	1,659	1,405	1,155	1,084	1,122	1,113	1,194	1,251	1,061
53	Local and highway passenger transportation	410	387	356	323	302	294	294	298	301	280
54	Local railways and buslines	280	263	239	214	199	201	202	204	207	187
55	Highway passenger transportation, n. e. c.	130	124	117	109	103	93	92	94	94	93
56	Highway freight transportation and warehousing	252	249	235	218	215	232	254	268	289	270
57	Water transportation	167	159	144	130	135	145	148	142	151	134
58	Air transportation (common carriers)	2	4	5	6	6	6	8	10	12	13
59	Pipeline transportation	25	24	21	17	20	22	23	25	26	23
60	Services allied to transportation	172	150	114	85	79	89	93	109	129	116
61	**Communications and public utilities**	**1,031**	**1,031**	**930**	**828**	**784**	**799**	**803**	**850**	**898**	**862**
62	Telephone, telegraph, and related services	534	524	459	412	383	379	376	393	422	400
63	Radio broadcasting and television	4	6	8	9	8	11	13	15	18	18
64	Utilities: electric and gas	465	473	437	384	371	386	392	418	437	423
65	Local utilities and public services, n. e. c.	28	28	26	23	22	23	22	24	21	21
66	**Services**	**5,112**	**4,928**	**4,547**	**4,068**	**3,919**	**4,280**	**4,448**	**4,748**	**5,000**	**4,800**
67	Hotels and other lodging places	387	371	331	282	266	313	327	349	373	373
68	Personal services	617	606	566	525	513	549	575	613	647	616
69	Private households	2,348	2,193	1,962	1,680	1,592	1,797	1,878	2,008	2,128	1,942
70	Commercial and trade schools and employment agencies	20	18	16	12	11	12	15	17	19	18
71	Business services, n. e. c.	157	153	137	141	147	172	172	201	204	208
72	Miscellaneous repair services and hand trades	59	58	57	56	56	56	56	57	57	58
73	Motion pictures	142	143	140	122	119	135	148	164	177	171
74	Amusement and recreation, except motion pictures	253	235	205	156	135	147	150	164	182	163
75	Medical and other health services	429	434	419	399	390	403	420	455	491	516
76	Legal services	90	94	99	100	101	100	104	105	108	112
77	Engineering and other professional services, n. e. c.	35	37	29	21	21	23	25	29	31	33
78	Educational services, n. e. c. [4]	224	228	232	233	233	234	240	244	251	259
79	Nonprofit membership organizations, n. e. c.	351	358	354	341	335	339	338	342	332	331
80	**Government and government enterprises**	**3,184**	**3,318**	**3,399**	**3,361**	**3,872**	**4,731**	**5,031**	**6,148**	**5,530**	**6,153**
81	Federal—general government	528	571	553	541	916	1,394	1,440	3,145	2,457	2,963
82	Civilian, except work relief [5]	267	310	296	290	294	357	449	521	517	507
83	Military [6]	261	261	257	251	249	250	263	290	313	326
84	Work relief [7]	0	0	0	0	373	787	728	2,334	1,627	2,130
85	Federal—government enterprises	299	300	298	297	300	323	336	343	349	366
86	State and local—general government	2,247	2,331	2,431	2,419	2,557	2,909	3,145	2,541	2,599	2,698
87	Public education [4]	1,082	1,110	1,120	1,109	1,084	1,083	1,112	1,134	1,165	1,196
88	Nonschool, except work relief	1,165	1,217	1,267	1,223	1,174	1,223	1,268	1,352	1,401	1,496
89	Work relief	0	4	44	87	299	603	765	55	33	6
90	State and local—government enterprises	110	116	117	104	99	105	110	119	125	126
91	**Rest of the world [8]**	**0**	**0**	**1**	**1**	**1**	**1**	**1**	**1**	**1**	**1**
92	**Addendum: All private industries**	**32,712**	**30,451**	**27,290**	**23,853**	**23,808**	**26,173**	**27,231**	**29,264**	**31,131**	**28,791**

1. Full-time equivalent employment measures man-years of full-time employment of wage and salary earners and its equivalent in work performed by part-time workers. Full-time employment is defined simply in terms of the number of hours which is customary at a particular time and place. For a full explanation of the concept, see *Survey of Current Business*, June 1945, pp. 17–18.

2. For certain manufacturing industries, the 1929–47 employment data shown are not comparable with those given for 1948 and subsequent years. The discontinuities stem from changes in the industrial classification basis on which the underlying social insurance employment tabulations are prepared. (See the Introduction to Part III.) Of the series principally involved here, five have been terminated in 1947; the others are indicated by footnotes.

3. See note 2. Estimates of 1948 employment comparable to those shown for 1947 in the specified industries are as follows (in thousands): Lumber and furniture products, 1,220;

Table 25.—Number of Full-Time Equivalent Employees, by Industry, 1939–53 [1]

[Data in thousands]

1939	1940	1941	1942	1943	1944	1945	1946	1947	1948	1949	1950	1951	1952	1953	Line
36,339	38,336	43,022	48,045	54,239	55,421	53,713	47,466	47,453	48,401	47,134	48,705	52,623	53,971	55,151	1
2,831	2,781	2,751	2,660	2,535	2,340	2,229	2,309	2,392	2,466	2,381	2,220	2,124	2,064	2,074	2
2,727	2,679	2,652	2,555	2,436	2,231	2,119	2,189	2,267	2,337	2,252	2,090	1,988	1,921	1,935	3
104	102	99	105	99	109	110	120	125	129	129	130	136	143	139	4
832	927	975	985	917	879	829	871	938	986	914	916	921	895	854	5
103	118	131	132	132	107	89	88	99	101	95	97	102	103	107	6
88	91	92	89	84	80	73	82	80	81	77	75	70	64	54	7
381	439	452	480	434	415	388	391	429	452	398	395	372	332	288	8
187	196	204	183	177	198	206	221	235	255	248	251	273	289	297	9
73	83	96	101	90	79	73	89	95	97	96	98	104	107	108	10
1,219	1,285	1,774	2,131	1,566	1,110	1,135	1,739	2,062	2,274	2,148	2,359	2,620	2,649	2,616	11
9,967	10,882	13,137	15,284	17,402	17,050	15,186	14,493	15,215	15,285	14,183	14,969	16,122	16,411	17,230	12
1,175	1,223	1,303	1,385	1,406	1,441	1,431	1,500	1,530	1,528	1,509	1,517	1,548	1,545	1,551	13
107	104	103	96	102	100	102	104	100	99	101	97	103	103	103	14
1,215	1,223	1,383	1,388	1,321	1,217	1,163	1,313	1,327	1,366	1,229	1,292	1,272	1,195	1,188	15
903	918	1,043	1,079	1,073	1,049	1,021	1,117	1,128	1,175	1,157	1,183	1,190	1,207	1,239	16
815	906	1,069	1,077	1,006	965	926	1,064	1,210	[3] 1,187	1,057	1,171	1,209	1,153	1,132	17
—	—	—	—	—	—	—	—	—	838	732	798	846	789	760	18
—	—	—	—	—	—	—	—	—	349	325	373	363	364	372	19
431	500	609	633	585	559	524	578	658	—	—	—	—	—	—	20
384	406	460	444	421	406	402	486	552	—	—	—	—	—	—	21
314	336	378	380	393	390	394	449	464	470	453	484	510	503	531	22
577	568	581	555	550	550	569	668	705	721	727	741	752	765	790	23
414	439	580	780	849	790	776	705	723	[3] 692	659	677	748	768	806	24
135	151	168	183	186	197	207	219	228	[3] 243	236	238	251	251	255	25
146	156	189	189	224	239	234	265	270	254	232	245	265	267	279	26
372	367	410	403	375	355	356	411	406	403	388	393	379	382	385	27
343	369	433	436	413	386	381	474	503	523	487	518	553	534	546	28
1,739	2,001	2,473	2,889	3,492	3,413	3,018	2,704	2,882	[3] 2,971	2,664	2,920	3,200	3,244	3,541	29
—	—	—	—	—	—	—	—	—	1,231	1,090	1,192	1,318	1,253	1,339	30
—	—	—	—	—	—	—	—	—	1,029	922	1,024	1,134	1,227	1,373	31
—	—	—	—	—	—	—	—	—	249	227	247	286	307	330	32
—	—	—	—	—	—	—	—	—	462	425	457	462	457	499	33
1,155	1,331	1,641	1,960	2,460	2,424	2,072	1,670	1,863	—	—	—	—	—	—	34
284	328	410	461	508	492	457	498	482	—	—	—	—	—	—	35
300	342	422	468	524	497	489	536	537	—	—	—	—	—	—	36
661	792	1,087	1,363	1,457	1,405	1,331	1,393	1,549	[3] 1,541	1,317	1,362	1,621	1,697	1,727	37
398	455	607	757	960	1,037	925	847	929	[3] 875	765	874	1,002	1,087	1,220	38
186	301	675	1,749	3,271	3,175	2,044	593	512	471	459	447	668	911	1,016	39
467	543	655	575	325	341	308	667	749	766	743	810	851	799	921	40
6,165	6,526	7,027	6,823	6,678	6,667	6,938	8,226	8,698	8,934	8,840	9,005	9,296	9,514	9,729	41
1,776	1,840	1,952	1,857	1,752	1,771	1,868	2,215	2,408	2,498	2,451	2,487	2,580	2,645	2,723	42
4,389	4,686	5,075	4,966	4,926	4,896	5,070	6,011	6,280	6,436	6,389	6,518	6,716	6,869	7,006	43
1,376	1,422	1,462	1,439	1,389	1,364	1,393	1,594	1,643	1,707	1,724	1,790	1,856	1,916	1,992	44
288	296	309	319	328	336	343	374	393	407	411	420	447	474	500	45
62	58	50	41	38	39	42	53	49	48	46	49	53	53	54	46
98	105	113	105	86	78	81	94	102	106	112	122	129	141	151	47
414	425	435	428	406	392	404	475	514	551	573	594	615	638	671	48
119	118	120	121	118	115	118	143	146	154	157	166	173	177	183	49
395	420	435	425	413	404	405	455	439	441	425	439	439	433	433	50
1,990	2,072	2,257	2,410	2,631	2,817	2,894	2,886	2,869	2,815	2,617	2,652	2,792	2,765	2,763	51
1,114	1,160	1,285	1,429	1,534	1,616	1,628	1,564	1,543	1,503	1,349	1,373	1,433	1,382	1,358	52
276	270	271	294	332	345	354	402	406	385	374	354	350	345	340	53
184	170	161	169	184	188	189	203	198	171	166	157	151	144	141	54
92	100	110	125	148	157	165	199	208	214	208	197	199	201	199	55
290	321	376	397	395	390	398	440	461	482	479	525	566	584	615	56
140	142	144	107	139	205	247	200	163	159	139	126	140	140	134	57
15	19	24	34	46	47	53	82	83	80	79	79	90	103	110	58
22	23	24	25	25	26	25	27	28	30	29	27	28	29	28	59
133	137	133	124	160	188	189	171	185	176	168	168	185	182	178	60
868	898	952	944	909	887	911	1,100	1,177	1,269	1,280	1,269	1,308	1,347	1,386	61
402	410	450	474	490	486	500	613	643	693	688	667	692	719	744	62
21	23	26	27	28	30	33	36	41	47	49	53	57	59	62	63
423	443	454	422	373	353	359	429	470	506	520	527	536	545	556	64
22	22	22	21	18	18	19	22	23	23	23	22	23	24	24	65
4,967	5,274	5,347	5,518	5,226	5,165	5,181	5,452	5,732	5,867	5,900	6,152	6,327	6,375	6,517	66
377	388	404	404	412	420	417	462	461	457	445	440	447	453	460	67
597	661	718	750	756	731	746	857	863	847	824	815	823	821	821	68
2,075	2,200	2,057	2,092	1,739	1,655	1,632	1,503	1,605	1,590	1,606	1,768	1,785	1,695	1,717	69
17	16	24	40	50	35	21	25	31	34	37	39	38	35	31	70
220	225	241	236	229	243	264	324	351	376	372	387	412	444	474	71
58	57	64	66	78	81	84	107	116	113	106	102	116	124	123	72
172	174	184	193	204	214	215	228	229	225	226	224	220	216	209	73
173	186	202	204	193	196	197	233	235	242	238	235	231	229	233	74
522	549	580	614	655	665	661	701	767	818	850	923	1,005	1,071	1,144	75
116	116	117	111	104	95	90	103	104	108	110	113	119	123	128	76
37	41	53	78	63	59	66	82	93	106	102	104	130	157	167	77
265	271	276	282	288	292	295	313	337	400	431	441	435	432	432	78
328	390	427	448	455	479	493	514	540	551	553	561	566	575	578	79
6,133	6,267	7,337	9,846	14,979	17,137	17,012	8,791	6,732	6,793	7,142	7,368	9,252	10,029	9,985	80
2,898	2,980	3,984	6,457	11,573	13,885	13,722	5,276	3,015	2,864	3,020	3,130	4,918	5,528	5,334	81
560	642	944	1,702	2,497	2,520	2,420	1,842	1,416	1,396	1,416	1,436	1,794	1,890	1,789	82
342	549	1,676	4,154	9,029	11,365	11,302	3,434	1,599	1,468	1,604	1,694	3,124	3,638	3,545	83
1,996	1,789	1,364	601	47	—	—	—	—	—	—	—	—	—	—	84
375	389	431	522	616	481	495	526	483	505	528	516	527	555	543	85
2,732	2,752	2,764	2,714	2,635	2,622	2,647	2,828	3,053	3,209	3,369	3,484	3,557	3,677	3,830	86
1,224	1,235	1,249	1,245	1,227	1,216	1,224	1,276	1,364	1,418	1,491	1,536	1,581	1,657	1,734	87
1,497	1,506	1,509	1,467	1,408	1,406	1,423	1,552	1,689	1,791	1,878	1,948	1,976	2,020	2,096	88
11	11	6	2	—	—	—	—	—	—	—	—	—	—	—	89
128	146	158	153	155	149	148	161	181	215	225	238	250	269	278	90
1	2	3	5	7	5	5	5	5	5	5	5	5	6	5	91
30,205	32,067	35,682	38,194	39,253	38,279	36,696	38,670	40,716	41,603	39,987	41,332	43,366	43,936	45,161	92

Chemicals and allied products, 723; Products of petroleum and coal, 235; Metals, metal products, and miscellaneous, 2,873; Machinery, except electrical, 1,562; and Electrical machinery, 889.

4. School teachers are considered to be employed during vacation periods.

5. Includes United States citizens, but not foreigners, employed abroad by the U. S. Government.

6. Includes personnel stationed abroad, but personnel recruited from the territories is excluded.

7. Because of the exceptional character of work relief employment, full-time equivalent employment has been computed for all years by use of a 40-hour week as a measure of full-time employment.

8. Represents the estimated number of permanent United States residents employed in the United States by foreign governments and international organizations.

Table 27.—*Average Annual Earnings per Full-Time Employee, by Industry, 1929–38* [1]

[Dollars]

Line		1929	1930	1931	1932	1933	1934	1935	1936	1937	1938
1	**All industries, total**	**1,405**	**1,368**	**1,275**	**1,120**	**1,048**	**1,091**	**1,137**	**1,184**	**1,258**	**1,230**
2	**Agriculture, forestry, and fisheries**	**397**	**388**	**312**	**247**	**230**	**251**	**286**	**307**	**360**	**369**
3	Farms	378	369	291	228	213	235	268	290	338	348
4	Agricultural services, forestry, and fisheries	898	893	844	755	685	679	759	788	854	870
5	**Mining**	**1,526**	**1,424**	**1,221**	**1,016**	**990**	**1,108**	**1,154**	**1,263**	**1,366**	**1,282**
6	Metal mining	1,613	1,551	1,291	1,060	1,040	1,133	1,239	1,380	1,630	1,453
7	Anthracite mining	1,728	1,750	1,602	1,452	1,435	1,500	1,414	1,408	1,388	1,315
8	Bituminous and other soft-coal mining	1,293	1,119	909	723	748	900	957	1,103	1,170	1,050
9	Crude petroleum and natural gas	2,019	1,980	1,890	1,600	1,427	1,472	1,558	1,594	1,734	1,734
10	Nonmetallic mining and quarrying	1,409	1,358	1,186	945	852	903	968	1,100	1,211	1,134
11	**Contract construction**	**1,674**	**1,526**	**1,233**	**907**	**869**	**942**	**1,027**	**1,178**	**1,278**	**1,193**
12	**Manufacturing**	**1,543**	**1,488**	**1,369**	**1,150**	**1,086**	**1,153**	**1,216**	**1,287**	**1,376**	**1,296**
13	Food and kindred products	1,503	1,489	1,451	1,303	1,204	1,221	1,253	1,290	1,351	1,331
14	Tobacco manufactures	979	985	908	787	726	750	778	817	883	870
15	Textile-mill products	1,155	1,096	1,039	847	829	883	926	952	994	926
16	Apparel and other finished fabric products	1,361	1,265	1,162	941	900	987	1,016	1,013	1,025	999
17	Lumber and furniture products [3]	1,267	1,224	1,106	881	820	865	907	987	1,037	1,015
18	Lumber and wood products, except furniture	----	----	----	----	----	----	----	----	----	----
19	Furniture and fixtures	----	----	----	----	----	----	----	----	----	----
20	Lumber and timber basic products	1,172	1,156	1,010	787	737	791	833	911	963	940
21	Furniture and finished lumber products	1,398	1,310	1,196	962	900	948	988	1,074	1,123	1,102
22	Paper and allied products	1,514	1,487	1,404	1,208	1,143	1,186	1,235	1,313	1,403	1,359
23	Printing, publishing, and allied industries	2,010	2,011	1,943	1,740	1,599	1,644	1,698	1,702	1,722	1,697
24	Chemicals and allied products [3]	1,673	1,647	1,608	1,419	1,312	1,341	1,385	1,455	1,559	1,621
25	Products of petroleum and coal [3]	1,844	1,904	1,810	1,619	1,505	1,513	1,587	1,629	1,833	1,863
26	Rubber products	1,597	1,563	1,392	1,191	1,137	1,248	1,358	1,472	1,528	1,457
27	Leather and leather products	1,327	1,215	1,152	970	950	1,017	1,043	1,045	1,085	1,017
28	Stone, clay, and glass products	1,557	1,525	1,386	1,167	1,071	1,088	1,171	1,262	1,357	1,303
29	Metals, metal products, and miscellaneous [3]	1,700	1,609	1,427	1,098	1,098	1,177	1,284	1,409	1,540	1,351
30	Primary metal industries	----	----	----	----	----	----	----	----	----	----
31	Fabricated metal products, including ordnance	----	----	----	----	----	----	----	----	----	----
32	Instruments	----	----	----	----	----	----	----	----	----	----
33	Miscellaneous manufacturing	----	----	----	----	----	----	----	----	----	----
34	Iron and steel and their products, including ordnance	1,740	1,640	1,410	1,044	1,073	1,166	1,295	1,446	1,591	1,359
35	Nonferrous metals and their products	1,665	1,554	1,455	1,177	1,132	1,209	1,277	1,361	1,492	1,402
36	Miscellaneous manufacturing	1,568	1,535	1,466	1,230	1,166	1,195	1,244	1,298	1,359	1,274
37	Machinery, except electrical [3]	1,827	1,748	1,521	1,311	1,260	1,345	1,425	1,550	1,693	1,534
38	Electrical machinery [3]	1,655	1,658	1,461	1,182	1,203	1,282	1,364	1,478	1,616	1,527
39	Transportation equipment, except automobiles	1,747	1,728	1,590	1,463	1,310	1,317	1,381	1,496	1,614	1,589
40	Automobiles and automobile equipment	1,813	1,571	1,455	1,234	1,170	1,314	1,489	1,600	1,672	1,653
41	**Wholesale and retail trade**	**1,594**	**1,569**	**1,465**	**1,315**	**1,183**	**1,228**	**1,279**	**1,275**	**1,352**	**1,352**
42	Wholesale trade	2,072	2,039	1,934	1,672	1,477	1,550	1,640	1,652	1,693	1,686
43	Retail trade and automobile services	1,409	1,384	1,324	1,173	1,066	1,102	1,139	1,159	1,218	1,217
44	**Finance, insurance, and real estate**	**2,062**	**1,973**	**1,858**	**1,652**	**1,555**	**1,601**	**1,632**	**1,713**	**1,788**	**1,731**
45	Banking	1,949	1,909	1,881	1,817	1,726	1,768	1,830	1,891	1,919	1,941
46	Security and commodity brokers, dealers, and exchanges	3,172	3,097	3,011	2,925	2,742	2,807	2,770	2,941	3,048	2,809
47	Finance, n. e. c.	1,862	1,828	1,767	1,632	1,574	1,660	1,759	1,886	2,009	2,039
48	Insurance carriers	2,268	2,226	2,127	1,800	1,677	1,718	1,745	1,823	1,901	1,846
49	Insurance agents and combination offices	1,975	1,877	1,748	1,581	1,464	1,575	1,679	1,781	1,887	1,880
50	Real estate	1,575	1,446	1,237	979	906	981	1,021	1,078	1,176	1,121
51	**Transportation**	**1,643**	**1,610**	**1,549**	**1,373**	**1,334**	**1,393**	**1,492**	**1,582**	**1,614**	**1,676**
52	Railroads	1,749	1,717	1,661	1,461	1,439	1,505	1,645	1,724	1,774	1,849
53	Local and highway passenger transportation	1,598	1,587	1,500	1,328	1,219	1,310	1,361	1,433	1,505	1,529
54	Local railways and buslines	1,721	1,719	1,678	1,533	1,422	1,473	1,515	1,583	1,633	1,674
55	Highway passenger transportation, n. e. c.	1,331	1,306	1,137	927	825	957	1,022	1,106	1,223	1,236
56	Highway freight transportation and warehousing	1,298	1,289	1,230	1,179	1,172	1,207	1,264	1,328	1,409	1,456
57	Water transportation	1,275	1,214	1,153	1,038	1,059	1,055	1,088	1,373	1,536	1,299
58	Air transportation (common carriers)	2,624	2,424	2,381	2,346	2,227	2,201	2,195	2,243	2,257	2,249
59	Pipeline transportation	1,927	1,802	1,794	1,691	1,443	1,521	1,575	1,609	1,822	1,909
60	Services allied to transportation	1,424	1,427	1,377	1,224	1,127	1,180	1,269	1,275	1,279	1,276
61	**Communications and public utilities**	**1,474**	**1,497**	**1,514**	**1,438**	**1,351**	**1,426**	**1,486**	**1,522**	**1,601**	**1,674**
62	Telephone, telegraph, and related services	1,386	1,410	1,436	1,335	1,245	1,338	1,378	1,420	1,481	1,580
63	Radio broadcasting and television	2,513	2,624	2,732	2,740	2,510	2,198	2,089	2,223	2,381	2,497
64	Utilities: electric and gas	1,589	1,603	1,600	1,542	1,453	1,510	1,589	1,615	1,705	1,749
65	Local utilities and public services, n. e. c.	1,116	1,124	1,122	1,081	1,021	1,061	1,116	1,135	1,197	1,228
66	**Services**	**1,079**	**1,066**	**1,006**	**918**	**854**	**857**	**873**	**898**	**938**	**942**
67	Hotels and other lodging places	1,098	1,097	1,030	908	816	863	878	897	941	946
68	Personal services	1,219	1,200	1,136	996	889	905	915	940	978	972
69	Private households	731	676	584	497	460	473	485	506	558	527
70	Commercial and trade schools and employment agencies	1,650	1,778	1,625	1,500	1,364	1,417	1,400	1,471	1,528	1,500
71	Business services, n. e. c.	2,274	2,412	2,255	1,844	1,653	1,709	1,884	1,915	1,966	1,899
72	Miscellaneous repair services and hand trades	1,814	1,793	1,684	1,464	1,286	1,339	1,429	1,456	1,544	1,552
73	Motion pictures	2,169	2,175	2,179	1,959	1,891	1,844	1,892	1,896	1,972	1,942
74	Amusement and recreation, except motion pictures	1,273	1,268	1,244	1,218	1,185	1,190	1,193	1,232	1,269	1,270
75	Medical and other health services	925	933	919	865	810	801	829	851	876	899
76	Legal services	1,378	1,394	1,333	1,260	1,168	1,160	1,163	1,200	1,231	1,205
77	Engineering and other professional services, n. e. c.	2,314	2,027	1,897	1,714	1,619	1,609	1,600	1,759	1,774	1,909
78	Educational services, n. e. c.	1,312	1,329	1,323	1,279	1,189	1,175	1,162	1,180	1,211	1,228
79	Nonprofit membership organizations, n. e. c.	1,712	1,698	1,653	1,545	1,442	1,440	1,435	1,465	1,497	1,529
80	**Government and government enterprises**	**1,551**	**1,583**	**1,547**	**1,477**	**1,328**	**1,284**	**1,292**	**1,279**	**1,355**	**1,336**
81	Federal—general government	1,561	1,504	1,564	1,518	1,217	1,180	1,183	1,112	1,189	1,149
82	Civilian, except work relief	1,933	1,768	1,895	1,824	1,673	1,717	1,759	1,896	1,797	1,832
83	Military	1,180	1,192	1,183	1,163	1,072	1,072	1,152	1,152	1,131	1,120
84	Work relief	0	0	0	0	954	971	839	931	1,007	991
85	Federal—government enterprises	1,903	1,907	1,913	1,791	1,577	1,635	1,780	1,869	1,851	1,811
86	State and local—general government	1,499	1,517	1,497	1,427	1,333	1,289	1,283	1,397	1,436	1,467
87	Public education	1,445	1,455	1,463	1,399	1,300	1,265	1,293	1,329	1,367	1,406
88	Nonschool, except work relief	1,549	1,576	1,541	1,479	1,413	1,391	1,425	1,457	1,493	1,517
89	Work relief	0	1,000	1,045	1,057	1,140	1,128	1,035	1,345	1,454	1,333
90	State and local—government enterprises	1,600	1,595	1,573	1,529	1,455	1,438	1,473	1,487	1,536	1,563
91	**Rest of the world**	**2,000**	**1,900**	**1,900**	**1,800**	**1,700**	**1,800**	**1,800**	**1,900**	**1,900**	**1,900**
92	**Addendum: All private industries**	**1,390**	**1,348**	**1,241**	**1,070**	**1,002**	**1,056**	**1,109**	**1,164**	**1,240**	**1,207**

1. Average annual earnings per full-time employee are obtained by dividing wages and salaries, as given in table 15, by the number of full-time equivalent employees, as given in table 25. Footnotes to tables 15 and 25 are, therefore, relevant also to table 27. For a full explanation of the concept of "average annual earnings per full-time employee", see *Survey of Current Business*, June 1945, pp. 17–18.

Table 27.—*Average Annual Earnings per Full-Time Employee, by Industry, 1939–53* [1]

[Dollars]

1939	1940	1941	1942	1943	1944	1945	1946	1947	1948	1949	1950	1951	1952	1953	Line
1,264	**1,300**	**1,443**	**1,709**	**1,961**	**2,108**	**2,189**	**2,356**	**2,589**	**2,793**	**2,850**	**3,008**	**3,247**	**3,428**	**3,598**	1
385	**468**	**498**	**673**	**867**	**1,027**	**1,127**	**1,297**	**1,288**	**1,345**	**1,319**	**1,362**	**1,534**	**1,629**	**1,653**	2
362	385	473	643	837	992	1,089	1,166	1,243	1,296	1,268	1,303	1,469	1,560	1,577	3
981	1,010	1,162	1,410	1,616	1,743	1,855	1,950	2,104	2,233	2,209	2,308	2,485	2,566	2,705	4
1,367	**1,388**	**1,579**	**1,796**	**2,162**	**2,499**	**2,621**	**2,719**	**3,113**	**3,387**	**3,207**	**3,448**	**3,891**	**4,069**	**4,364**	5
1,515	1,610	1,771	2,045	2,333	2,458	2,551	2,636	3,000	3,327	3,400	2,567	4,098	4,544	4,879	6
1,409	1,297	1,467	1,753	2,119	2,525	2,685	2,890	3,125	3,420	2,896	3,107	3,386	3,500	3,389	7
1,197	1,235	1,500	1,715	2,115	2,535	2,629	2,724	3,212	3,383	2,930	3,268	3,831	3,780	4,198	8
1,684	1,714	1,779	1,940	2,299	2,601	2,762	2,819	3,157	3,584	3,746	3,861	4,143	4,471	4,043	9
1,178	1,217	1,375	1,634	1,911	2,089	2,205	2,371	2,663	2,928	3,021	3,255	3,587	3,766	4,019	10
1,268	**1,330**	**1,635**	**2,191**	**2,503**	**2,602**	**2,600**	**2,537**	**2,829**	**3,119**	**3,230**	**3,354**	**3,735**	**4,022**	**4,244**	11
1,363	**1,432**	**1,653**	**2,023**	**2,349**	**2,517**	**2,517**	**2,517**	**2,793**	**3,040**	**3,092**	**3,300**	**3,612**	**3,834**	**4,061**	12
1,372	1,385	1,472	1,650	1,878	2,044	2,170	2,385	2,669	2,853	2,925	3,068	3,307	3,478	3,676	13
916	1,000	1,117	1,240	1,431	1,580	1,676	1,779	1,950	2,040	2,089	2,258	2,447	2,592	2,709	14
960	986	1,159	1,385	1,556	1,681	1,817	2,056	2,338	2,584	2,564	2,762	2,898	2,987	3,026	15
1,025	1,022	1,159	1,331	1,595	1,788	1,943	2,192	2,327	2,442	2,385	2,496	2,585	2,653	2,747	16
1,042	1,034	1,146	1,332	1,571	1,702	1,779	1,984	2,305	[3] 2,399	2,446	2,647	2,849	3,052	3,170	17
----	----	----	----	----	----	----	----	----	2,242	2,272	2,477	2,681	2,876	2,975	18
----	----	----	----	----	----	----	----	----	2,777	2,837	3,011	3,242	3,434	3,570	19
956	934	1,026	1,205	1,446	1,564	1,618	1,813	2,046	----	----	----	----	----	----	20
1,138	1,158	1,304	1,514	1,743	1,892	1,988	2,187	2,395	----	----	----	----	----	----	21
1,414	1,458	1,646	1,850	2,076	2,254	2,365	2,535	2,903	3,196	3,232	3,479	3,763	3,974	4,169	22
1,718	1,764	1,852	1,971	2,156	2,376	2,576	2,862	3,210	3,499	3,655	3,800	4,003	4,220	4,420	23
1,611	1,723	1,893	2,131	2,386	2,608	2,670	2,765	3,119	[3] 3,399	3,539	3,768	4,075	4,297	4,560	24
1,852	1,954	2,113	2,410	2,806	3,046	3,097	3,183	3,610	[3] 4,054	4,174	4,315	4,629	4,952	5,204	25
1,548	1,583	1,778	2,116	2,478	2,699	2,722	2,826	3,085	3,200	3,228	3,543	3,819	4,127	4,290	26
1,038	1,041	1,236	1,447	1,659	1,831	1,972	2,131	2,313	2,414	2,405	2,545	2,670	2,861	2,940	27
1,359	1,393	1,554	1,771	2,024	2,174	2,249	2,380	2,672	2,925	3,008	3,239	3,595	3,702	3,956	28
1,508	1,590	1,841	2,210	2,560	2,705	2,720	2,649	2,972	[3] 3,245	3,287	3,527	3,904	4,134	4,376	29
----	----	----	----	----	----	----	----	----	3,431	3,435	3,728	4,162	4,401	4,712	30
----	----	----	----	----	----	----	----	----	3,247	3,324	3,532	3,886	4,142	4,363	31
----	----	----	----	----	----	----	----	----	3,157	3,291	3,530	3,892	4,147	4,355	32
----	----	----	----	----	----	----	----	----	2,790	2,826	2,987	3,219	3,372	3,527	33
1,549	1,643	1,923	2,283	2,637	2,781	2,792	2,696	3,063	----	----	----	----	----	----	34
1,521	1,594	1,824	2,230	2,581	2,724	2,735	2,717	2,969	----	----	----	----	----	----	35
1,337	1,380	1,540	1,882	2,176	2,320	2,401	2,442	2,657	----	----	----	----	----	----	36
1,681	1,813	2,144	2,630	2,857	2,975	2,930	2,862	3,112	[3] 3,433	3,477	3,755	4,228	4,466	4,692	37
1,601	1,688	1,919	2,287	2,466	2,578	2,584	2,615	2,876	[3] 3,153	3,2[illegible]	3,370	3,714	3,959	4,133	38
1,667	1,764	2,160	2,695	2,982	3,188	3,175	2,971	3,146	3,594	3,59[illegible]	3,736	4,251	4,470	4,761	39
1,762	1,934	2,243	2,880	2,978	3,103	2,968	2,814	3,143	3,381	3,608	4,010	4,224	4,608	4,947	40
1,360	**1,382**	**1,478**	**1,608**	**1,781**	**1,946**	**2,114**	**2,378**	**2,632**	**2,832**	**2,899**	**3,034**	**3,225**	**3,338**	**3,476**	41
1,698	1,754	1,943	2,177	2,416	2,600	2,751	3,021	3,322	3,566	3,619	3,834	4,138	4,284	4,465	42
1,224	1,236	1,299	1,395	1,555	1,709	1,879	2,141	2,368	2,547	2,623	2,729	2,875	2,974	3,092	43
1,729	**1,725**	**1,777**	**1,885**	**2,041**	**2,191**	**2,347**	**2,570**	**2,740**	**2,947**	**3,046**	**3,244**	**3,426**	**3,592**	**3,761**	44
1,969	1,963	1,977	2,069	2,134	2,258	2,408	2,650	2,860	3,039	3,173	3,340	3,506	3,656	3,798	45
2,806	2,845	3,040	3,073	3,947	4,179	5,280	5,226	4,714	4,958	5,043	6,122	6,132	6,094	6,130	46
2,102	2,114	2,177	2,352	2,605	2,808	2,914	3,213	3,412	3,670	3,795	3,893	4,194	4,390	4,543	47
1,826	1,838	1,910	2,044	2,224	2,380	2,490	2,655	2,811	2,953	3,082	3,237	3,434	3,647	3,855	48
1,882	1,890	1,975	2,140	2,331	2,513	2,661	2,923	3,103	3,364	3,478	3,711	3,896	4,056	4,262	49
1,144	1,145	1,198	1,285	1,412	1,550	1,642	1,864	2,052	2,317	2,301	2,481	2,595	2,684	2,792	50
1,723	**1,756**	**1,885**	**2,183**	**2,493**	**2,679**	**2,734**	**2,948**	**3,145**	**3,440**	**3,556**	**3,699**	**4,033**	**4,254**	**4,441**	51
1,877	1,906	2,030	2,303	2,585	2,714	2,711	3,055	3,216	3,581	3,706	3,789	4,171	4,342	4,407	52
1,569	1,559	1,664	1,990	2,280	2,458	2,596	2,689	2,833	2,935	2,987	3,096	3,293	3,429	3,556	53
1,701	1,700	1,795	2,018	2,288	2,468	2,619	2,729	2,965	3,146	3,277	3,376	3,623	3,833	4,000	54
1,304	1,320	1,473	1,952	2,270	2,446	2,570	2,648	2,707	2,766	2,755	2,873	3,025	3,139	3,241	55
1,521	1,551	1,630	1,859	2,147	2,374	2,545	2,752	3,063	3,355	3,545	3,811	4,069	4,375	4,709	56
1,557	1,648	1,854	2,729	3,388	3,624	3,583	3,415	3,748	4,006	4,129	4,413	4,779	5,214	6,022	57
2,328	2,239	2,258	2,265	2,457	2,766	2,830	2,829	3,265	3,662	3,873	4,089	4,344	4,650	4,864	58
1,930	1,928	2,099	2,280	2,720	3,038	3,240	3,259	3,750	4,100	4,172	4,296	4,679	5,000	5,250	59
1,271	1,365	1,579	1,782	2,100	2,314	2,388	2,550	2,762	2,852	2,911	3,077	3,459	3,676	3,882	60
1,692	**1,718**	**1,766**	**1,883**	**2,075**	**2,248**	**2,425**	**2,567**	**2,792**	**3,002**	**3,153**	**3,321**	**3,554**	**3,802**	**4,034**	61
1,600	1,610	1,633	1,715	1,878	2,035	2,246	2,413	2,583	2,776	2,907	3,033	3,218	3,441	3,645	62
2,427	2,554	2,581	2,667	2,929	3,333	3,515	3,972	4,073	4,234	4,469	4,698	5,175	5,559	5,855	63
1,766	1,795	1,870	2,040	2,284	2,467	2,596	2,697	2,994	3,223	3,383	3,571	3,849	4,123	4,387	64
1,240	1,286	1,344	1,544	1,715	1,855	1,951	2,040	2,230	2,380	2,519	2,606	2,776	2,988	3,191	65
952	**953**	**1,020**	**1,132**	**1,347**	**1,538**	**1,688**	**1,872**	**2,005**	**2,112**	**2,166**	**2,220**	**2,362**	**2,529**	**2,650**	66
958	997	1,025	1,097	1,269	1,455	1,612	1,779	1,924	2,031	2,094	2,150	2,246	2,355	2,435	67
1,034	1,042	1,075	1,196	1,384	1,570	1,709	1,854	1,978	2,096	2,154	2,236	2,348	2,474	2,585	68
544	554	601	706	919	1,140	1,312	1,411	1,463	1,498	1,502	1,509	1,587	1,686	1,777	69
1,529	1,625	1,833	2,175	2,520	2,714	2,571	2,520	2,903	3,147	3,243	3,410	3,421	3,514	3,742	70
1,886	1,889	1,967	2,072	2,332	2,584	2,739	2,861	3,023	3,226	3,309	3,457	3,699	3,878	4,046	71
1,603	1,579	1,891	2,152	2,641	2,901	2,810	2,766	2,974	3,150	3,236	3,441	3,845	4,097	4,325	72
1,971	1,948	2,016	2,124	2,250	2,379	2,567	2,978	3,031	2,911	2,912	2,915	3,059	3,190	3,244	73
1,277	1,280	1,292	1,328	1,461	1,663	1,888	2,185	2,345	2,455	2,492	2,566	2,719	2,900	3,052	74
908	927	955	1,036	1,127	1,262	1,401	1,605	1,821	1,952	2,044	2,137	2,260	2,394	2,503	75
1,198	1,224	1,265	1,324	1,423	1,653	1,856	1,757	1,971	2,093	2,218	2,301	2,445	2,618	2,773	76
1,973	1,902	2,245	2,654	3,063	3,237	3,258	3,280	3,495	3,745	3,931	4,106	4,531	4,847	5,054	77
1,234	1,240	1,264	1,344	1,469	1,562	1,641	1,802	2,113	2,185	2,225	2,290	2,372	2,521	2,625	78
1,546	1,408	1,379	1,492	1,679	1,795	1,876	2,070	2,172	2,339	2,490	2,626	2,807	2,997	3,161	79
1,337	**1,344**	**1,388**	**1,623**	**1,777**	**1,924**	**2,052**	**2,341**	**2,574**	**2,758**	**2,863**	**3,015**	**3,114**	**3,270**	**3,351**	80
1,137	1,127	1,240	1,632	1,792	1,929	2,057	2,437	2,793	2,930	2,983	3,205	3,144	3,252	3,290	81
1,843	1,894	1,970	2,226	2,628	2,677	2,646	2,736	3,074	3,168	3,362	3,504	3,778	3,975	4,103	82
1,135	1,026	1,113	1,485	1,565	1,763	1,931	2,277	2,543	2,704	2,648	2,951	2,780	2,877	2,879	83
939	883	889	965	1,064	----	----	----	----	----	----	----	----	----	----	84
1,819	1,820	1,777	1,676	1,778	2,372	2,412	2,644	2,865	3,095	3,284	3,512	3,797	4,092	4,195	85
1,471	1,497	1,522	1,574	1,687	1,797	1,938	2,091	2,298	2,533	2,668	2,755	2,947	3,142	3,277	86
1,403	1,435	1,462	1,512	1,608	1,730	1,822	2,025	2,261	2,538	2,671	2,794	2,998	3,169	3,315	87
1,530	1,552	1,574	1,628	1,756	1,855	1,986	2,144	2,327	2,528	2,665	2,725	2,906	3,119	3,245	88
909	909	1,000	1,000	----	----	----	----	----	----	----	----	----	----	----	89
1,578	1,610	1,734	1,908	2,142	2,255	2,405	2,590	2,818	3,023	3,182	3,227	3,464	3,688	3,888	90
2,000	**2,000**	**2,000**	**2,100**	**2,100**	**2,200**	**2,400**	**3,400**	**3,400**	**3,200**	**3,200**	**3,600**	**4,000**	**4,167**	**4,000**	91
1,250	**1,291**	**1,454**	1,731	2,018	**2,190**	**2,253**	**2,359**	**2,591**	**2,798**	**2,848**	**3,007**	**3,276**	**3,465**	**3,643**	92

2. See note 1, table 15 and note 2, table 25. Estimates of 1948 average annual earnings approximately comparable to those shown for 1947 in the specified industries are as follows: Lumber and furniture products, $2,411; Chemicals and allied products, $3,389; Products of petroleum and coal, $4,072; Metals, metal products and miscellaneous, $3,252; Machinery, except electrical, $3,431; and Electrical machinery, $3,154.

Table 30.—*Personal Consumption Expenditures, by Type of Product, 1929–38*[*]

[Millions of dollars]

Line		1929	1930	1931	1932	1933	1934	1935	1936	1937	1938
1	**I. Food [1] and tobacco**	**21,230**	**19,414**	**16,220**	**12,704**	**12,757**	**15,549**	**17,621**	**19,955**	**21,552**	**20,585**
2	1. Food purchased for off-premise consumption (n. d. c.)	14,777	13,500	10,833	8,203	8,626	10,757	12,150	13,929	14,792	14,082
3	2. Purchased meals and beverages [2] (n. d. c.)	2,911	2,788	2,541	2,102	1,816	2,248	2,610	2,985	3,528	3,392
4	3. Food furnished government (including military) and commercial employees (n. d. c.).	257	245	198	160	155	185	214	236	271	247
5	4. Food produced and consumed on farms (n. d. c.)	1,590	1,431	1,159	917	927	992	1,213	1,270	1,288	1,167
6	5. Tobacco products (n. d. c.)	1,695	1,450	1,489	1,322	1,233	1,367	1,434	1,535	1,673	1,697
7	**II. Clothing, accessories, and jewelry**	**11,193**	**9,713**	**8,217**	**6,042**	**5,438**	**6,562**	**7,010**	**7,661**	**8,092**	**7,991**
8	1. Shoes and other footwear (n. d. c.)	1,675	1,375	1,207	1,022	887	1,072	1,031	1,145	1,279	1,257
9	2. Shoe cleaning and repair (s.)	164	141	114	100	98	102	106	113	122	118
10	3. Clothing and accessories except footwear [3]	7,682	6,659	5,713	4,022	3,731	4,585	4,982	5,403	5,546	5,495
11	a. Women s and children's (n. d. c.)	4,662	4,100	3,528	2,446	2,254	2,801	3,080	3,226	3,277	3,337
12	b. Men's and boys' (n. d. c.)	3,020	2,559	2,185	1,576	1,477	1,784	1,902	2,177	2,289	2,158
13	4. Standard clothing issued to military personnel (n. d. c.)	12	11	9	10	11	7	9	12	13	14
14	5. Cleaning, dyeing, pressing, alteration, storage, and repair of garments including furs (in shops) not elsewhere classified (s).	473	420	352	252	230	265	302	339	383	391
15	6. Laundering in establishments (s.)	475	458	392	310	252	262	272	304	323	308
16	7. Jewelry and watches (d. c.)	560	513	328	252	172	198	233	265	333	323
17	8. Other [4] (s.)	152	136	102	74	57	71	75	80	93	85
18	**III. Personal care**	**1,116**	**1,039**	**979**	**817**	**660**	**760**	**802**	**864**	**961**	**951**
19	1. Toilet articles and preparations (n. d. c.)	591	515	504	420	320	377	374	395	428	442
20	2. Barbershops, beauty parlors, and baths (s.)	525	524	475	397	340	383	428	469	533	509
21	**IV. Housing**	**11,446**	**11,015**	**10,270**	**9,002**	**7,880**	**7,577**	**7,640**	**7,938**	**8,436**	**8,813**
22	1. Owner-occupied nonfarm dwellings—space-rental value [5] (s.)	5,868	5,552	5,101	4,416	3,844	3,643	3,646	3,759	3,950	4,104
23	2. Tenant-occupied nonfarm dwellings (including lodging houses)—space rent [5] (s.).	4,500	4,397	4,200	3,753	3,296	3,158	3,199	3,365	3,639	3,870
24	3. Rental value of farm houses (s.)	829	830	754	655	587	615	621	620	636	622
25	4. Other [6] (s.)	249	236	215	178	153	161	174	194	211	217
26	**V. Household operation**	**10,735**	**9,585**	**8,425**	**6,779**	**6,466**	**7,209**	**7,737**	**8,821**	**9,525**	**8,865**
27	1. Furniture (d. c.)	1,201	937	796	509	462	514	666	848	923	827
28	2. Kitchen and other household appliances [7] (d. c.)	768	671	565	344	408	518	614	733	845	711
29	3. China, glassware, tableware, and utensils (d. c.)	628	442	429	406	364	404	407	456	515	472
30	4. Other durable house furnishings [8] (d. c.)	1,148	937	783	562	472	573	617	827	885	800
31	5. Semidurable house furnishings [9] (n. d. c.)	717	570	497	374	391	449	478	591	639	568
32	6. Cleaning and polishing preparations, and miscellaneous household supplies and paper products (n. d. c.)	485	471	419	328	332	386	403	449	488	485
33	7. Stationery and writing supplies (n. d. c.)	143	133	103	71	69	87	101	112	131	129
34	8. Household utilities	3,044	3,058	2,844	2,615	2,561	2,729	2,792	2,979	3,042	2,971
35	a. Electricity (s.)	616	660	674	662	645	671	697	726	766	810
36	b. Gas (s.)	542	560	556	537	495	494	503	516	528	523
37	c. Water (s.)	278	296	296	278	269	301	311	326	331	327
38	d. Other fuel and ice (n. d. c.)	1,608	1,542	1,318	1,138	1,152	1,263	1,281	1,411	1,417	1,311
39	9. Telephone, telegraph, cable, and wireless (s.)	569	577	554	482	436	443	472	511	542	542
40	10. Domestic service (s.)	1,716	1,483	1,146	835	732	850	911	1,016	1,187	1,023
41	11. Other [10] (s.)	316	306	289	253	239	256	276	299	328	337
42	**VI. Medical care and death expenses**	**3,544**	**3,382**	**3,029**	**2,542**	**2,370**	**2,581**	**2,728**	**2,978**	**3,180**	**3,172**
43	1. Drug preparations and sundries (n. d. c.)	604	568	517	449	427	468	474	509	558	578
44	2. Ophthalmic products and orthopedic appliances (d. c.)	131	133	117	93	92	124	131	140	165	157
45	3. Physicians (s.)	959	924	819	661	617	678	731	820	854	833
46	4. Dentists (s.)	482	463	408	312	276	295	302	331	350	356
47	5. Other professional services [11] (s.)	250	233	201	154	138	145	151	165	168	163
48	6. Privately controlled hospitals and sanitariums [12] (s.)	403	404	395	386	363	369	406	422	454	467
49	7. Medical care and hospitalization insurance [13] (s.)	108	110	92	72	70	85	93	106	123	134
50	8. Funeral and burial expenses (s.)	607	547	480	415	387	417	440	485	508	484
51	**VII. Personal business**	**5,086**	**4,035**	**3,497**	**2,986**	**2,912**	**2,927**	**3,119**	**3,391**	**3,663**	**3,472**
52	1. Brokerage charges and interest, and investment counseling (s.)	1,707	759	418	269	372	227	228	296	281	195
53	2. Bank service charges, trust services, and safe-deposit box rental (s.).	76	79	80	78	79	92	104	116	126	130
54	3. Services furnished without payment by financial intermediaries except insurance companies (s.).	1,278	1,141	1,017	872	757	793	792	843	876	818
55	4. Expense of handling life insurance [14] (s.)	874	901	884	853	846	875	974	981	1,025	1,001
56	5. Legal services (s.)	402	397	410	348	334	359	371	383	402	392
57	6. Interest on personal debt (s.)	584	614	566	481	435	452	501	612	703	669
58	7. Other [15] (s.)	165	144	122	85	89	129	149	160	250	267
59	**VIII. Transportation**	**7,612**	**6,147**	**5,003**	**3,981**	**3,987**	**4,596**	**5,281**	**6,131**	**6,517**	**5,633**
60	1. User-operated transportation	5,960	4,662	3,747	2,935	3,035	3,584	4,217	4,956	5,288	4,453
61	a. New cars and net purchases of used cars (d. c.)	2,588	1,642	1,144	635	779	1,024	1,508	1,921	1,988	1,228
62	b. Tires, tubes, accessories, and parts (d. c.)	648	523	433	314	280	346	368	402	433	398
63	c. Automobile repair, greasing, washing, parking, storage, and rental (s.).	776	624	509	385	392	445	457	520	543	517
64	d. Gasoline and oil (n. d. c.)	1,814	1,749	1,540	1,476	1,466	1,640	1,743	1,945	2,143	2,145
65	e. Bridge, tunnel, ferry, and road tolls (s.)	40	43	45	43	42	43	42	44	44	41
66	f. Automobile insurance premiums less claims paid (s.)	94	81	76	82	76	86	99	124	137	124
67	2. Purchased local transportation	1,117	1,053	921	786	720	761	790	845	871	842
68	a. Street and electric railway and local bus (s.)	820	772	705	624	578	605	626	674	684	660
69	b. Taxicab (s.)	220	208	152	109	96	111	119	127	145	141
70	c. Railway (commutation) (s.)	77	73	64	53	46	45	45	44	42	41
71	3. Purchased intercity transportation	535	432	335	260	232	251	274	330	358	338
72	a. Railway (excluding commutation) and sleeping and parlor car (s.).	413	333	247	170	154	169	173	210	232	209
73	b. Intercity bus (s.)	52	53	50	48	46	44	62	74	80	89
74	c. Airline (s.)	3	2	2	3	3	4	6	8	8	8
75	d. Other [16] (s.)	67	44	36	39	29	34	33	38	38	32
76	**IX. Recreation**	**4,331**	**3,990**	**3,302**	**2,442**	**2,202**	**2,441**	**2,630**	**3,020**	**3,381**	**3,241**
77	1. Books and maps (d. c.)	309	264	253	153	152	165	183	208	243	221
78	2. Magazines, newspapers, and sheet music (n. d. c.)	538	512	479	428	419	441	456	490	518	514
79	3. Nondurable toys and sport supplies [17] (n. d. c.)	336	281	266	207	181	200	216	242	269	268
80	4. Wheel goods, durable toys, sport equipment, boats, and pleasure aircraft [17] (d. c.).	219	172	159	110	93	118	136	171	210	210
81	5. Radio and television receivers, records, and musical instruments (d. c.).	1,012	921	478	268	195	229	248	333	385	339
82	6. Radio and television repair (s.)	26	27	24	19	14	17	21	21	23	25
83	7. Flowers, seeds, and potted plants (n. d. c.)	221	190	134	89	90	116	130	159	186	176
84	8. Admissions to specified spectator amusements	913	892	854	631	573	625	672	759	818	816
85	a. Motion picture theaters (s.)	720	732	719	527	482	518	556	626	676	663
86	b. Legitimate theaters and opera, and entertainments of nonprofit institutions (except athletics) (s.)	127	95	78	57	41	42	44	50	53	58
87	c. Spectator sports [18] (s.)	66	65	57	47	50	65	72	83	89	95
88	9. Clubs and fraternal organizations except insurance [19] (s.)	302	294	277	242	208	199	197	198	203	200
89	10. Commercial participant amusements [20] (s.)	207	203	175	132	121	135	141	165	194	164
90	11. Pari-mutuel net receipts (s.)	8	7	6	4	6	19	26	29	38	44
91	12. Other [21] (s.)	240	227	197	159	150	177	204	245	294	264

See footnotes at end of table.

Table 30.—*Personal Consumption Expenditures, by Type of Product, 1939–53**

[Millions of dollars]

1939	1940	1941	1942	1943	1944	1945	1946	1947	1948	1949	1950	1951	1952	1953	Line
20,931	22,223	25,741	31,168	36,353	40,133	44,573	52,284	58,040	61,441	60,737	63,250	71,236	75,065	77,154	1
14,163	14,954	17,089	20,328	22,586	24,503	26,689	33,332	38,677	41,671	41,513	43,760	49,376	52,175	53,915	2
3,633	3,974	4,738	5,865	7,392	8,472	10,063	11,709	11,939	12,036	11,830	12,019	13,246	13,811	14,161	3
254	278	470	933	1,677	2,398	2,753	1,349	1,023	1,082	1,070	1,175	1,772	1,940	1,831	4
1,114	1,134	1,336	1,661	2,021	2,043	2,096	2,396	2,532	2,505	2,072	1,895	2,141	2,047	1,937	5
1,767	1,883	2,108	2,381	2,677	2,717	2,972	3,478	3,869	4,147	4,252	4,401	4,701	5,092	5,310	6
8,406	8,857	10,521	13,082	16,026	17,512	19,706	22,215	22,952	23,878	22,676	22,705	24,246	24,803	24,604	7
1,226	1,265	1,446	1,793	1,872	1,958	2,263	2,781	2,955	2,988	2,928	3,052	3,274	3,285	3,362	8
114	124	142	153	223	218	210	241	227	216	205	201	211	207	204	9
5,893	6,153	7,132	8,537	10,486	11,647	13,109	15,097	15,610	16,450	15,371	15,154	16,086	16,588	16,269	10
3,607	3,766	4,348	5,341	6,940	7,838	8,796	9,728	9,963	10,736	9,929	9,655	10,275	10,675	10,603	11
2,286	2,387	2,784	3,196	3,546	3,809	4,313	5,369	5,647	5,714	5,442	5,499	5,811	5,913	5,666	12
16	32	219	657	1,031	1,041	1,087	364	229	191	213	274	418	259	197	13
397	423	492	571	716	809	936	1,198	1,349	1,434	1,444	1,466	1,565	1,639	1,703	14
312	340	397	466	523	561	600	715	796	837	842	854	870	902	939	15
355	414	562	743	968	1,050	1,243	1,506	1,463	1,435	1,360	1,385	1,477	1,561	1,560	16
93	106	131	162	207	228	258	313	323	327	313	319	339	362	370	17
1,004	1,036	1,162	1,354	1,616	1,834	1,982	2,086	2,253	2,286	2,259	2,355	2,488	2,573	2,641	18
486	507	607	728	874	992	1,087	1,109	1,245	1,256	1,233	1,306	1,393	1,434	1,466	19
518	529	555	626	742	842	895	977	1,008	1,030	1,026	1,019	1,095	1,139	1,175	20
9,018	9,327	10,046	10,820	11,333	11,885	12,407	13,609	15,436	17,548	19,439	21,356	23,367	25,631	27,710	21
4,179	4,310	4,706	5,192	5,588	6,060	6,492	7,343	8,471	9,776	10,962	12,195	13,430	14,818	16,194	22
3,994	4,154	4,438	4,692	4,737	4,729	4,596	4,759	5,113	5,745	6,422	7,062	7,595	8,311	8,898	23
620	625	646	684	727	791	980	1,103	1,316	1,421	1,445	1,448	1,616	1,715	1,751	24
225	238	256	252	281	305	339	404	536	606	610	651	726	787	867	25
9,624	10,479	11,951	12,727	13,110	14,032	15,530	20,023	23,878	25,617	24,642	27,414	28,592	28,877	30,070	26
949	1,060	1,320	1,285	1,242	1,314	1,559	2,248	2,552	2,758	2,664	3,010	3,122	3,229	3,291	27
774	881	1,158	809	291	171	362	1,811	3,179	3,344	2,928	3,590	3,406	3,354	3,488	28
475	510	623	658	612	643	800	1,263	1,348	1,405	1,324	1,395	1,439	1,380	1,398	29
908	991	1,214	1,266	1,369	1,398	1,519	2,194	2,453	2,548	2,315	2,533	2,623	2,433	2,420	30
681	749	913	1,119	1,330	1,481	1,545	2,039	2,135	2,287	2,178	2,402	2,472	2,406	2,461	31
508	544	607	704	756	776	722	924	1,523	1,556	1,478	1,555	1,659	1,550	1,613	32
149	162	191	230	287	353	410	426	440	445	450	450	469	503	538	33
3,128	3,391	3,582	3,875	4,079	4,242	4,507	4,872	5,611	6,299	6,124	6,741	7,209	7,500	7,830	34
849	910	965	1,017	1,045	1,125	1,194	1,270	1,406	1,564	1,746	1,955	2,192	2,426	2,692	35
538	573	575	623	648	667	705	754	862	958	1,031	1,177	1,335	1,457	1,550	36
343	359	368	384	391	407	419	433	464	491	512	554	593	651	715	37
1,398	1,549	1,674	1,851	1,995	2,043	2,189	2,415	2,879	3,286	2,835	3,055	3,089	2,966	2,873	38
576	615	695	825	973	1,077	1,180	1,312	1,383	1,617	1,761	1,966	2,182	2,410	2,640	39
1,129	1,218	1,237	1,477	1,598	1,887	2,142	2,120	2,348	2,382	2,412	2,668	2,833	2,858	3,051	40
347	358	411	479	573	690	775	814	906	996	1,008	1,074	1,178	1,254	1,337	41
3,347	3,533	3,852	4,312	4,832	5,383	5,756	6,893	7,685	8,307	8,660	9,257	9,843	10,486	11,169	42
612	635	725	848	1,014	1,072	1,138	1,271	1,313	1,358	1,350	1,406	1,516	1,569	1,615	43
172	186	227	258	307	333	349	396	400	427	448	479	532	561	577	44
866	913	957	1,048	1,092	1,321	1,370	1,720	2,020	2,203	2,312	2,435	2,528	2,676	2,815	45
386	419	459	505	539	573	620	772	784	833	857	869	888	906	943	46
167	173	179	196	206	245	266	338	390	423	448	476	498	532	562	47
492	527	555	649	752	846	925	1,163	1,397	1,591	1,730	1,975	2,167	2,398	2,602	48
153	165	196	231	279	315	374	444	513	550	557	636	651	740	887	49
499	515	554	577	643	678	714	789	868	922	958	981	1,063	1,101	1,168	50
3,548	3,646	3,894	3,743	3,831	4,141	4,431	4,993	5,707	6,574	7,113	8,181	8,726	9,403	10,620	51
183	151	131	105	207	215	317	320	244	291	256	459	446	375	403	52
135	142	151	159	176	196	207	234	260	293	314	341	367	387	413	53
817	792	852	904	948	1,186	1,325	1,499	1,532	1,710	1,880	2,028	2,198	2,524	2,839	54
1,014	1,029	1,040	1,025	1,074	1,106	1,090	1,292	1,549	1,684	1,779	2,035	2,058	2,210	2,428	55
407	423	450	475	493	541	590	609	668	799	857	889	935	962	1,004	56
709	815	930	706	486	445	457	618	904	1,210	1,444	1,820	2,030	2,274	2,817	57
283	294	340	369	447	452	445	421	550	587	583	609	692	671	716	58
6,365	7,143	8,438	5,529	5,539	5,848	6,845	12,066	15,390	17,525	20,053	23,225	22,828	23,392	26,821	59
5,128	5,872	7,031	3,581	2,859	3,045	3,992	9,004	12,316	14,313	16,939	20,182	19,586	20,054	23,461	60
1,679	2,217	2,706	415	410	322	357	2,436	4,587	5,646	7,768	10,078	8,693	8,315	10,696	61
484	530	673	303	366	449	652	1,492	1,674	1,671	1,707	2,275	2,166	2,263	2,416	62
596	647	772	594	558	695	957	1,717	1,975	2,152	2,108	2,138	2,418	2,563	2,727	63
2,181	2,273	2,649	2,090	1,339	1,384	1,809	3,034	3,630	4,294	4,741	5,012	5,542	6,006	6,619	64
46	50	58	43	31	35	42	65	69	74	80	87	97	119	123	65
142	155	173	136	155	160	175	260	381	476	535	562	670	788	874	66
878	907	978	1,294	1,646	1,726	1,746	1,951	2,007	2,115	2,086	2,075	2,128	2,170	2,171	67
684	714	760	980	1,237	1,299	1,316	1,334	1,326	1,418	1,421	1,388	1,413	1,440	1,423	68
153	153	177	261	353	370	372	554	614	621	586	608	632	611	655	69
41	40	41	53	56	57	58	63	67	76	79	79	83	89	93	70
359	364	429	654	1,034	1,077	1,107	1,111	1,067	1,097	1,028	968	1,114	1,168	1,189	71
216	214	234	364	664	677	676	627	589	603	517	446	500	513	500	72
98	101	137	241	315	336	339	341	321	324	325	315	343	342	331	73
12	18	23	23	24	33	55	106	120	134	152	177	213	287	330	74
33	31	35	26	31	31	37	37	37	36	34	30	28	26	28	75
3,452	3,761	4,239	4,677	4,961	5,422	6,139	8,621	9,352	9,603	9,801	10,768	10,961	11,368	11,892	76
226	234	255	291	366	450	520	594	536	513	490	476	495	501	531	77
554	589	636	703	838	880	965	1,099	1,243	1,360	1,434	1,470	1,528	1,616	1,708	78
285	306	362	404	393	459	553	843	910	948	924	999	1,080	1,164	1,209	79
228	254	314	306	271	323	400	809	972	1,010	906	978	1,040	1,115	1,193	80
420	494	607	634	403	311	344	1,143	1,429	1,457	1,663	2,379	2,155	2,100	2,176	81
28	32	36	46	60	72	88	115	140	174	213	324	420	476	533	82
191	201	229	241	274	327	378	447	475	484	506	527	587	641	681	83
821	904	995	1,204	1,455	1,563	1,714	2,066	2,004	1,920	1,885	1,792	1,739	1,687	1,660	84
659	735	809	1,022	1,275	1,341	1,450	1,692	1,594	1,506	1,468	1,391	1,338	1,284	1,252	85
64	71	79	92	118	142	148	174	188	182	179	177	183	181	185	86
98	98	107	90	62	80	116	200	222	232	238	221	218	222	223	87
199	203	203	205	217	236	281	359	399	439	460	470	487	511	530	88
183	197	210	213	215	241	284	379	415	437	457	467	482	512	539	89
41	55	65	69	79	131	153	241	255	257	247	239	263	327	377	90
276	292	327	361	390	429	459	526	574	604	616	647	685	715	752	91

Table 30.—*Personal Consumption Expenditures, by Type of Product, 1929-38*—Continued*

[Millions of dollars]

Line		1929	1930	1931	1932	1933	1934	1935	1936	1937	1938
92	**X. Private education and research**	664	683	665	571	481	483	507	546	600	619
93	1. Higher education [22] (s.)	219	242	251	227	205	213	228	242	249	256
94	2. Elementary and secondary schools [22] (s.)	162	170	185	158	121	121	122	140	174	192
95	3. Other [23] (s.)	283	271	229	186	155	149	157	164	177	171
96	**XI. Religious and welfare activities** [24] (s.)	1,196	1,209	1,125	973	872	870	862	899	900	923
97	**XII. Foreign travel and remittances—net**	799	756	601	467	367	339	352	412	452	376
98	1. Foreign travel by United States residents (s.)	632	611	445	334	258	276	303	368	433	379
99	2. Expenditures abroad by United States Government personnel (military and civilian) (n. d. c.).	21	20	20	20	18	16	20	18	18	18
100	3. Personal cash remittances to foreign countries less personal cash remittances to the United States by foreigners (s.).	288	257	234	182	161	132	135	148	141	114
101	4. Less: expenditures in the United States by foreigners (s.)	142	132	98	69	70	85	106	122	140	135
102	**Total personal consumption expenditures**	78,952	70,968	61,333	49,306	46,392	51,894	56,289	62,616	67,259	64,641
103	**Durable commodities** (d. c.)	9,212	7,155	5,485	3,646	3,469	4,213	5,111	6,304	6,925	5,686
104	**Nondurable commodities** (n. d. c.)	37,677	34,010	28,946	22,758	22,251	26,656	29,319	32,836	35,185	33,985
105	**Services** (s.)	32,063	29,803	26,902	22,902	20,672	21,025	21,859	23,476	25,149	24,970

*Consumer durable commodities are designated (d. c.), nondurable commodities (n. d. c.), and services (s.) following group titles.

1. Expenditures for food (items 1–4) include consumer expenditures for alcoholic beverages of the following amounts in millions of dollars: 1933, $665; 1934, $2,000; 1935, $2,555; 1936, $3,175; 1937, $3,465; 1938, $3,270; 1939, $3,420; 1940, $3,600; 1941, $4,185; 1942, $5,080; 1943, $5,840; 1944, $6,775; 1945, $7,485; 1946, $8.360; 1947, $8,620; 1948, $7,930; 1949, $7,730; 1950, $7,880; 1951, $8,200; 1952, $8,725; and 1953, $8,865. Expenditures for food (items 1–4) excluding alcoholic beverages are as follows in millions of dollars: 1929, $19,535; 1930, $17,964; 1931, $14,731; 1932, $11,382; 1933 $10,859; 1934, $12,182; 1935, $13,632; 1936, $15,245; 1937, $16,414; 1938. $15,618; 1939, $15,744; 1940, $16,740; 1941, $19,448; 1942, $23,707; 1943, $27,836; 1944, $30.641; 1945, $34,116; 1946, $40,426; 1947, $45,551; 1948, $49,364; 1949, $48,755; 1950, $50,969; 1951, $58,335; 1952, $61,248; and 1953, $62,979.

2. Comprises purchases of meals and beverages from retail, service, and amusement establishments, hotels, dining and buffet cars, schools, school fraternities, institutions, clubs, and industrial lunchrooms, and also tips.

3. Includes luggage.

4. Comprises watch, clock, and jewelry repairs, dressmakers and seamstresses not in shops, costume and dress suit rental, and miscellaneous personal services related to clothing.

5. Space rent covers heating and plumbing facilities, water heaters, lighting fixtures, kitchen cabinets, linoleum, storm windows and doors, window screens, screen doors, and window blinds or shades, but excludes other furnishings, equipment, and related services—furniture, stoves and ranges, refrigerators, repairs of furniture and appliances, fuel, electricity, etc.

6. Comprises transient hotels, tourist cabins, clubs, schools, and institutions.

7. Includes refrigerators, cooking ranges, dish washers, laundry equipment, heating stoves, air conditioners, sewing machines, vacuum cleaners, and other small electric appliances.

8. The principal house furnishings included are floor coverings, bedding, picture frames, mirrors, art products, portable lamps, and clocks. Also includes writing equipment, technical equipment such as microscopes, drafting, and surveying instruments, and hand, power, and garden tools.

9. Consists mainly of textile house furnishings (except those specified in group V–4) including piece goods allocated to house furnishings use. Among other products covered are lamp shades, brooms, and brushes.

10. Comprises maintenance services for appliances and house furnishings, moving and warehouse expenses, postage and express charges, premiums for fire and theft insurance on personal property less claims paid, and miscellaneous household operation services.

11. Comprises services of osteopathic physicians, chiropractors, chiropodists and podiatrists, private duty trained nurses, and miscellaneous curative and healing professions.

12. Comprises current expenditures (including depreciation) of nonprofit hospitals and sanitariums and payments by patients to proprietary hospitals and sanitariums.

Table 31.—*New Construction Activity, by Type, 1929–38* [1]

[Millions of dollars]

Line		1929	1930	1931	1932	1933	1934	1935	1936	1937	1938
1	**Total new construction activity**	10,793	8,741	6,427	3,538	2,879	3,720	4,232	6,497	6,999	6,980
2	**New private construction activity**	8,307	5,883	3,768	1,676	1,231	1,509	1,999	2,981	3,903	3,560
3	Residential building (excluding farm)	3,625	2,075	1,565	630	470	625	1,010	1,565	1,875	1,990
4	New dwelling units	3,040	1,570	1,320	485	290	380	710	1,210	1,475	1,620
5	Additions and alterations	340	305	175	105	145	200	250	295	320	295
6	Nonhousekeeping units	245	200	70	40	35	45	50	60	80	75
7	Nonresidential building (excluding farm) [2]	2,694	2,003	1,099	502	406	456	472	713	1,085	764
8	Industrial buildings [3]	949	532	221	74	176	191	158	266	492	232
9	Warehouses, office and loft buildings [3]	619	596	276	117	44	66	75	111	137	95
10	Stores, restaurants, and garages [3]	516	297	178	106	86	107	136	179	250	190
11	Other nonresidential buildings	610	578	424	205	100	92	103	157	206	247
12	Religious	147	135	87	45	22	21	28	34	44	51
13	Educational	120	118	100	53	15	14	17	40	42	40
14	Hospital and institutional	104	109	71	34	10	9	10	17	31	35
15	Social and recreational	173	148	123	60	34	33	34	54	73	97
16	Miscellaneous	66	68	43	13	19	15	14	12	16	24
17	Public utility	1,578	1,527	946	467	261	326	363	518	705	605
18	Railroads	510	521	292	139	94	128	116	149	199	119
19	Telephone and telegraph	354	333	166	87	45	47	52	67	102	92
20	Other public utility [4]	714	673	488	241	122	151	195	302	404	394
21	Farm construction	307	193	97	37	49	66	126	161	207	171
22	Residential	147	107	59	24	29	36	61	76	100	79
23	Nonresidential	160	86	38	13	20	30	65	85	107	92
24	All other private [5]	103	85	61	40	45	36	28	24	31	30
25	**New public construction activity**	2,486	2,858	2,659	1,862	1,648	2,211	2,233	3,516	3,096	3,420
26	Residential building	----	----	----	----	----	1	9	61	93	35
27	Nonresidential building	659	660	612	415	230	363	328	701	550	672
28	Industrial	----	----	----	----	2	11	2	4	2	12
29	Educational	389	364	285	130	52	148	153	366	253	311
30	Hospital and institutional	101	118	110	83	49	51	38	74	73	97
31	Other nonresidential building [6]	169	178	217	202	127	153	135	257	222	252
32	Military facilities	19	29	40	34	36	47	37	29	37	62
33	Highway	1,266	1,516	1,355	958	847	1,000	845	1,362	1,226	1,421
34	Sewer and water	253	343	270	156	95	173	175	342	311	355
35	Miscellaneous public service enterprises	151	157	209	135	65	55	71	167	134	137
36	Conservation and development	115	137	156	150	359	518	700	658	605	551
37	All other public [7]	23	16	17	14	16	54	68	196	140	187
38	**Petroleum and natural gas well drilling**	(8)	(8)	(8)	(8)	(8)	(8)	(8)	(8)	(8)	(8)

1. These construction data are published by the Building Materials and Construction Division of the Department of Commerce. For an explanation of the differences between the series shown in this table and the new construction series in the other tables of this report, see the first paragraph of section 9 on New construction in Part III.

2. Excludes nonresidential building by privately owned public utilities.

3. Public industrial and commercial building not segregable from private construction, 1929–32; amount believed negligible.

4. Consists of local transit, petroleum pipeline, electric light and power (including construction with Rural Electrification Administration funds), and manufactured and natural gas.

Table 30.—*Personal Consumption Expenditures, by Type of Product, 1939–53*—Continued*

[Millions of dollars]

1939	1940	1941	1942	1943	1944	1945	1946	1947	1948	1949	1950	1951	1952	1953	Line
628	641	702	813	957	972	974	1,162	1,411	1,589	1,789	1,959	2,139	2,319	2,476	92
267	280	288	312	366	404	415	501	649	715	787	822	876	935	999	93
195	198	208	221	239	266	299	350	420	495	584	681	758	812	853	94
166	163	206	280	352	302	260	311	342	379	418	456	505	572	624	95
938	1,012	1,060	1,207	1,428	1,667	1,735	1,915	2,032	2,256	2,294	2,463	2,607	2,855	2,964	96
317	223	269	316	555	1,004	1,621	770	837	985	1,135	1,093	1,315	1,652	1,969	97
333	172	189	128	143	175	267	450	597	696	828	893	889	1,014	1,144	98
20	27	77	251	417	822	1,394	388	450	417	501	444	705	960	1,157	99
108	129	97	59	135	176	163	234	169	216	195	187	197	208	229	100
144	105	94	122	140	169	203	302	379	344	389	431	476	560	571	101
67,578	71,881	81,875	89,748	100,541	109,833	121,699	146,617	164,973	177,609	180,598	194,026	208,342	218,424	230,060	102
6,670	7,771	9,659	6,968	6,605	6,764	8,105	15,892	20,593	22,214	23,573	28,608	27,148	26,815	29,749	103
35,131	37,215	43,208	51,324	59,259	65,368	73,222	84,501	93,077	98,741	96,879	100,386	111,054	116,012	118,925	104
25,777	26,895	29,008	31,456	34,677	37,701	40,372	46,224	51,303	56 654	60,146	65,082	70,140	75,597	81,406	105

13. Premiums less claims: accident and health insurance, mutual accident and sick benefit associations, and group hospitalization associations. Also covers administrative and medical expenses of group health associations and student fees for medical care.

14. Comprises total operating expenses of life insurance companies and fraternal and assessment associations, excluding payments to policyholders and expenses allocated to accident and health insurance.

15. Comprises total payments to labor unions minus cash benefits, employment agency fees, employees' payments to professional associations, miners' expenditures (for explosives, lamps, and smithing), money order fees, classified advertisements, net purchases from pawnbrokers and miscellaneous second-hand stores, and other personal business services.

16. Comprises baggage charges and coastal and inland waterway and ferry foot passenger fares.

17. Groups IX-3 and IX-4 include games, toys, sporting, athletic, and photographic goods, and related products. These commodities are divided roughly between the two groups on the basis of durability.

18. Comprises professional baseball, football, and hockey, horse and dog race tracks, college football, and other amateur spectator sports.

19. Comprises gross receipts less cash benefits of fraternal, patriotic, and women's organizations except insurance; and dues and fees of athletic, social, and luncheon clubs, and school fraternities.

20. Comprises billiard parlors, bowling alleys, dancing, riding, shooting, skating, and swimming places, amusement devices and parks, daily fee golf course greens fees, golf instruction, club rental, and caddy fees, sightseeing buses and guides, and private flying operations.

21. Comprises photo developing and printing, photographic studies, collectors' net acquisitions of stamps and coins, hunting dog purchase and training, sports guide service, veterinary service, purchase of pets, camp fees, nonvending coin machine receipts minus payoff, and other commercial amusements.

22. The estimates represent current expenditures (including depreciation) net of receipts accounted for separately in consumer expenditures, such as receipts from meals, rooms, and entertainments.

23. Comprises fees paid to commercial, business, trade, and correspondence schools; fees for musical, dancing, and other instruction except athletics; and current expenditures (including depreciation) of foundations for education and research.

24. Comprises religious bodies, social welfare and foreign relief agencies, political organizations, museums and libraries, and foundations (except foundation expenditures for education and research). The estimates represent current expenditures (including depreciation but excluding relief payments within the United States), and are net of receipts accounted for separately in consumer expenditures, such as receipts from meals, rooms, and entertainments.

Table 31.—*New Construction Activity, by Type, 1939–53* [1]

[Millions of dollars]

1939	1940	1941	1942	1943	1944	1945	1946	1947	1948	1949	1950	1951	1952	1953	Line
8,198	8,682	11,957	14,075	8,301	5,259	5,633	12,000	16,689	21,678	22,789	28,454	31,182	33,008	35,256	1
4,389	5,054	6,206	3,415	1,979	2,186	3,235	9,638	13,256	16,853	16,384	21,454	21,764	22,107	23,877	2
2,680	2,985	3,510	1,715	885	815	1,100	4,015	6,310	8,580	8,267	12,600	10.973	11,100	11,930	3
2,270	2,560	3,040	1,440	710	570	720	3,300	5,450	7,500	7,257	11,525	9,819	9,870	10.555	4
320	335	375	225	160	220	340	570	735	925	825	900	934	1,015	1,108	5
90	90	95	50	15	25	40	145	125	155	185	175	190	185	267	6
786	1,025	1,482	635	233	351	1,020	3,341	3,142	3,621	3,228	3,777	5,152	5,014	5,680	7
254	442	801	346	156	208	642	1,689	1,702	1,397	972	1,062	2,117	2,320	2,229	8
81	91	123	62	14	17	56	331	237	352	321	402	544	515	739	9
211	257	286	93	19	39	147	801	619	901	706	886	827	622	1,052	10
240	235	272	134	44	87	175	520	584	971	1,229	1,427	1,661	1,557	1,660	11
48	59	62	31	6	11	26	76	126	251	360	409	452	399	472	12
39	50	58	24	6	11	31	123	174	253	269	294	345	351	426	13
31	33	46	29	11	26	37	85	110	126	202	344	419	394	317	14
100	67	72	30	7	17	27	125	99	224	262	247	164	125	163	15
22	26	34	20	14	22	54	111	75	117	136	133	284	288	282	16
683	771	872	786	570	725	827	1,874	2,338	3,043	3,323	3,330	3,729	4,003	4,416	17
137	167	187	197	211	247	264	258	318	379	352	315	399	438	442	18
93	122	179	155	61	83	117	305	510	713	533	440	487	570	615	19
453	482	506	434	298	395	446	811	1,510	1,951	2,438	2,575	2,843	2,995	3,359	20
212	240	310	260	284	283	267	856	1,397	1,644	1,488	1,635	1,846	1,905	1,731	21
106	145	182	135	121	108	100	409	683	738	695	763	863	890	809	22
106	95	128	125	163	175	167	447	714	806	793	872	983	1,015	922	23
28	33	32	19	7	12	21	52	69	65	78	112	64	85	120	24
3,809	3,628	5,751	10,660	6,322	3,073	2,398	2,362	3,433	4,825	6,405	7,000	9,418	10,901	11,379	25
65	200	430	545	739	211	80	374	200	156	359	345	595	654	556	26
970	615	1,646	3,685	2,010	1,361	937	354	599	1,301	2,068	2,384	3,497	4,136	4,352	27
23	164	1,280	3,437	1,870	1,230	755	113	96	196	177	224	974	1,681	1,771	28
468	156	158	128	63	41	59	101	287	618	934	1,133	1,513	1,619	1,728	29
127	54	42	35	44	58	85	85	85	223	477	496	528	473	353	30
352	241	166	85	33	32	38	55	131	264	480	531	482	360	500	31
125	385	1,620	5,016	2,550	837	690	188	204	158	137	177	887	1,388	1,307	32
1,381	1,302	1,066	734	446	362	398	895	1,451	1,774	2,131	2,272	2,518	2,820	3,165	33
371	338	252	169	107	79	97	194	351	535	619	659	775	790	861	34
136	131	141	85	49	46	55	99	164	185	203	185	213	193	201	35
570	528	500	357	285	163	130	240	394	629	793	881	853	851	830	36
191	129	96	69	136	14	11	18	70	87	95	97	80	66	107	37
368	398	423	306	347	526	598	653	773	1,051	1,069	1,279	1,568	1,616	1,659	38

5. Consists of sewer and water, roads, bridges, and miscellaneous nonstructural items such as parks and playgrounds.

6. Consists of public administration, social and recreational, commercial, and miscellaneous nonresidential.

7. Includes publicly owned parks and playgrounds, memorials, etc. Includes petroleum pipelines as follows: $25 million in 1942, $125 million in 1943, and $4 million in 1944.

8. Estimates for this item by the Building Materials and Construction Division for the years 1929–38 are not available. Rough approximations, in billions of dollars, are as follows: 1929, $0.4; 1930, $0.3; 1931, $0.2; 1932, $0.2; 1933, $0.2; 1934, $0.2; 1935, $0.3; 1936, $0.3; 1937, $0.5; 1938, $0.4.

Table 32.—*Private Purchases of Producers' Durable Equipment, 1929–38*

[Millions of dollars]

Line		1929	1930	1931	1932	1933	1934	1935	1936	1937	1938
1	**Total producers' durable equipment**	**5,850**	**4,465**	**2,839**	**1,593**	**1,589**	**2,304**	**3,066**	**4,169**	**5,095**	**3,644**
2	Furniture and fixtures	361	292	193	113	98	141	154	181	236	197
3	Cutlery and hand tools	94	73	49	32	35	46	54	63	77	60
4	Fabricated metal products (except cutlery and hand tools)	190	160	114	81	76	101	106	122	153	120
5	Engines and turbines	54	45	26	12	10	17	25	43	64	44
6	Tractors	186	174	112	56	30	69	131	208	270	204
7	Agricultural machinery (except tractors)	265	252	114	62	49	71	136	176	229	229
8	Construction machinery	90	71	41	7	7	17	31	54	72	62
9	Mining and oilfield machinery	143	87	41	30	33	51	77	117	119	79
10	Metalworking machinery	270	171	101	41	45	86	147	220	301	172
11	Special-industry machinery, n. e. c.	407	288	210	133	151	186	227	309	368	276
12	General industrial machinery	440	314	225	134	130	173	240	335	400	292
13	Office and store machines	201	144	104	73	72	88	115	140	172	143
14	Service-industry and household machines	186	147	117	65	61	74	92	134	168	127
15	Electrical machinery	443	339	230	108	80	132	193	246	396	263
16	Trucks, buses, and trailers	590	423	291	155	186	307	388	508	523	360
17	Passenger cars	1,105	701	488	271	331	436	643	822	849	524
18	Aircraft	41	17	9	1	8	15	8	7	19	15
19	Ships and boats	75	109	83	18	12	21	9	57	65	122
20	Railroad equipment	374	374	82	45	22	101	97	196	356	142
21	Instruments	81	69	51	34	29	32	41	51	75	57
22	Miscellaneous equipment	254	215	158	122	124	140	152	180	183	156

Table 33.—*Net Change in Business Inventories, 1929–38*

[Millions of dollars]

Line		1929	1930	1931	1932	1933	1934	1935	1936	1937	1938
1	**Net change in business inventories, total**	**1,674**	**−383**	**−1,234**	**−2,556**	**−1,629**	**−1,125**	**912**	**954**	**2,249**	**−943**
2	Farm	−162	−300	324	34	−259	−1,320	536	−1,112	523	103
3	Nonfarm	1,836	−83	−1,608	−2,590	−1,370	195	376	2,066	1,726	−1,046
4	**Net change in nonfarm inventories**	**1,836**	**−83**	**−1,608**	**−2,590**	**−1,370**	**195**	**376**	**2,066**	**1,726**	**−1,046**
5	Corporate	1,558	191	−1,149	−1,816	−871	182	217	1,589	1,520	−920
6	Noncorporate	278	−274	−459	−774	−499	13	159	477	206	−126
7	Change in book value	1,222	−4,098	−4,633	−3,932	1,298	874	653	2,924	1,786	−2,230
8	Corporate	1,086	−3,069	−3,563	−2,863	1,272	807	444	2,327	1,551	−1,883
9	Noncorporate	136	−1,029	−1,070	−1,069	26	67	209	597	235	−347
10	Inventory valuation adjustment	614	4,015	3,025	1,342	−2,668	−679	−277	−858	−60	1,184
11	Corporate	472	3,260	2,414	1,047	−2,143	−625	−227	−738	−31	963
12	Noncorporate	142	755	611	295	−525	−54	−50	−120	−29	221
13	**Net change in nonfarm inventories by industrial group**	**1,836**	**−83**	**−1,608**	**−2,590**	**−1,370**	**195**	**376**	**2,066**	**1,726**	**−1,046**
14	Manufacturing	911	747	−594	−1,155	−578	136	213	1,095	1,344	−631
15	Change in book value	598	−1,553	−2,239	−1,846	828	598	381	1,586	1,340	−1,268
16	Inventory valuation adjustment	313	2,300	1,645	691	−1,406	−462	−168	−491	4	637
17	Wholesale trade	31	54	−413	−175	−89	66	1	286	210	−198
18	Change in book value	−74	−527	−832	−358	268	226	9	487	70	−403
19	Inventory valuation adjustment	105	581	419	183	−357	−160	−8	−201	140	205
20	Retail trade	250	−457	−316	−695	−488	−48	297	668	53	−164
21	Change in book value	77	−1,314	−1,087	−1,078	220	−17	378	796	198	−467
22	Inventory valuation adjustment	173	857	771	383	−708	−31	−81	−128	−145	303
23	All other	644	−427	−285	−565	−215	41	−135	17	119	−53
24	Change in book value	621	−704	−475	−650	−18	67	−115	55	178	−92
25	Inventory valuation adjustment	23	277	190	85	−197	−26	−20	−38	−59	39

Table 32.—*Private Purchases of Producers' Durable Equipment, 1939–52*

[Millions of dollars]

1939	1940	1941	1942	1943	1944	1945	1946	1947	1948	1949	1950	1951	1952	Line
4,180	**5,531**	**6,942**	**4,343**	**4,027**	**5,438**	**7,654**	**10,733**	**16,667**	**19,110**	**17,833**	**21,135**	**23,177**	**23,307**	1
210	252	332	248	200	213	287	500	690	639	551	704	878	855	2
70	99	147	97	128	181	161	353	348	373	341	375	433	381	3
144	151	166	144	191	238	298	317	506	510	414	463	533	505	4
54	62	56	26	47	91	193	52	148	215	198	255	280	268	5
195	240	341	189	84	303	324	298	544	757	854	913	1,096	976	6
183	209	309	280	180	349	414	351	676	985	1,075	1,077	1,210	1,161	7
57	80	88	74	66	38	273	323	408	503	343	511	576	640	8
90	119	215	117	112	164	293	301	352	567	485	544	735	792	9
240	531	744	701	699	606	704	779	834	776	610	875	1,107	1,393	10
297	335	356	297	232	360	529	837	1,340	1,453	1,189	1,403	1,667	1,574	11
322	344	367	249	290	504	738	863	1,170	1,300	1,069	1,162	1,531	1,585	12
149	173	215	167	119	174	229	443	588	648	565	634	663	750	13
143	162	179	150	174	245	345	456	873	1,276	891	941	831	926	14
328	493	549	359	325	672	776	1,129	2,061	1,968	1,730	2,104	2,[illegible]97	2,865	15
489	562	737	126	140	343	901	1,376	2,283	2,613	2,138	2,861	2,825	2,629	16
715	948	1,158	251	253	167	172	995	1,889	2,316	3,269	4,237	3,613	3,399	17
23	39	35	6	0	0	12	156	145	75	103	63	86	167	18
57	133	185	197	232	130	195	174	236	123	108	111	168	192	19
170	313	408	394	268	346	331	359	631	1,004	1,030	796	1,075	935	20
71	61	59	32	67	69	179	226	335	355	315	389	517	588	21
173	225	296	239	220	245	300	445	610	654	555	717	753	726	22

Table 33.—*Net Change in Business Inventories, 1939–53*

[Millions of dollars]

1939	1940	1941	1942	1943	1944	1945	1946	1947	1948	1949	1950	1951	1952	1953	Line
372	**2,172**	**4,501**	**1,811**	**−753**	**−1,020**	**−1,057**	**6,101**	**−991**	**4,162**	**−2,737**	**7,351**	**10,355**	**3,625**	**1,494**	1
56	270	452	1,159	−176	−445	−462	−249	−2,289	1,136	−875	923	1,404	654	−675	2
316	1,902	4,049	652	−577	−575	−595	6,350	1,298	3,026	−1,862	6,428	8,951	2,971	2,169	3
316	**1,902**	**4,049**	**652**	**−577**	**−575**	**−595**	**6,350**	**1,298**	**3,026**	**−1,862**	**6,428**	**8,951**	**2,971**	**2,169**	4
251	1,586	3,318	470	−458	−1,070	−1,027	5,967	1,240	2,055	−1,635	4.924	8,080	2,781	1,621	5
65	316	731	182	−119	495	432	383	58	971	−227	1,504	871	190	548	6
1,196	2,147	7,135	2,223	352	−219	75	13,318	8,668	5,588	−4,273	12,426	10.555	1,782	3,328	7
965	1,786	5,789	1,674	315	−783	−463	11,230	7,139	4,205	−3,578	9,788	9.310	1,800	2,585	8
231	361	1,346	549	37	564	538	2,088	1,529	1,383	−695	2,638	1,215	−18	743	9
−880	−245	−3,086	−1,571	−929	−356	−670	−6,968	−7,370	−2,562	2,411	−5,998	−1,604	1,189	−1,159	10
−714	−200	−2,471	−1,204	−773	−287	−564	−5,263	−5,899	−2,150	1,943	−4,864	−1,260	981	−964	11
−166	−45	−615	−367	−156	−69	−106	−1,705	−1,471	−412	468	−1,134	−314	208	−195	12
316	**1,902**	**4,049**	**652**	**−577**	**−575**	**−595**	**6,350**	**1,298**	**3,026**	**−1,862**	**6,428**	**8,951**	**2,971**	**2,169**	13
214	1,218	2,567	1,553	244	−814	−1,556	2,901	450	1,274	−1,494	2,265	7.400	2,024	1,699	14
713	1,357	4,151	2,324	823	−593	−1,121	6,163	4,412	2,750	−2,744	5,496	8,066	1,359	2,324	15
−499	−139	−1,584	−771	−579	−221	−435	−3,262	−3,962	−1,476	1,250	−3,231	−666	665	−625	16
77	183	221	−554	−234	202	560	815	−21	566	4	1,356	308	721	451	17
236	173	846	−279	−66	233	665	2,081	1,084	706	−401	2,458	604	391	594	18
−159	10	−625	−275	−168	−31	−105	−1,266	−1,105	−140	405	−1,102	−296	330	−143	19
97	482	851	−411	−462	−58	272	2,048	603	1,229	−147	2,404	336	187	−1	20
291	563	1,633	87	−316	17	358	4,094	2,249	1,777	−690	3,653	836	−45	264	21
−194	−81	−782	−498	−146	−75	−86	−2,046	−1,646	−548	543	−1,249	−500	232	−265	22
−72	19	410	64	−125	95	129	586	266	−43	−225	403	907	39	20	23
−44	54	505	91	−89	124	173	990	923	355	−438	819	1,019	77	146	24
−28	−35	−95	−27	−36	−29	−44	−394	−657	−398	213	−416	−142	−38	−126	25

Table 36.—*Transfer Payments, 1929–38*

[Millions of dollars]

Line		1929	1930	1931	1932	1933	1934	1935	1936	1937	1938
1	**Total transfer payments**	1,496	1,533	2,714	2,170	2,116	2,194	2,400	3,520	2,418	2,834
2	**Federal Government**	691	735	1,716	931	698	600	634	2,064	828	1,196
3	Benefits from social insurance funds	44	51	60	72	82	94	93	95	142	606
4	Old-age and survivors insurance benefits	----	----	----	----	----	----	----	*	1	10
5	State unemployment insurance benefits	----	----	----	----	----	----	----	----	2	393
6	Railroad retirement insurance benefits	----	----	----	----	----	----	----	1	40	98
7	Railroad unemployment insurance benefits	----	----	----	----	----	----	----	----	----	----
8	Federal civilian pensions	18	22	27	32	42	52	57	60	63	65
9	Government life insurance benefits	26	29	33	40	40	42	36	34	36	40
10	Direct relief [1]	----	----	----	----	----	----	2	20	36	23
11	Military pension, disability, and retirement payments	443	468	548	571	456	382	418	433	434	446
12	Adjusted compensation benefits [2]	93	106	996	170	58	28	29	1,430	134	59
13	Mustering-out payments to discharged servicemen and terminal-leave benefits.	----	----	----	----	----	----	----	----	----	----
14	Readjustment, self-employment, and subsistence allowances to veterans.	----	----	----	----	----	----	----	----	[6]	----
15	Other [3]	111	110	112	118	102	96	92	86	82	62
16	**State and local government**	218	264	349	502	759	953	1,172	862	1,023	1,209
17	Benefits from social insurance funds	72	78	86	95	110	119	127	137	144	151
18	Government pensions	72	78	86	95	110	119	127	137	144	151
19	Cash sickness compensation	----	----	----	----	----	----	----	----	----	----
20	Direct relief	71	105	176	317	558	745	954	635	787	965
21	Special types of public assistance	71	105	176	317	72	80	115	218	397	509
22	General assistance					486	665	839	417	390	456
23	Other [4]	75	81	87	90	91	89	91	90	92	93
24	**Business**	587	534	649	737	659	641	594	594	567	429
25	Corporate gifts to nonprofit institutions	32	35	40	31	27	27	28	30	33	27
26	Consumer bad debts	452	390	497	598	530	508	458	461	428	296
27	Other [5]	103	109	112	108	102	106	108	103	106	106

1. Consists of Farm Security Administration grants and the value of free stamps issued under the surplus food and cotton stamp programs.

2. Covers benefits under the World War Veterans Adjusted Compensation Act of May 19, 1924, as amended, and under the Adjusted Compensation Payment Act of Jan. 27, 1936. For the period 1929 through May 1936 this series represents very largely net loans to veterans on the security of their adjusted service certificates from the U. S. Government Life Insurance Fund and the Adjusted Service Certificate Fund; for the period since June 1936 it consists almost entirely of cash redemptions by veterans of their adjusted service bonds. Additionally, the series includes (1) payments to beneficiaries on certificates matured by death of veterans; (2) "adjusted service dependent pay", which comprises cash payments (negligible in amount) to veterans and their beneficiaries where, under certain circumstances, no certificates were issued; (3) payments to veterans in settlement of adjusted service certificates not

Table 36.—*Transfer Payments, 1939–53*

[Millions of dollars]

1939	1940	1941	1942	1943	1944	1945	1946	1947	1948	1949	1950	1951	1952	1953	Line
2,963	3,114	3,113	3,143	2,954	3,588	6,165	11,411	11,787	11,281	12,403	15,147	12,575	13,090	13,801	1
1,240	1,421	1,369	1,419	1,239	1,841	4,310	9,214	8,887	7,652	8,754	10,884	8,663	8,940	9,660	2
696	835	707	747	538	655	1,322	2,348	2,123	2,226	3,492	6,100	4,352	4,791	5,607	3
14	35	88	130	165	209	273	378	463	552	664	954	1,872	2,178	2,979	4
429	518	344	344	80	62	446	1,094	775	790	1,730	1,367	837	992	951	5
110	118	124	128	132	137	146	159	212	283	320	337	345	476	515	6
6	16	14	6	1	1	2	40	39	28	103	60	20	42	46	7
68	73	78	83	93	130	183	349	282	220	242	273	288	328	395	8
69	75	59	56	67	116	272	328	352	353	433	3,109	990	775	718	9
22	63	137	108	9											10
462	476	474	476	491	649	1,013	1,623	2,181	2,297	2,402	2,478	2,431	2,553	2,720	11
36	28	19	10	6	7	189	18	6	3	2	2	1	0	1	12
					230	1,404	2,131	1,577	431	167	116	153	455	352	13
					5	142	2,780	2,605	2,284	2,280	1,708	1,222	652	499	14
24	19	32	78	195	295	240	244	395	411	411	480	504	489	481	15
1,272	1,262	1,242	1,229	1,220	1,241	1,323	1,640	2,226	2,890	2,868	3,420	2,927	3,151	3,125	16
157	163	175	194	213	223	240	260	297	326	356	398	466	542	610	17
157	163	175	194	210	218	235	255	275	300	325	360	430	500	560	18
				3	5	5	5	22	26	31	38	36	42	50	19
1,024	1,013	985	956	929	939	986	1,177	1,478	1,727	2,169	2,345	2,267	2,297	2,357	20
566	630	718	778	818	850	900	1,057	1,314	1,529	1,889	2,055	2,075	2,129	2,207	21
458	383	267	178	111	89	86	120	164	198	280	290	192	168	150	22
91	86	82	79	78	79	97	203	451	837	343	677	194	312	158	23
451	431	502	455	505	506	532	557	674	739	781	843	985	999	1,016	24
31	38	58	98	159	234	266	214	241	239	223	253	343	343	343	25
316	287	332	283	246	165	150	193	258	298	353	328	328	328	328	26
104	106	112	114	100	107	116	150	175	202	205	262	314	328	345	27

covered by issuance of bonds; and (4) payments to veterans holding certificates to maturity.

3 Consists of military and naval insurance payments, payments to nonprofit institutions, profits of military post exchanges and navy exchanges and ships' stores, payments under the Panama Canal Construction Annuity Act, enemy alien and civilian war assistance, payments to United States military and civilian prisoners of war, and Atomic Energy Commission fellowships.

4. Consists of veterans' aid and bonuses, payments for the care of foster children in private family homes, and payments to nonprofit institutions.

5. Consists of cash prizes, unrecovered thefts from business of cash and capital assets, and personal-injury payments from business other than to employees.

Table 40.—*Gross National Product or Expenditure in Constant Dollars, 1929–38* [1]

[Billions of 1947 dollars]

Line		1929	1930	1931	1932	1933	1934	1935	1936	1937	1938
1	**Gross national product**	**149.3**	**135.2**	**126.6**	**107.6**	**103.7**	**113.4**	**127.8**	**142.5**	**153.5**	**145.9**
2	**Personal consumption expenditures**	**107.3**	**100.9**	**98.0**	**88.9**	**86.6**	**91.5**	**97.3**	**107.6**	**111.5**	**109.8**
3	Durable goods	13.0	10.5	9.1	6.9	6.7	7.6	9.4	11.6	12.2	10.0
4	Nondurable goods	58.1	55.2	55.0	50.7	49.2	52.5	55.4	61.8	63.8	64.9
5	Services	36.2	35.2	33.9	31.4	30.8	31.4	32.5	34.3	35.5	34.9
6	**Gross private domestic investment**	**26.8**	**17.9**	**12.0**	**3.3**	**2.1**	**4.3**	**13.6**	**15.2**	**22.5**	**12.1**
7	New construction	16.1	11.8	8.3	4.6	3.5	3.9	5.2	7.3	8.7	7.8
8	Residential nonfarm	6.9	4.0	3.4	1.7	1.3	1.5	2.5	3.6	3.9	4.0
9	Other	9.3	7.8	5.0	2.9	2.3	2.4	2.7	3.7	4.8	3.8
10	Producers' durable equipment	8.5	6.8	4.6	2.7	2.9	3.9	5.2	7.1	8.1	5.6
11	Change in business inventories	2.1	–.7	–.9	–4.1	–4.2	–3.5	3.2	.9	5.7	–1.2
12	Nonfarm	2.6	–.2	–3.0	–5.1	–3.0	.3	.7	3.7	3.0	–1.8
13	Farm	–.4	–.6	2.1	1.1	–1.3	–3.9	2.6	–2.8	2.8	.6
14	**Net foreign investment**	**1.6**	**1.2**	**.6**	**.3**	**.1**	**.5**	**–.5**	**–.7**	**–.2**	**1.9**
15	**Government purchases of goods and services**	**13.6**	**15.1**	**15.9**	**15.1**	**14.9**	**17.2**	**17.4**	**20.3**	**19.7**	**22.1**
16	Federal	2.3	2.7	2.9	3.0	4.3	5.7	5.4	8.3	7.8	9.6
17	State and local	11.2	12.5	13.0	12.1	10.6	11.6	11.9	12.0	11.8	12.5
18	**Gross government product** [2]	**7.0**	**7.4**	**7.5**	**7.4**	**8.1**	**9.5**	**10.2**	**12.2**	**11.3**	**12.3**
19	**Other gross product** [3]	**142.3**	**127.8**	**119.1**	**100.3**	**95.6**	**103.9**	**117.6**	**130.3**	**142.1**	**133.6**

1. Detail will not necessarily add to totals because of rounding.
2. Compensation of general government employees.
3. Gross national product less compensation of general government employees; i. e., gross product accruing from domestic business, households, and institutions, and from the rest of the world.

Table 41.—*Implicit Price Deflators for Gross National Product by Major Segments, 1929–38*

[Index numbers, 1947=100]

Line		1929	1930	1931	1932	1933	1934	1935	1936	1937	1938
1	**Gross national product**	**70.0**	**67.4**	**60.3**	**54.3**	**54.0**	**57.3**	**56.7**	**58.1**	**59.2**	**58.4**
2	**Personal consumption expenditures**	**73.6**	**70.3**	**62.6**	**55.4**	**53.6**	**56.7**	**57.8**	**58.2**	**60.3**	**58.9**
3	Durable goods	70.7	67.9	60.6	53.0	52.0	55.4	54.5	54.5	56.9	57.0
4	Nondurable goods	64.8	61.6	52.6	44.9	45.3	50.8	52.9	53.2	55.1	52.3
5	Services	88.6	84.8	79.3	73.0	67.2	66.9	67.2	68.4	70.8	71.6
6	**Gross private domestic investment**	----	----	----	----	----	----	----	----	----	----
7	New construction	53.9	52.2	47.7	40.8	40.6	43.4	44.2	45.0	50.4	50.7
8	Residential nonfarm	52.6	51.3	46.7	37.7	37.5	41.7	41.1	43.2	47.6	49.2
9	Other	54.9	52.6	48.4	42.5	42.4	44.4	47.0	46.8	52.8	52.3
10	Producers' durable equipment	68.5	65.8	62.3	58.8	55.7	59.3	59.1	59.0	63.3	65.4
11	Change in business inventories	----	----	----	----	----	----	----	----	----	----
12	**Net foreign investment**	----	----	----	----	----	----	----	----	----	----
13	**Government purchases of goods and services**	**62.4**	**60.7**	**57.9**	**53.4**	**54.0**	**56.7**	**57.5**	**58.3**	**59.6**	**57.9**
14	Federal	56.0	52.8	53.2	48.9	47.3	52.9	53.8	58.3	58.0	55.1
15	State and local	63.8	62.4	58.9	54.5	56.7	58.6	59.2	58.4	60.6	60.1
16	**Gross government product** [1]	**61.5**	**61.3**	**62.0**	**60.5**	**58.3**	**58.7**	**58.3**	**59.7**	**61.0**	**61.8**
17	**Other gross product** [2]	**70.4**	**67.7**	**60.2**	**53.9**	**53.6**	**57.2**	**56.6**	**57.9**	**59.0**	**58.1**

1. Compensation of general government employees.
2. Gross national product less compensation of general government employees; i. e., gross product accruing from domestic business, households, and institutions, and from the rest of the world.

Table 40.—*Gross National Product or Expenditure in Constant Dollars, 1939–53* [1]

[Billions of 1947 dollars]

1939	1940	1941	1942	1943	1944	1945	1946	1947	1948	1949	1950	1951	1952	1953	Line
157.5	**171.6**	**198.2**	**223.6**	**248.9**	**268.2**	**263.1**	**233.8**	**232.2**	**243.9**	**241.5**	**264.7**	**282.9**	**294.2**	**306.6**	1
116.3	**122.5**	**130.9**	**128.1**	**131.4**	**135.9**	**145.2**	**162.4**	**165.0**	**168.0**	**172.3**	**182.8**	**183.6**	**189.2**	**196.7**	2
11.8	13.5	15.6	10.1	8.7	7.9	8.9	17.2	20.6	21.3	22.4	27.2	24.2	23.8	26.5	3
68.5	71.6	76.4	78.0	80.8	84.3	90.6	95.4	93.1	93.3	94.7	97.2	99.0	102.4	105.2	4
36.0	37.4	38.9	40.1	42.0	43.7	45.6	49.8	51.3	53.5	55.2	58.4	60.4	63.0	65.0	5
16.8	**22.8**	**28.9**	**14.7**	**7.4**	**9.2**	**13.0**	**32.4**	**29.7**	**38.8**	**28.1**	**45.3**	**45.2**	**39.9**	**39.3**	6
9.4	10.6	11.8	6.0	3.4	3.6	5.0	12.3	14.0	16.1	15.8	20.0	19.0	18.9	19.9	7
5.4	5.8	6.2	2.9	1.4	1.1	1.4	4.8	6.3	7.7	7.6	11.1	9.0	8.9	9.4	8
4.0	4.8	5.6	3.2	2.0	2.5	3.6	7.5	7.7	8.4	8.2	8.9	10.0	10.0	10.5	9
6.5	8.4	9.8	5.7	5.2	6.9	9.7	12.3	16.7	17.7	15.7	18.3	18.4	18.3	18.8	10
.8	3.9	7.3	3.0	−1.2	−1.3	−1.6	7.8	−1.0	5.1	−3.5	7.0	7.8	2.8	.6	11
.5	3.1	6.0	.6	−.8	−.8	−.7	7.7	1.3	2.8	−1.7	6.0	7.1	2.4	1.7	12
.3	.8	1.2	2.4	−.3	−.6	−.9	.0	−2.3	2.3	−1.8	1.0	.6	.4	−1.1	13
1.6	**2.2**	**1.1**	**−1.1**	**−4.1**	**−4.0**	**−2.9**	**5.0**	**8.9**	**2.1**	**.8**	**−1.1**	**2.3**	**1.6**	**−.3**	14
22.8	**24.1**	**37.3**	**81.8**	**114.2**	**127.1**	**107.8**	**34.0**	**28.6**	**34.9**	**40.3**	**37.7**	**51.8**	**63.5**	**70.8**	15
9.0	11.0	25.1	70.8	104.3	117.4	97.9	22.7	15.8	20.8	24.3	20.5	34.2	45.7	52.1	16
13.8	13.0	12.2	11.0	9.9	9.7	9.9	11.2	12.8	14.0	16.0	17.3	17.5	17.8	13.7	17
12.4	**13.0**	**16.5**	**24.8**	**39.9**	**46.2**	**45.1**	**22.6**	**16.7**	**16.6**	**17.4**	**18.1**	**23.0**	**24.9**	**24.7**	18
145.0	**158.6**	**181.7**	**198.7**	**209.0**	**222.0**	**218.0**	**211.2**	**215.6**	**227.3**	**224.0**	**246.6**	**259.9**	**269.3**	**281.9**	19

Table 41.—*Implicit Price Deflators for Gross National Product by Major Segments, 1939–53*

[Index numbers, 1947=100]

1939	1940	1941	1942	1943	1944	1945	1946	1947	1948	1949	1950	1951	1952	1953	Line
57.9	**58.6**	**63.5**	**71.2**	**77.3**	**78.8**	**81.2**	**89.5**	**100.0**	**105.5**	**106.6**	**107.7**	**116.0**	**117.6**	**119.0**	1
58.1	**58.7**	**62.6**	**70.0**	**76.5**	**80.8**	**83.8**	**90.3**	**100.0**	**105.7**	**104.8**	**106.2**	**113.5**	**115.5**	**117.0**	2
56.5	57.4	61.9	69.2	76.2	85.6	90.6	92.2	100.0	104.3	105.1	105.1	112.0	112.6	112.2	3
51.3	52.0	56.6	65.8	73.4	77.6	80.8	88.6	100.0	105.9	102.3	103.3	112.2	113.3	113.1	4
71.6	72.0	74.5	78.5	82.7	86.3	88.5	92.9	100.0	105.9	108.9	111.4	116.1	120.0	125.2	5
------	------	------	------	------	------	------	------	------	------	------	------	------	------	------	6
50.6	51.7	56.0	61.6	69.2	74.7	76.8	83.3	100.0	111.4	110.7	113.9	122.8	125.5	128.3	7
49.9	51.5	56.3	59.9	65.2	71.6	77.0	83.4	100.0	112.0	109.2	113.8	121.6	124.6	126.8	8
51.5	51.9	55.6	63.1	71.9	76.1	76.8	83.3	100.0	110.9	112.0	113.9	123.9	126.4	129.7	9
64.0	66.0	70.6	76.4	77.2	78.3	79.3	87.4	100.0	108.1	113.3	115.7	125.7	127.5	130.0	10
------	------	------	------	------	------	------	------	------	------	------	------	------	------	------	11
------	------	------	------	------	------	------	------	------	------	------	------	------	------	------	12
58.3	**58.5**	**66.3**	**73.0**	**77.6**	**76.0**	**76.9**	**91.0**	**100.0**	**104.9**	**108.2**	**111.3**	**121.3**	**121.6**	**120.3**	13
57.3	55.9	67.3	73.4	77.9	75.8	76.4	92.2	100.0	100.8	104.6	108.0	119.9	118.0	115.4	14
59.0	60.7	64.3	70.0	74.8	77.8	81.8	88.8	100.0	110.8	113.6	115.3	124.3	130.7	134.2	15
61.2	**59.9**	**57.2**	**60.9**	**64.1**	**69.7**	**77.9**	**91.9**	**100.0**	**104.5**	**111.0**	**115.0**	**118.3**	**124.4**	**127.5**	16
57.6	**58.5**	**64.1**	**72.5**	**79.9**	**80.7**	**81.8**	**89.2**	**100.0**	**105.6**	**106.2**	**107.2**	**115.8**	**117.0**	**118.3**	17

Bei Fragen zur Produktsicherheit wenden Sie sich bitte an:
If you have any questions regarding product safety,
please contact:

Walter de Gruyter GmbH
Genthiner Straße 13
10785 Berlin
productsafety@degruyterbrill.com